# Financial and Managerial Accounting

## TENTH EDITION

**Carl S. Warren**
Professor Emeritus of Accounting
University of Georgia, Athens

**James M. Reeve**
Professor Emeritus of Accounting
University of Tennessee, Knoxville

**Jonathan E. Duchac**
Professor of Accounting
Wake Forest University

SOUTH-WESTERN
CENGAGE Learning

Australia • Brazil • Japan • Korea • Mexico • Singapore • Spain • United Kingdom • United States

**SOUTH-WESTERN**
CENGAGE Learning

ISBN-13: 978-0-324-66465-2
ISBN-10: 0-324-66465-6

South-Western, Cengage Learning
2640 Eagan Woods Drive
Suite 220
Eagan, MN 55121

Cengage Learning is a leading provider of customized learning solutions with office locations around the globe, including Singapore, the United Kingdom, Australia, Mexico, Brazil, and Japan. Locate your local office at:
**www.cengage.com/international**

Cengage Learning products are represented in Canada by Nelson Education, Ltd.

To learn more about South-Western, visit
**www.cengage.com/southwestern**

Purchase any of our products at your local college store or at our preferred online store
**www.ichapters.com**

Printed in the United States of America
1 2 3 4 5 6 7 12 10 09

# CONTENTS

# 16 Managerial Accounting Concepts and Principles

## QUIZ AND TEST HINTS

The following hints may be helpful to you in preparing for a quiz or test over the material covered in Chapter 16.

1. You should be able to identify and explain the common differences between managerial and financial accounting highlighted in Exhibit 1. You should be prepared to write a short answer describing these differences.

2. This chapter introduces managerial accounting concepts and terminology. There are many new terms in this chapter that will be used throughout the remaining chapters. Thus, instructors will test your understanding of these terms. Instructors normally test this material using true/false and multiple-choice questions. Review the "Key Terms" section at the end of the chapter and be sure you understand each term. Do the Matching and Fill-in-the-Blank exercises included in this Study Guide.

3. The third objective of the chapter illustrating the financial statements of a manufacturing business is often emphasized in homework assignments and exams by instructors. Give special attention to the statement of cost of goods manufactured and its link to the income statement (Exhibit 10 in the text). Common test questions will ask you to construct these statements from raw data, much like illustrated in the text.

4. Review the "At A Glance" section at the end of the chapter. Read and review each of the Key Points and related Learning Outcomes. For each Learning Outcome that has an Example Exercise, locate the Example Exercise in the chapter and be sure that you understand the solution and can work a similar item on a test. If you have any questions about an Example Exercise, read the section of the chapter immediately preceding the Example Exercise.

## MATCHING

*Instructions:* Match each of the statements below with its proper term. Some terms may not be used.

A. continuous process improvement
B. controller
C. controlling
D. conversion costs
E. cost
F. cost object
G. cost of finished goods available
H. cost of goods manufactured
I. cost of goods sold
J. cost of merchandise sold
K. decision making
L. direct costs
M. direct labor cost
N. direct materials cost
O. directing
P. factory overhead cost
Q. feedback
R. financial accounting

S. finished goods inventory
T. indirect costs
U. line department
V. management by exception
W. management process
X. managerial accounting
Y. material inventory
Z. objectives
AA. period costs
BB. planning
CC. prime costs
DD. product costs
EE. staff department
FF. statement of costs of goods manufactured
GG. strategic planning
HH. strategies
II. work in process inventory

_____ 1. The chief management accountant of a division or other segment of a business.

_____ 2. The branch of accounting that is concerned with the recording of transactions using generally accepted accounting principles (GAAP) for a business or other economic unit and with a periodic preparation of various statements from such records.

_____ 3. The branch of accounting that uses both historical and estimated data in providing information that management uses in conducting daily operations, in planning future operations, and in developing overall business strategies.

_____ 4. A payment of cash (or a commitment to pay cash in the future) for the purpose of generating revenues.

_____ 5. All of the costs of operating the factory except for direct materials and direct labor, also termed factory burden or manufacturing overhead.

_____ 6. The cost of materials that are an integral part of the finished product.

_____ 7. Wages of factory workers who are directly involved in converting materials into a finished product.

_____ 8. The combination of direct labor and factory overhead costs.

____ 9. The three components of manufacturing cost: direct materials, direct labor, and factory overhead costs.

____ 10. The direct materials costs, the direct labor costs, and the factory overhead costs that have entered into the manufacturing process but are associated with products that have not been finished.

____ 11. The cost of materials that have not yet entered into the manufacturing process.

____ 12. The cost of finished products on hand that have not been sold.

____ 13. Those costs that are used up in generating revenue during the current period and that are not involved in the manufacturing process.

____ 14. A management approach that is part of the overall total quality management philosophy. The approach requires all employees to constantly improve processes of which they are a part or for which they have managerial responsibility.

____ 15. A phase in the management process that consists of monitoring the operating results of implemented plans and comparing the actual results with the expected results.

____ 16. The object or segment of operations to which costs are related for management's use, such as a product or department.

____ 17. The total cost of making and finishing a product during the period.

____ 18. The cost that is reported as an expense when merchandise is sold.

____ 19. A component inherent in the management processes of planning, directing, controlling, and improving.

____ 20. Costs that can be traced directly to a cost object.

____ 21. The process by which managers, given their assigned level of responsibilities, run day-to-day operations.

____ 22. Measures provided to operational employees or managers on the performance of subunits of the organization. These measures are used by employees to adjust a process or a behavior to achieve goals.

____ 23. Costs that cannot be traced directly to a cost object.

____ 24. A unit that is directly involved in the basic objectives of an organization.

____ 25. The philosophy of managing which involves monitoring the operating results of implemented plans and comparing the expected results with the actual results. This feedback allows management to isolate significant variations for further investigation and possible remedial action.

____ 26. The five basic management functions of (1) planning, (2) directing, (3) controlling, (4) improving, and (5) decision making.

_____ **27.** Developed in the planning stage, these reflect the direction and desired outcomes of certain courses of action.

_____ **28.** A phase of the management process whereby objectives are outlined and courses of action determined.

_____ **29.** The combination of direct materials and direct labor costs.

_____ **30.** A unit that provides services, assistance, and advice to the departments with line or other staff responsibilities.

_____ **31.** The income statement of manufacturing companies.

_____ **32.** The development of a long-range course of action to achieve business goals.

_____ **33.** The means by which business goals and objectives will be achieved.

_____ **34.** The cost of manufactured product that is sold.

_____ **35.** The cost of making products that are available for sale during the period added to the beginning finished goods inventory.

## FILL IN THE BLANK—PART A

*Instructions:* Answer the following questions or complete the statements by writing the appropriate words or amounts in the answer blanks.

1. _____ accounting information is prepared in accordance to generally accepted accounting principles for the use of government agencies, creditors, and public investors.

2. A(n) _____ department is one that provides services and assistance to other departments.

3. _____ is a part of the management process by which managers, given their assigned level of operations, run day-to-day operations.

4. _____ allows management to isolate significant departures from plans for further investigation and possible remedial action.

5. A(n) _____ is a payment of cash or its equivalent or the commitment to pay cash in the future for the purpose of generating revenues.

6. If a technician is directly involved in converting materials into finished products, his or her salary should be classified as a(n) _____ _____ cost.

7. Cost that are not directly associated with a cost object are known as _____ costs.

8. Shark Company owns dozens of machines used on its product assembly line. Depreciation expenses for these assets should be classified as _____ _____ costs.

9. _____ costs consist of the grouping of direct labor and direct material costs.

10. Expenses that are not incurred to support the manufacturing process, and which are incurred during the current period of time, are called _____ costs.

11. _____ expenses are incurred in the administration of the business and are not related to the manufacturing or selling functions.

12. Product costs are first recognized on the _____ _____ before being expensed in the income statement.

13. _____ _____ consists of the direct and indirect materials that have not yet entered the manufacturing process.

14. _____ _____ inventory consists of completed products that have not been sold.

15. For a merchandising company the expense associated with sold product is known as _____ ___ _____ _____.

16. The total cost of making and finishing product is called the _____ ____ _____ _____.

17. The total manufacturing costs added to production will be greater than the cost of goods manufactured when the work in process inventory at the beginning of the period is _____ _____ the work in process inventory at the end of the period.

18. The total materials purchased during the period will be less than the cost of materials placed into production when the materials inventory at the beginning of the period is _____ _____ the materials inventory at the end of the period.

19. The total manufacturing costs added to production are equal to the cost of _____ _____ _____ _____, direct labor, and factory overhead.

20. The statement of _____ ____ _____ _____ provides the details of the costs for making and finishing product.

## FILL IN THE BLANK—PART B

*Instructions:* Answer the following questions or complete the statements by writing the appropriate words or amounts in the answer blanks.

1. _____ accounting information includes both historical and estimated data used by a company to conduct daily operations, plan future operations, and develop an overall business strategy.

2. Managerial accounting reports do not need to be prepared according to _____ _____ _____ _____.

3. If a department is directly involved in manufacturing activities, it is known as a(n) _____ department.

4. Another title for a firm's chief management accountant is the firm's _____.

5. Within the management process _____ is used to develop the organization's goals (objectives).

6. _____ is a step in the management process that consists of monitoring the operating results of implemented plans and comparing the actual results with the expected results.

7. _____ _____ _____ is the management philosophy of continually improving employees, business processes, and products.

8. A company uses an electric furnace to melt iron ore. Costs of running the furnace, a necessary step in converting iron ore into steel, are known as _____ _____ costs.

9. Woods Company, a manufacturer of air compressors, regularly buys flow regulators from an outside vendor. If they are an integral component for the final product, flow regulators should be classified as _____ _____ costs.

10. Labor costs that do not enter directly into the manufacture of a product are classified as _____ _____ and are recorded as factory overhead.

11. The cost of the insurance on the factory building would be classified as a _____ _____ cost.

12. _____ costs consist of the grouping of direct labor and factory overhead costs.

13. _____ costs consists of the three elements of manufacturing cost.

14. _____ expenses are incurred in marketing the product and delivering the sold product to customers.

15. _____ _____ _____ inventory consists of the direct materials costs, direct labor costs, and factory overhead costs that have entered the manufacturing process but are associated with products that have not been completed.

16. The cost of product sold for a manufacturer is generally called the _____ ____ _____ _____.

17. The total manufacturing costs added to production will be less than the cost of goods manufactured when the work in process inventory at the beginning of the period is _____ _____ the work in process inventory at the end of the period.

18. The total materials purchased during the period will be greater than the cost of materials placed into production when the materials inventory at the beginning of the period is _____ _____ the materials inventory at the end of the period.

19. The cost of goods manufactured is equal to the total manufacturing costs less the ending _____ _____ _____ _____.

20. The cost of goods sold of a manufacturer is equal to the cost of _____ _____ _____ ____ _____ less the ending finished goods inventory.

## MULTIPLE CHOICE

*Instructions:* Circle the best answer for each of the following questions.

1. Which of the following is not a characteristic of managerial accounting reports?
   a. both objective and subjective
   b. required to be prepared according to generally accepted accounting principles (GAAP)
   c. prepared at fixed intervals, or as needed
   d. reported to company as a whole or segment

2. A characteristic of managerial accounting is:
   a. strict adherence to GAAP
   b. a focus on external decision maker needs
   c. a focus on management decision needs
   d. all of the above

3. Which of the following would be considered a staff department of a manufacturing company?
   a. Accounting Department
   b. Assembly Department
   c. Sales Department
   d. Fabrication Department

4. Which phase of the management process is inherent to all the others?
   a. planning
   b. directing
   c. controlling
   d. decision making

5. Which of the following items would be classified as a factory overhead cost?
   a. depreciation on the general offices
   b. utility and power costs of the factory
   c. the wages of a machine operator
   d. advertising costs

6. Which of the following would not be considered a cost object?
   a. common stock
   b. product
   c. sales territory
   d. organizational department

7. Which of the following would not be considered part of factory overhead costs?
   a. property taxes on factory building
   b. insurance on factory building
   c. sales salaries
   d. depreciation on factory plant and equipment

8. Conversion costs consist of:
   a. direct materials and direct labor
   b. direct materials and factory overhead cost
   c. period costs and product costs
   d. direct labor and factory overhead cost

9. Which of the following inventory classifications would be included in a Statement of Cost of Goods Manufactured?
   a. materials inventory
   b. work in process inventory
   c. finished goods inventory
   d. a. and b.

10. The total manufacturing costs added to production during the period is $110,000. The materials inventory increased from the beginning to the end of the period by $12,000, while the work in process inventory decreased from the beginning to the end of the period by $5,000. What is the cost of goods manufactured?
    a. $103,000
    b. $105,000
    c. $115,000
    d. $117,000

11. The cost of goods manufactured is $245,000. The finished goods inventory increased from the beginning to the end of the period by $8,000, while the work in process inventory increased from the beginning to the end of the period by $3,000. What is the cost of goods sold?

    a. $234,000

    b. $237,000

    c. $253,000

    d. $256,000

## TRUE/FALSE

*Instructions:*   Indicate whether each of the following statements is true or false by placing a check mark in the appropriate column.

|  | | True | False |
|---|---|---|---|
| 1. | Managerial accounting reports are intended for use by external users, such as bankers. | ____ | ____ |
| 2. | The sales department is a staff department. | ____ | ____ |
| 3. | The controlling phase of the management process consists of monitoring the operating results of implemented plans. | ____ | ____ |
| 4. | The paper for a textbook would be classified as direct material. | ____ | ____ |
| 5. | The cost of electricity for running machinery in a factory would be classified as a direct manufacturing cost. | ____ | ____ |
| 6. | The salary of the production engineer is a direct labor cost. | ____ | ____ |
| 7. | The cost of cheese for a pizza would be classified as a product cost. | ____ | ____ |
| 8. | The conversion cost is equal to the cost of goods manufactured. | ____ | ____ |
| 9. | The balance sheet of a manufacturing business would include materials, work in process, and finished goods inventory. | ____ | ____ |
| 10. | If the work in process inventory increased during the period, then the cost of goods manufactured will be less than the total manufacturing costs added to production. | ____ | ____ |

## EXERCISE 16-1

**Instructions:** Indicate whether the following costs of the Ford Motor Company would be classified as direct materials cost, direct labor cost, or factory overhead cost:

(a)  Console assembly wages

_____

(b)  Salary of plant manager

_____

(c)  Factory insurance

_____

(d)  Tires

_____

(e)  Paint

_____

(f)  Factory and equipment power costs

_____

(g)  Factory maintenance costs

_____

(h)  Factory controller salary

_____

(i)  Paint department wages

_____

(j)  Steel

_____

(k)  Final assembly line inspection wages

_____

(l)  Seats and interior trim

_____

(m)  Interior trim assembly wages

_____

(n)  Paint department supervisor salary

_____

# EXERCISE 16-2

***Instructions:*** Determine whether the following costs are properly classified as part of factory overhead for Apple Computer, Inc.:

**(a)** Keyboard                                     _____

**(b)** Quality manager salary          _____

**(c)** Factory property taxes          _____

**(d)** LCD monitor                         _____

**(e)** Circuit board assembly wages   _____

**(f)** Robotic assembly depreciation   _____

**(g)** Plant manager's salary          _____

**(h)** General office depreciation      _____

**(i)** Final assembly wages           _____

**(j)** Computer mouse                   _____

**(k)** Packaging wages                  _____

**(l)** Test equipment depreciation    _____

**(m)** CEO salary                          _____

**(n)** Plant controller salary         _____

## EXERCISE 16-3

*Instructions:* Classify each of the following costs as either a product or period cost for Kellogg's cereal company:

(a)  Television advertising costs

(b)  Chief financial officer (CFO) salary

(c)  Oats

(d)  Salesperson salaries

(e)  Packaging equipment depreciation

(f)  Mixing department wages

(g)  Interest expense

(h)  Cereal boxes

(i)  Sugar

(j)  Plant depreciation

(k)  Promotion coupon costs

(l)  Vice-President of Human Resources salary

(m)  CEO salary

(n)  Packing department wages

## EXERCISE 16-4

The following events took place for Swift Manufacturing Company during May, the first month of its operations as a producer of athletic shoes.

**(a)** Purchased $80,000 of rubber.
**(b)** Used $55,000 of rubber in production.
**(c)** Incurred $34,000 of assembly wages.
**(d)** Incurred $41,000 of factory overhead.
**(e)** Transferred $121,000 of work in process to finished goods.
**(f)** Sold goods with a cost of $114,000.
**(g)** Earned revenues of $195,000.
**(h)** Incurred $29,000 of selling expenses.
**(i)** Incurred $38,000 administrative expenses.

### Instructions:

**(1)** Prepare a May income statement for Swift Manufacturing Company.

| Swift Manufacturing Company | | |
|---|---|---|
| Income Statement | | |
| For the Month Ended May 31, 20-- | | |
|  |  |  |
|  |  |  |
|  |  |  |
|  |  |  |
|  |  |  |
|  |  |  |
|  |  |  |
|  |  |  |
|  |  |  |
|  |  |  |

**(2)** Determine the inventory balances at the end of May.

# PROBLEM 16-1

Several items are omitted from each of the following income statement and cost of goods manufactured statement data for the month of March:

| | Scenario 1 | Scenario 2 |
|---|---|---|
| Materials inventory, January 1 | $ 18,000 | $  42,000 |
| Materials inventory, January 31 | 23,000 | (a) |
| Materials purchased | (a) | 245,000 |
| Materials placed into production | (b) | 247,000 |
| Direct labor | 95,000 | 128,000 |
| Factory overhead | 156,000 | 202,000 |
| Total manufacturing costs added | 431,000 | (b) |
| Total manufacturing costs | 457,000 | 610,000 |
| Work in process inventory, January 1 | 26,000 | 33,000 |
| Work in process inventory, January 31 | (c) | 40,000 |
| Cost of goods manufactured | 435,000 | (c) |
| Finished goods inventory, January 1 | 87,000 | 102,000 |
| Finished goods inventory, January 31 | (d) | 109,000 |
| Sales | 810,000 | 1,100,000 |
| Cost of goods sold | 443,000 | (d) |
| Gross profit | (e) | (e) |
| Operating expenses | (f) | 367,000 |
| Net income | 72,000 | (f) |

## Instructions:

(1) Determine the amounts of the missing items, for each independent scenario, identifying them by letter.

Scenario 1

(a)

(b)

(c)

(d)

(e)

(f)

Scenario 2

**(a)**

**(b)**

**(c)**

**(d)**

**(e)**

**(f)**

**(2)** Prepare a statement of cost of goods manufactured for Scenario 1.

*Scenario 1*

*Statement of Cost of Goods Manufactured*

*For the Month Ended March 31, 20--*

| | | | |
|---|---|---|---|
| | | | |
| | | | |
| | | | |
| | | | |
| | | | |
| | | | |
| | | | |
| | | | |
| | | | |
| | | | |
| | | | |
| | | | |
| | | | |
| | | | |
| | | | |
| | | | |
| | | | |
| | | | |

**(3)** Prepare an income statement for Scenario 1.

*Scenario 1*

*Income Statement*

*For the Month Ended March 31, 20--*

| | | |
|---|---|---|
| | | |
| | | |
| | | |
| | | |
| | | |
| | | |
| | | |
| | | |
| | | |
| | | |
| | | |
| | | |
| | | |
| | | |
| | | |
| | | |
| | | |
| | | |

## PROBLEM 16-2

The following information is available for the Ginza Manufacturing Company for October.

| Inventories | October 1 | October 31 |
|---|---|---|
| Materials | $19,000 | $16,000 |
| Work in process | 32,000 | 36,000 |
| Finished goods | 42,000 | 40,000 |

| | |
|---|---|
| Advertising expense | $ 97,000 |
| Depreciation expense – Factory equipment | 48,000 |
| Depreciation expense – Office furniture | 31,000 |
| Direct labor | 178,000 |
| Heat, light, and power – Factory | 26,000 |
| Indirect labor | 112,000 |
| Materials purchased during October | 302,000 |
| Office salaries expense | 189,000 |
| Property taxes – Factory | 36,000 |
| Property taxes – Headquarters building | 24,000 |
| Rent expense – Factory | 67,000 |
| Sales | 1,350,000 |
| Sales salaries expense | 103,000 |
| Supplies – Factory | 11,000 |
| Miscellaneous cost – Factory | 16,000 |

**(1)** Prepare the October statement of cost of goods manufactured.

*Ginza Manufacturing Company*

*Statement of Cost of Goods Manufactured*

*For the Month Ended October 31, 20--*

| | | | |
|---|---|---|---|
| | | | |
| | | | |
| | | | |
| | | | |
| | | | |
| | | | |
| | | | |
| | | | |
| | | | |
| | | | |
| | | | |
| | | | |
| | | | |
| | | | |
| | | | |
| | | | |
| | | | |
| | | | |
| | | | |
| | | | |
| | | | |
| | | | |
| | | | |
| | | | |
| | | | |
| | | | |
| | | | |
| | | | |
| | | | |

**(2)** Prepare the October income statement.

*Ginza Manufacturing Company*

*Income Statement*

*For the Month Ended October 31, 20--*

| | | | |
|---|---|---|---|
| | | | |
| | | | |
| | | | |
| | | | |
| | | | |
| | | | |
| | | | |
| | | | |
| | | | |
| | | | |
| | | | |
| | | | |
| | | | |
| | | | |
| | | | |
| | | | |
| | | | |
| | | | |
| | | | |
| | | | |
| | | | |
| | | | |
| | | | |
| | | | |
| | | | |
| | | | |
| | | | |
| | | | |
| | | | |
| | | | |
| | | | |
| | | | |
| | | | |
| | | | |
| | | | |
| | | | |
| | | | |

# 17        Job Order Costing

## QUIZ AND TEST HINTS

The following hints may be helpful to you in preparing for a quiz or a test over the material covered in Chapter 17.

1. It is important to be able to distinguish between direct and indirect materials, labor, and overhead; and between product and period costs.

2. You should be able to prepare journal entries for the recording of transactions using a job order cost system. Carefully review the chapter illustration of the job order cost system. Also, the Illustrative Problem provided in the text chapter is a useful study aid.

3. Instructors will often require you to calculate the ending balance of materials, work in process, and finished goods inventories. These calculations are based on understanding the flow of costs through T-accounts. Thus, an understanding of Exhibit 8 is useful for this chapter.

4. You should be able to calculate factory overhead application rates using activity bases.

5. Review the "Key Terms" section at the end of the chapter and be sure you understand each term. Do the Matching and Fill-in-the-Blank exercises included in this Study Guide.

6. Review the "At A Glance" section at the end of the chapter. Read and review each of the Key Points and related Learning Outcomes. For each Learning Outcome that has an Example Exercise, locate the Example Exercise in the chapter and be sure that you understand the solution and can work a similar item on a test. If you have any questions about an Example Exercise, read the section of the chapter immediately preceding the Example Exercise.

## MATCHING

***Instructions:*** Match each of the statements below with its proper term. Some terms may not be used.

| | | | |
|---|---|---|---|
| **A.** | activity base | **J.** | overapplied factory overhead |
| **B.** | activity-based costing | **K.** | period costs |
| **C.** | cost accounting system | **L.** | predetermined factory overhead rate |
| **D.** | cost allocation | | |
| **E.** | finished goods ledger | **M.** | process cost system |
| **F.** | job cost sheet | **N.** | receiving report |
| **G.** | job order cost system | **O.** | time tickets |
| **H.** | materials ledger | **P.** | underapplied factory overhead |
| **I.** | materials requisitions | | |

_____ 1. A type of cost accounting system that provides for a separate record of the cost of each particular quantity of product that passes through the factory.

_____ 2. An account in the work in process subsidiary ledger in which the costs charged to a particular job order are recorded.

_____ 3. The form or electronic transmission used by a manufacturing department to authorize the issuance of materials from the storeroom.

_____ 4. The subsidiary ledger containing the individual accounts for each type of material.

_____ 5. The form or electronic transmission used by the receiving personnel to indicate that materials have been received and inspected.

_____ 6. The form on which the amount of time spent by each employee and the labor cost incurred for each individual job, or for factory overhead, are recorded.

_____ 7. The process of assigning indirect costs to a cost object, such as a job.

_____ 8. A measure of activity that is related to changes in cost and is used in the denominator in calculating the predetermined factory overhead rate to assign factory overhead costs to cost objects.

_____ 9. The rate used to apply factory overhead costs to the goods manufactured. The rate is determined from budgeted overhead cost and estimated activity usage data at the beginning of the fiscal period.

_____ 10. The amount of factory overhead applied in excess of the actual factory overhead costs incurred for production during a period.

_____ 11. An accounting framework based on determining the cost of activities.

_____ 12. The subsidiary ledger that contains the individual accounts for each kind of commodity or product produced.

_____ 13. Those costs that are used up in generating revenue during the current period and that are not involved in the manufacturing process.

_____  **14.** A type of cost accounting system in which costs are accumulated by department or process within a factory.

## FILL IN THE BLANK—PART A

*Instructions:*  Answer the following questions or complete the statements by writing the appropriate words or amounts in the answer blanks.

1. Under a(n) _____ system, costs are accumulated for each of the departments or processes within a factory.

2. In a job order cost system, perpetual inventory controlling accounts and subsidiary ledgers are maintained for _____, _____ ___ _____, and _____ _____ inventories.

3. The three components of manufacturing cost are classified as _____ costs.

4. If a technician is directly involved in converting materials into finished products, his or her salary should be classified as a(n) _____ _____ cost.

5. Shark Company owns dozens of machines used on its product assembly line. Depreciation expenses for these assets should be classified as _____ _____ costs.

6. A company uses an electric furnace to melt iron ore. Costs of running the furnace, a necessary step in converting iron ore into steel, are known as factory burden or _____ _____ costs.

7. Beta Company manufactures customized fiber-optic systems for NASA's space missions. If separate records are kept for the cost of each individual product that the company produces, Beta's accountants are using a(n) _____ _____ cost system.

8. If 1,000 springs are moved out of the storeroom and into the assembly line, the company's accounting system will reflect this flow of materials by _____ the materials account and _____ the work in process account.

9. With a job order cost system, factory workers record the hours they spend working on specific jobs using forms known as _____ _____.

10. Cost _____ is the process of assigning factory overhead costs to a cost object, such as a job.

11. Amber Company estimates that its total factory overhead costs will amount to $75,600 this year. If the company expects to operate its only machine for 1,800 hours this year, the predetermined factory overhead rate per hour of machine time is _____ (round your answer to the nearest whole dollar).

12. A new method of allocating factory overhead costs using different rates corresponding to different activities is known as _____-_____ costing.

13. If the factory overhead account has a credit balance at the end of the period, the credit is described as _____ overhead.

14. During one month, Smith Company had a beginning debit balance of $13,200 in its factory overhead account. By the end of the month, the account had increased 75%, ending with a debit balance of $23,100. The company's accountant should investigate the overhead _____ to determine whether it needs revision.

15. One approach for disposing of the balance of factory overhead at the end of the year is to transfer the entire balance to the _____ _____ _____ _____ account.

16. Direct materials costs are debited to Work in Process based on data obtained from a summary of _____ _____.

17. The finished goods account is a controlling account with a subsidiary ledger called a finished goods ledger or _____ _____.

18. Expenses that are not incurred to support the manufacturing process, and which are incurred during the current period of time, are called _____ costs.

19. _____ expenses are incurred in the administration of the business and are not related to the manufacturing or selling functions.

20. A job order cost system is useful for both manufacturing and _____ businesses.

## FILL IN THE BLANK—PART B

*Instructions:* Answer the following questions or complete the statements by writing the appropriate words or amounts in the answer blanks.

1. _____ _____ systems accumulate manufacturing costs for the goods that are produced.

2. A(n) _____ _____ system provides a separate record for the cost of each quantity of product that passes through the factory.

3. Sandpaper used by a guitar company would be classified as _____ _____ cost.

4. Woods Company, a manufacturer of air compressors, regularly buys flow regulators from an outside vendor. If they are an integral component for the final product, flow regulators should be classified as _____ _____ costs.

5. Labor costs that do not enter directly into the manufacture of a product are classified as _____ _____ and are recorded as factory overhead.

6. Managerial accountants gather information related to product costs. Managers frequently use this information to establish _____ _____, control operations, and develop financial statements.

7. Each inventory account, including Raw Materials Inventory, Work in Process Inventory, and Finished Goods Inventory, is _____ for all additions and _____ for all deductions.

8. Materials are released from the storeroom to the factory in response to materials _____ received from the production department.

9. Under the job order cost system, a(n) _____ _____ sheet is used to keep track of the resources consumed during the production of a specific customer order.

10. A summary of the _____ _____ at the end of each month is the basis for recording the direct and indirect labor costs incurred in production.

11. The measure used to allocate factory overhead is frequently called a(n) _____ _____.

12. Green Company has a predetermined factory overhead rate of $3.75 per direct labor hour. If Green Company uses 1,500 hours as the activity base, the estimated total factory overhead cost is _____.

13. Gold Company uses $4.00 per hour as a predetermined factory overhead rate for allocating direct labor costs as factory overhead. If Job A requires a total of 16½ hours of direct labor, the amount of factory overhead to be applied to Job A is _____.

14. Factory overhead costs applied to production are periodically debited to the _____ _____ _____ account and credited to the factory overhead account.

15. If the factory overhead account has a debit balance at the end of the period, the debit is described as _____ overhead.

16. Direct labor and factory overhead costs are debited to Work in Process based on data obtained from a summary of _____ _____.

17. Each account in the _____ _____ ledger contains cost data including the units manufactured, units sold, and the units on hand for each of the individual product types which the company manufactures.

18. Randolph Company completed 20,000 units at a cost of $175,000. The beginning finished goods inventory was 3,500 units, costing a total of $26,600. The cost of goods sold for 12,000 units, assuming a fifo cost flow, is _____.

19. _____ expenses are incurred in marketing the product and delivering the sold product to customers.

20. The Silver Agency sells advertising services. When the agency completes a job and a client is billed, the accountant will transfer the job's costs from a work in process account to a(n) _____ _____ _____ account.

## MULTIPLE CHOICE

*Instructions:*    Circle the best answer for each of the following questions.

1. For which of the following businesses would the process cost system be most appropriate?
   a. building contractor
   b. cookie processor
   c. plumber
   d. textbook publisher

2. The production department requests that materials be released from the storeroom to the factory based on which of the following forms?
   a. receiving report
   b. purchase order
   c. purchase requisition
   d. materials requisition

3. The amount of time spent by each employee on an individual job is recorded on a(n):
   a. clock card
   b. time ticket
   c. in-and-out card
   d. labor requisition

4. For which of the following businesses would the job order cost system be most appropriate?
   a. oil refinery
   b. meat processor
   c. a hotel
   d. textbook publisher

5. The subsidiary ledger that contains the individual accounts for each product produced is called the:
   a. work in process ledger
   b. finished goods ledger
   c. factory overhead ledger
   d. materials ledger

6. Which of the following would not be considered part of factory overhead costs?

    a. property taxes on factory building

    b. insurance on factory building

    c. sales salaries

    d. depreciation on factory plant and equipment

7. Factory overhead is applied to jobs in a job order cost system using:

    a. a predetermined factory overhead rate

    b. a direct labor wage rate

    c. material requisitions

    d. all of the above

8. The amount of actual factory overhead in excess of the factory overhead applied to production during a period is called:

    a. underapplied factory overhead

    b. excess factory overhead

    c. overapplied factory overhead

    d. excess capacity

9. A method of accumulating and allocating factory overhead costs to products using many overhead rates is:

    a. variable costing

    b. flexible costing

    c. activity-based costing

    d. service function allocation

10. Job order cost information can be used by management to:

    a. control costs

    b. establish product prices

    c. prepare financial statements

    d. all of the above

11. Total budgeted factory overhead is $360,000, while the budgeted direct labor hours are 15,000 hours. Job 115 took 16 direct labor hours at a direct labor rate of $12 per hour. What is the amount of factory overhead applied to this job?

    a. $24

    b. $192

    c. $384

    d. $576

## TRUE/FALSE

*Instructions:* Indicate whether each of the following statements is true or false by placing a check mark in the appropriate column.

|  |  | True | False |
|---|---|---|---|

1. A cost accounting system uses perpetual inventory procedures in accounting for manufacturing costs. ..................... ____  ____

2. A process cost system provides for a separate record of cost of each particular quantity of product that passes through the factory. ................................................. ____  ____

3. A publishing company which produces a variety of different publication titles would normally use a process cost accounting system. ................................................. ____  ____

4. The two principal types of cost systems for manufacturing operations are job order cost accounting and process cost accounting systems. ................................................. ____  ____

5. Materials are transferred from the storeroom to the factory in response to purchase requisitions. ................................. ____  ____

6. As a practical matter, unless the total amount of the underapplied or overapplied overhead balance is large, it is transferred to Cost of Goods Sold. ...................................... ____  ____

7. If the factory overhead account has a debit balance, the factory overhead is said to be overapplied. ........................ ____  ____

8. The subsidiary ledger that contains the individual accounts for each kind of product is the finished goods ledger........... ____  ____

9. A manufacturer that uses a job order cost system for one product must use that system for all products. .................... ____  ____

10. The predetermined factory overhead rate is calculated by relating the estimated amount of factory overhead for the period to an activity base. ................................................. ____  ____

## EXERCISE 17-1

*Instructions:*   Indicate the flow of costs through the perpetual inventory accounts and into the cost of goods sold account for a cost accounting system by connecting with arrows the letters that should be paired together in the following diagram.

| Materials | |
|---|---|
| Purchased | Dir. used a |
|  | Indir. used b |

| Work in Process | |
|---|---|
| e | Finished k |
| f |  |
| g |  |

| Finished Goods | |
|---|---|
| l | Sold m |

| Wages Payable | |
|---|---|
| Paid | Dir. used c |
|  | Indir. used d |

| Factory Overhead | |
|---|---|
| h | Applied j |
| i |  |
| Other costs |  |

| Cost of Goods Sold | |
|---|---|
| n |  |

## EXERCISE 17-2

*Instructions:*   Indicate the flow of costs through a service business using a job order cost accounting system by connecting with arrows the letters that should be paired together in the following diagram.

| Wages Payable | |
|---|---|
| Paid | Dir. labor a |
|  | Indir. labor b |

| Work in Process | |
|---|---|
| d | Completed |
| g | jobs i |

| Cost of Services | |
|---|---|
| j |  |

| Supplies | |
|---|---|
| Purchased | Used c |

| Overhead | |
|---|---|
| e | Applied h |
| f |  |
| Other costs |  |

# EXERCISE 17-3

Foley Company operates two factories. It applies factory overhead to jobs on the basis of machine hours in Factory 1 and on the basis of direct labor costs in Factory 2. Estimated factory overhead costs, direct labor costs, and machine hours for the year and actual amounts for January are as follows:

|  | Factory 1 | Factory 2 |
|---|---|---|
| Estimated factory overhead cost for year ............... | $65,000 | $243,600 |
| Estimated direct labor costs for year ...................... |  | $580,000 |
| Estimated machine hours for year .......................... | 20,000 |  |
| Actual factory overhead costs for January ............. | $6,050 | $20,100 |
| Actual direct labor costs for January ........,............ |  | $48,500 |
| Actual machine hours for January .......................... | 1,800 |  |

## Instructions:

**(1)** Determine the factory overhead rate for Factory 1. _____

**(2)** Determine the factory overhead rate for Factory 2. _____

**(3)** Journalize the entries to apply factory overhead to production in each factory for January.

**JOURNAL**                                                               PAGE

| | DATE | DESCRIPTION | POST. REF. | DEBIT | CREDIT | |
|---|---|---|---|---|---|---|
| 1 | | | | | | 1 |
| 2 | | | | | | 2 |
| 3 | | | | | | 3 |
| 4 | | | | | | 4 |
| 5 | | | | | | 5 |
| 6 | | | | | | 6 |
| 7 | | | | | | 7 |
| 8 | | | | | | 8 |
| 9 | | | | | | 9 |
| 10 | | | | | | 10 |

**(4)** Determine the balance of the factory overhead account in each factory as of January 31, and indicate whether the amounts represent overapplied or underapplied factory overhead.

## EXERCISE 17-4

D'Amato CPAs use a job order cost system to determine the cost of serving clients. The following client information is available for work completed in February of the current year:

| Client | Service | Job Costs | Billable Hours | Job Cost per Billable Hour |
|--------|---------|-----------|----------------|----------------------------|
| Astor Co. | Audit | $11,040 | 240 | |
| Brown, Inc. | Audit | 11,750 | 250 | |
| Singhal Co. | Audit | 14,880 | 310 | |
| Martinez Co. | Compilation | 1,875 | 75 | |
| Ng, Inc. | Compilation | 2,040 | 85 | |
| Wrigley Co. | Compilation | 2,185 | 95 | |
| Zane, Inc. | Compilation | 4,950 | 110 | |
| Howard Co. | Tax | 10,395 | 165 | |
| McNelly Co. | Tax | 9,000 | 150 | |

Audit services relate to annual financial statement audits for the client businesses; compilation refers to bookkeeping services; and tax services relate to preparing and advising clients on tax returns.

### Instructions:

(1) Determine the job cost per billable hour for each of the completed jobs in February and complete the table above.

(2) What can you determine from this information?

(3) Prepare the summary journal entry to close out the completed jobs for February.

### JOURNAL

PAGE

| | DATE | DESCRIPTION | POST. REF. | DEBIT | CREDIT | |
|---|------|-------------|------------|-------|--------|---|
| 1 | | | | | | 1 |
| 2 | | | | | | 2 |

## PROBLEM 17-1

**Instructions:** Below are listed some transactions of Zintor Inc., which uses a job order cost accounting system. Prepare the entries to record the transactions. (Omit dates and explanations.)

(1) Purchased materials costing $60,000 and incurred prepaid expenses amounting to $5,300, all on account.

(2) Requisitioned $23,200 worth of materials to be used directly in production ($15,400 on Job 101 and $7,800 on Job 102) and $1,200 worth of materials to be used indirectly for repairs and maintenance.

(3) Factory labor used as follows: direct labor, $35,900; indirect labor, $2,700.

(4) Other costs incurred on account as follows: factory overhead, $12,200; selling expenses, $21,950; administrative expenses, $15,300. (Credit Accounts Payable.)

(5) Prepaid expenses expired as follows: factory overhead, $5,000; selling expenses, $800; administrative expenses, $600.

(6) The predetermined rate for the application of factory overhead to jobs (work in process) was 70% of direct labor cost. (See transaction 3.)

(7) The cost of jobs completed was $53,000.

(8) The sales on account for the period amounted to $160,000. The cost of goods sold was $110,000.

## JOURNAL

PAGE

| | DATE | | DESCRIPTION | POST. REF. | DEBIT | CREDIT | |
|---|---|---|---|---|---|---|---|
| 1 | | | | | | | 1 |
| 2 | | | | | | | 2 |
| 3 | | | | | | | 3 |
| 4 | | | | | | | 4 |
| 5 | | | | | | | 5 |
| 6 | | | | | | | 6 |
| 7 | | | | | | | 7 |
| 8 | | | | | | | 8 |
| 9 | | | | | | | 9 |
| 10 | | | | | | | 10 |
| 11 | | | | | | | 11 |
| 12 | | | | | | | 12 |
| 13 | | | | | | | 13 |
| 14 | | | | | | | 14 |
| 15 | | | | | | | 15 |
| 16 | | | | | | | 16 |

## JOURNAL

PAGE

| | DATE | | DESCRIPTION | POST. REF. | DEBIT | CREDIT | |
|---|---|---|---|---|---|---|---|
| 1 | | | | | | | 1 |
| 2 | | | | | | | 2 |
| 3 | | | | | | | 3 |
| 4 | | | | | | | 4 |
| 5 | | | | | | | 5 |
| 6 | | | | | | | 6 |
| 7 | | | | | | | 7 |
| 8 | | | | | | | 8 |
| 9 | | | | | | | 9 |
| 10 | | | | | | | 10 |
| 11 | | | | | | | 11 |
| 12 | | | | | | | 12 |
| 13 | | | | | | | 13 |
| 14 | | | | | | | 14 |
| 15 | | | | | | | 15 |
| 16 | | | | | | | 16 |
| 17 | | | | | | | 17 |
| 18 | | | | | | | 18 |
| 19 | | | | | | | 19 |
| 20 | | | | | | | 20 |
| 21 | | | | | | | 21 |
| 22 | | | | | | | 22 |
| 23 | | | | | | | 23 |
| 24 | | | | | | | 24 |
| 25 | | | | | | | 25 |
| 26 | | | | | | | 26 |
| 27 | | | | | | | 27 |
| 28 | | | | | | | 28 |
| 29 | | | | | | | 29 |
| 30 | | | | | | | 30 |
| 31 | | | | | | | 31 |
| 32 | | | | | | | 32 |
| 33 | | | | | | | 33 |
| 34 | | | | | | | 34 |
| 35 | | | | | | | 35 |
| 36 | | | | | | | 36 |

# PROBLEM 17-2

*Instructions:* Post the following transactions to the proper T accounts below. Identify the postings with the transactions by using the number preceding each transaction.

**(1)** Purchased materials for $78,000 cash.

**(2)** Requisitioned $56,000 worth of direct materials and $2,400 worth of indirect materials from the storeroom.

**(3)** The factory labor cost for the period amounted to $75,000. (Credit Wages Payable.) The labor cost is determined to be $70,000 direct labor, $5,000 indirect labor.

**(4)** Paid $12,500 for factory overhead costs.

**(5)** Applied $24,000 of factory overhead to work in process.

**(6)** The cost of jobs completed amounted to $164,000.

|  | Cash |  | Finished Goods |
|---|---|---|---|
| Bal.    135,400 |  | Bal.    50,800 |  |

|  | Work in Process |  | Materials |
|---|---|---|---|
| Bal.    33,800 |  | Bal.    18,000 |  |

|  | Factory Overhead |  | Wages Payable |
|---|---|---|---|
| Bal.    3,000 |  |  |  |

# 18 Process Cost Systems

## QUIZ AND TEST HINTS

The following hints may be helpful to you in preparing for a quiz or a test over the material covered in Chapter 18.

1. The focus of this chapter is accounting for manufacturing operations using a process cost system. You can expect to see at least one problem requiring you to prepare journal entries for process costing or a cost of production report. The illustration of process costing in the chapter and the Illustrative Problem are good study aids.

2. You have to be able to compute equivalent units of production and cost per equivalent unit. In addition to a problem requiring the preparation of a cost of production report, expect to see some multiple-choice questions requiring equivalent unit computations.

3. Be prepared to explain the change in cost per equivalent unit between the previous period and the current period under the FIFO method.

4. Terminology is important. Study the highlighted terms in the chapter for possible true/false or multiple-choice questions. Review the "Key Terms" section at the end of the chapter and be sure you understand each term. Do the Matching and Fill-in-the-Blank exercises included in this Study Guide.

5. Review the "At A Glance" section at the end of the chapter. Read and review each of the Key Points and related Learning Outcomes. For each Learning Outcome that has an Example Exercise, locate the Example Exercise in the chapter and be sure that you understand the solution and can work a similar item on a test. If you have any questions about an Example Exercise, read the section of the chapter immediately preceding the Example Exercise.

## MATCHING

*Instructions:* Match each of the statements below with its proper term. Some terms may not be used.

A. cost of production report
B. cost per equivalent unit
C. equivalent units of production
D. first-in, first-out (FIFO) cost method
E. just-in-time processing
F. manufacturing cells

G. oil refinery
H. process cost system
I. process manufacturers
J. transferred-out costs
K. whole units
L. yield

_____ 1. A type of cost system that accumulates costs for each of the various departments within a manufacturing facility.

_____ 2. Manufacturers that use large machines to process a continuous flow of raw materials through various stages of completion into a finished state.

_____ 3. The number of production units that could have been completed within a given accounting period, given the resources consumed.

_____ 4. A method of inventory costing that assumes the unit product costs should be determined separately for each period in the order in which the costs were incurred.

_____ 5. The rate used to allocate costs between completed and partially completed production.

_____ 6. A report prepared periodically by a processing department, summarizing the costs incurred by the department and the allocation of those costs between completed and incomplete production.

_____ 7. A measure of materials usage efficiency.

_____ 8. A grouping of processes where employees are cross-trained to perform more than one function.

_____ 9. A processing approach that focuses on eliminating time, cost, and poor quality within manufacturing and nonmanufacturing processes.

_____ 10. The number of units in production during a period, whether completed or not.

# FILL IN THE BLANK—PART A

*Instructions:*   Answer the following questions or complete the statements by writing the appropriate words or amounts in the answer blanks.

1. A _____ (specify process or job order) cost system would be more appropriate for a shipbuilding company.

2. A _____ (specify process or job order) cost system would be more appropriate for an oil refining company.

3. Direct materials, direct labor, and _____ _____ are the three elements of product costs.

4. In a process cost system, the amount of work in process inventory is determined by _____ costs between completed and partially completed units within a department.

5. In a process cost system, product cost flows should reflect the _____ flow of materials passing through the manufacturing process.

6. Smith Company refines oil. If the company sells 5,000 gallons of oil, should the finished goods account be debited or credited?

   _____

7. The first step in determining the cost of goods completed and the ending inventory valuation is to determine the _____ _____ _____ _____ _____.

8. Omega Department had a beginning in-process inventory of 24,000 pounds. During the month, 58,500 pounds were completed and transferred to another department. The ending in-process inventory was 16,000 pounds. During the period, _____ pounds were started and completed.

9. The number of units that could have been completed during a given accounting period is called the _____ units of production.

10–13. Department G had 8,000 units in work in process that were 40% converted at the beginning of the period at a cost of $19,450. During the period, 18,000 units of direct materials were added at a cost of $54,000, 18,500 units were completed, and 7,500 units were 40% completed. Direct labor was $32,500, and factory overhead was $66,320 during the period.

10. The number of conversion equivalent units was _____.

11. The total conversion costs were _____.

12. The conversion costs of the units started and completed during the period were _____.

13. The conversion costs of the 7,500 units in process at the end of the period were _____.

14. The _____ _____ _____ _____ is determined by dividing the direct materials and conversion costs by the respective total equivalent units for direct materials and conversion costs.

15. The oxidation department had $68,000 of direct materials cost and 128 direct materials equivalent units. The cost per equivalent unit of direct materials is _____.

16. Department Z had $99,510 of conversion costs and $5.35 of cost per equivalent unit of conversion. The number of conversion equivalent units is _____.

17. The _____ _____ _____ report summarizes (1) the units for which the department is accountable and their disposition, and (2) the costs charged to the department and their allocation.

18. The ratio of the materials output quantity to the materials input quantity is known as the _____.

19. A production philosophy focused on reducing production time and costs and eliminating poor quality is known as _____-_____-_____ processing.

20. Separate process functions combined into "work centers" are sometimes called _____ _____.

# FILL IN THE BLANK—PART B

*Instructions:* Answer the following questions or complete the statements by writing the appropriate words or amounts in the answer blanks.

1. A _____ (specify process or job order) cost system would be more appropriate for a company that continually produces a homogenous product.

2. A _____ (specify process or job order) cost system would be more appropriate for a company that builds specialized products according to individual contracts with its customers.

3. In a process cost system, product costs are accumulated by _____.

4. The two elements of conversion costs are _____ _____ and _____ _____.

5. Costs transferred from one department to another normally include direct materials and _____ costs.

6. When the first units entering a production process are the first to be completed, the flow of production would be described as a(n) _____ flow.

7. The last step in determining the cost of goods completed and the ending inventory valuation is "to allocate costs to transferred and _____ _____ units."

8. The three categories of units to be assigned costs for an accounting period are (1) units in beginning in-process inventory, (2) units started and completed during the period, and (3) units in _____ _____-_____ _____.

9. This month, Alpha Department had 100 units in beginning in-process inventory that were completed during the month, 300 units started and completed, and 200 units in ending in-process inventory. In order to reflect this month's activity, _____ total units should be assigned costs.

10. The number of units in production during a period, regardless of whether they are completed or not, is called the _____ units of production.

11. On April 1, Department X had a beginning in-process inventory of 300 gallons of a special chemical. The 300 gallons should be counted as equivalent units of direct materials for the month of _____.

12. Conversion costs are usually incurred _____ throughout a process.

13. Department B had a beginning work in process inventory of 200 half-finished assemblies. This month the department completed 550 assemblies, leaving 120 half-finished assemblies in ending work in process inventory. The equivalent units for conversion costs are _____.

14. Echo Department had $25,000 in conversion costs and 1,000 conversion equivalent units. The cost per equivalent unit of conversion is _____.

15. Department 2 had $55,000 of conversion costs and $6.25 of cost per equivalent unit of conversion. The number of conversion equivalent units is _____.

16. The cost of transferred and partially completed units is calculated by _____ equivalent unit rates by the number of equivalent units.

17–19. A department calculated that it had 600 equivalent units for direct materials and 300 equivalent units for conversion in this month's ending inventory. Equivalent cost per unit of direct materials was $17.25, and equivalent cost per unit of conversion was $5.30.

17. The cost of direct materials in ending inventory is _____.

18. The cost of conversion in ending inventory is _____.

19. The total cost of ending inventory is _____.

20. In a JIT system, each work center may be connected to the other work centers through information contained on _____, which is a Japanese term for cards.

## MULTIPLE CHOICE

*Instructions:*   Circle the best answer for each of the following questions.

1. In the manufacture of 10,000 equivalent units of product for a period, direct materials cost incurred was $200,000, direct labor cost incurred was $75,000, and applied factory overhead cost was $185,000. What was the unit conversion cost for the period?

   a. $7.50

   b. $18.50

   c. $26

   d. $46

2. The Finishing Department had 6,000 units, 1/3 completed at the beginning of the period; 16,000 units were transferred to the Finishing Department from the Sanding Department during the period; and 2,500 units were 1/5 completed at the end of the period. What is the total units to be accounted for on the cost of production report for the Finishing Department for the period?

   a. 13,500

   b. 15,500

   c. 18,500

   d. 22,000

3. Material B is added after the processing is 60% completed. There were 2,400 units completed during the period. There were 300 units in beginning inventory (50% completed) and 100 units in process at the end of the period (20% completed). What was the total equivalent units of production for Material B?

   a. 2,400

   b. 2,200

   c. 2,500

   d. 2,700

4. If the Weaving Department had 900 units, 40% completed, in process at the beginning of the period; 9,000 units were completed during the period; and 600 units were 10% completed at the end of the period, what was the number of conversion equivalent units of production for the period using the fifo cost method?

   a. 8,520

   b. 8,700

   c. 8,900

   d. 9,060

5. The number of units that could have been completed within a given accounting period is called the:

   a. equivalent units of production

   b. optimal units of production

   c. theoretical units of production

   d. whole units

6. The combined direct labor and factory overhead per equivalent unit is called the:

   a. prime cost per unit

   b. processing cost per unit

   c. conversion cost per unit

   d. combined cost per unit

7. The ratio of the materials output quantity to the materials input quantity is the:

   a. materials consumption ratio

   b. materials absorption ratio

   c. capacity constraint

   d. yield

8. Cards that contain information to help work centers communicate with one another in a just-in-time processing system are called:

   a. pillars

   b. kanbans

   c. JIT cards

   d. flow cards

9. Work centers in a just-in-time processing system where processing functions are combined are:

   a. JIT centers

   b. combined processing centers

   c. master cells

   d. manufacturing cells

10. There were 2,000 pounds in process at the beginning of the period in the Finishing Department. The department received 22,000 pounds from the Blending Department during the period, and 3,000 pounds were in process at the end of the period. How many pounds were completed by the Finishing Department during the period?

   a. 27,000

   b. 24,000

   c. 21,000

   d. 19,000

11. At the beginning of the period, there were 3,000 tons in process, 30% complete with respect to materials. There were 12,000 tons transferred into the process, of which 1,000 tons were remaining in work in process at the end of the period. The ending work in process was 60% complete as to materials. Materials were introduced at the beginning of the process and had a total cost of $415,000. What was the cost per equivalent unit for materials?

   a. $28.23

   b. $30.29

   c. $33.20

   d. $33.74

12. The costs per equivalent unit for materials and conversion costs were $18 and $6, respectively. The 5,000 whole units of ending work in process were 40% complete with respect to processing. Materials were added at the beginning of the process. What was the cost of the ending work in process?

   a. $48,000

   b. $102,000

   c. $108,000

   d. $120,000

## TRUE/FALSE

*Instructions:* Indicate whether each of the following statements is true or false by placing a check mark in the appropriate column.

|  | True | False |
|---|---|---|
| 1. The number of units that could have been completed within a given accounting period is referred to as the equivalent units of production. | ___ | ___ |
| 2. A report prepared periodically for each processing department and which summarizes (a) the units for which the department is accountable and the disposition of those units and (b) the production costs incurred by the department and the allocation of those costs is called a cost of production report. | ___ | ___ |
| 3. The accumulated costs transferred from preceding departments and the costs of direct materials, direct labor, and applied factory overhead incurred in each processing department are debited to the related work in process accounts. | ___ | ___ |
| 4. The most important use of the cost of production report is to schedule production. | ___ | ___ |
| 5. Direct labor and factory overhead are referred to as primary costs. | ___ | ___ |

**True**    **False**

6. Equivalent units for materials and conversion costs are usually determined separately. ........................................... ____   ____

7. A cost of production report will normally list costs in greater detail to help management isolate problems and opportunities. ................................................................. ____   ____

8. If a material is introduced halfway through processing and the beginning inventory is 40% complete, then the equivalent units for beginning inventory for this material for the current period will be zero (assuming fifo). ......................... ____   ____

9. The first-in, first-out cost method is based on the assumption that the work in process at the beginning of the current period was started and completed during the current period. ................................................................................ ____   ____

10. If the work in process at the beginning of the period is 400 gallons, 1,600 gallons were started during the period, and 300 gallons remained in process at the end of the period, then the units started and completed are 1,700 gallons. ...... ____   ____

# EXERCISE 18-1

*Instructions:* Presented below is a diagram of the cost flows for Cortex Company, a process manufacturer. Cortex has two processing departments. All materials are placed into production in Department 1. In the spaces beneath the diagram identify each letter contained in the diagram.

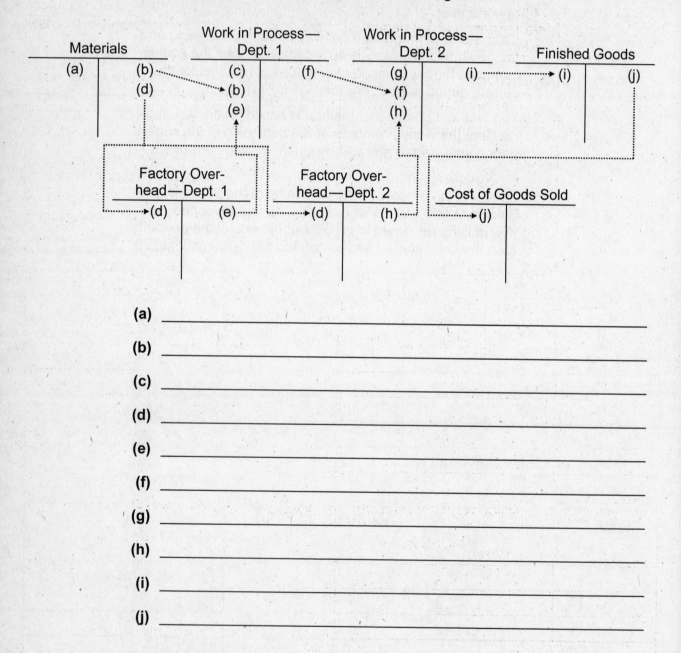

(a) _____

(b) _____

(c) _____

(d) _____

(e) _____

(f) _____

(g) _____

(h) _____

(i) _____

(j) _____

# EXERCISE 18-2

Ellis Company started April with 12,000 units in process that were 30% complete at a cost of $47,000. During April, the following costs were incurred: direct materials, $148,800; direct labor, $141,000; and factory overhead, $185,400. During April, 66,000 units were completed and transferred to finished goods. There were 8,000 units in process that were 20% completed at April 30. All materials are added at the beginning of the production process and conversion costs are incurred evenly throughout.

*Instructions:*  Use the work sheet presented below to determine the following:

(1)  Equivalent units of production for materials costs .......... _____

(2)  Equivalent units of production for conversion costs ....... _____

(3)  Materials cost per equivalent unit ..................................... $ _____

(4)  Conversion cost per equivalent unit ................................ $ _____

(5)  Work in process inventory, April 30 ................................. $ _____

(6)  Cost of goods transferred to finished goods warehouse . $ _____

| Units | Total Whole Units | % Material to be Completed in April | % Conversion to be Completed in April | (1) Equivalent Units for Materials | (2) Equivalent Units for Conversion |
|---|---|---|---|---|---|
|  |  |  |  |  |  |
|  |  |  |  |  |  |
|  |  |  |  |  |  |
|  |  |  |  |  |  |
| Total Equivalent Units to Account for ........................................... |  |  |  |  |  |

| Costs | (3) Direct Materials | (4) Conversion Costs | Total |
|---|---|---|---|
|  |  |  |  |
|  |  |  |  |
|  |  |  |  |
|  |  |  |  |
|  |  |  |  |
| (6) |  |  |  |
| (5) |  |  |  |
| Total Costs Charged to Department .................................................................. |  |  |  |

## EXERCISE 18-3

The following work in process account information was obtained from the Cooking Department of Southern Soup Company. All direct materials are introduced at the beginning of the process, and conversion costs are incurred evenly throughout the process. The beginning inventory consists of $75,600 of direct materials and $20,160 of conversion costs.

ACCOUNT    *Work In Process—Cooking Dept.*                    ACCOUNT NO.

| DATE | | ITEM | DEBIT | CREDIT | BALANCE DEBIT | BALANCE CREDIT |
|---|---|---|---|---|---|---|
| April | 1 | Bal., 4,200 units, 40% completed | | | 95,760.00 | |
| | 30 | Direct materials, 35,000 units | 647,500.00 | | 743,260.00 | |
| | 30 | Direct labor | 202,100.00 | | 945,360.00 | |
| | 30 | Factory overhead | 247,720.00 | | 1,193,080.00 | |
| | 30 | Goods transferred, 36,000 units | | 1,104,480.00 | 88,600.00 | |
| | 30 | Bal., 3,200 units, 75% completed | | | 88,600.00 | |

**Instructions:**  Determine the cost per equivalent unit of direct materials and conversion costs.

| | WHOLE UNITS | EQUIVALENT UNITS DIRECT MATERIALS | EQUIVALENT UNITS CONVERSION |
|---|---|---|---|
| | | | |
| | | | |
| | | | |
| | | | |
| | | | |
| | | | |
| | | | |

| | COSTS DIRECT MATERIALS | COSTS CONVERSION |
|---|---|---|
| | | |
| | | |
| | | |
| | | |

## EXERCISE 18-4

The Cooking Department of Southern Soup Company (Exercise 18-3) had April 1 inventory of $95,760, representing 4,200 whole units that were 40% complete as to conversion cost and 100% complete as to materials. The April 1 inventory consists of $75,600 of direct materials and $20,160 of conversion costs.

### Instructions:

(1) Prepare a table comparing the cost per equivalent unit of direct materials and conversion cost computed for April (from Exercise 18-3) with the cost per equivalent unit of direct materials and conversion cost for March.

| | Direct Materials Cost per Equivalent Unit | Conversion Cost per Equivalent Unit |
|---|---|---|
| March | | |
| April (from Exercise 18-3) | | |

Computations:

(2) Interpret your results.

## PROBLEM 18-1

Mirror Inc. is a small manufacturing company that uses a process cost accounting system. The firm has two processing departments.

*Instructions:*    Record the following transactions in the journals provided on the following pages. Any indirect cost such as indirect labor or indirect material incurred by a department should be charged to the department's overhead account. (Omit dates and explanations.)

(1) Materials purchased on account, $210,000.

(2) The following materials were requisitioned: Department 10, direct, $18,000; Department 10, indirect, $2,100; Department 20, direct, $24,000; Department 20, indirect, $600.

(3) The labor used by factory departments was as follows: Department 10, direct, $25,000; Department 10, indirect, $2,700; Department 20, direct, $20,000; Department 20, indirect, $2,700.

(4) The following other costs and expenses were incurred on account: factory overhead, Department 10, $1,500; factory overhead, Department 20, $2,250.

(5) Depreciation expenses were as follows: Department 10, $4,200; Department 20, $3,150.

(6) Factory overhead costs were applied to work in process on the basis of 102% of the direct labor cost of Department 10 and 75% of the direct labor cost of Department 20. (See transaction 3.)

(7) There was no beginning or ending inventory in Department 10. All costs accumulated in Department 10 work in process were transferred to Department 20.

(8) The work in process in Department 20 at the end of the period amounted to $12,500. The balance (representing 25,000 units) was transferred to finished goods. (There was no beginning inventory of work in process.)

(9) Sales of 21,000 units for $160,000 on account were made during the month. The cost of goods sold was $122,000.

## JOURNAL

PAGE

| | DATE | | DESCRIPTION | POST. REF. | DEBIT | CREDIT | |
|---|---|---|---|---|---|---|---|
| 1 | | | | | | | 1 |
| 2 | | | | | | | 2 |
| 3 | | | | | | | 3 |
| 4 | | | | | | | 4 |
| 5 | | | | | | | 5 |
| 6 | | | | | | | 6 |
| 7 | | | | | | | 7 |
| 8 | | | | | | | 8 |
| 9 | | | | | | | 9 |
| 10 | | | | | | | 10 |
| 11 | | | | | | | 11 |
| 12 | | | | | | | 12 |
| 13 | | | | | | | 13 |
| 14 | | | | | | | 14 |
| 15 | | | | | | | 15 |
| 16 | | | | | | | 16 |
| 17 | | | | | | | 17 |
| 18 | | | | | | | 18 |
| 19 | | | | | | | 19 |
| 20 | | | | | | | 20 |
| 21 | | | | | | | 21 |
| 22 | | | | | | | 22 |
| 23 | | | | | | | 23 |
| 24 | | | | | | | 24 |
| 25 | | | | | | | 25 |
| 26 | | | | | | | 26 |
| 27 | | | | | | | 27 |
| 28 | | | | | | | 28 |
| 29 | | | | | | | 29 |
| 30 | | | | | | | 30 |
| 31 | | | | | | | 31 |
| 32 | | | | | | | 32 |
| 33 | | | | | | | 33 |
| 34 | | | | | | | 34 |
| 35 | | | | | | | 35 |
| 36 | | | | | | | 36 |

# JOURNAL

PAGE

| | DATE | | DESCRIPTION | POST. REF. | DEBIT | CREDIT | |
|---|---|---|---|---|---|---|---|
| 1 | | | | | | | 1 |
| 2 | | | | | | | 2 |
| 3 | | | | | | | 3 |
| 4 | | | | | | | 4 |
| 5 | | | | | | | 5 |
| 6 | | | | | | | 6 |
| 7 | | | | | | | 7 |
| 8 | | | | | | | 8 |
| 9 | | | | | | | 9 |
| 10 | | | | | | | 10 |
| 11 | | | | | | | 11 |
| 12 | | | | | | | 12 |
| 13 | | | | | | | 13 |
| 14 | | | | | | | 14 |
| 15 | | | | | | | 15 |
| 16 | | | | | | | 16 |
| 17 | | | | | | | 17 |
| 18 | | | | | | | 18 |
| 19 | | | | | | | 19 |
| 20 | | | | | | | 20 |
| 21 | | | | | | | 21 |
| 22 | | | | | | | 22 |
| 23 | | | | | | | 23 |
| 24 | | | | | | | 24 |
| 25 | | | | | | | 25 |

## PROBLEM 18-2

**Instructions:** Using the following data prepare:

**(1)** a cost of production report for the Polishing Department of Ivy Inc. for March of the current fiscal year using the fifo cost method and

**(2)** an analysis of the change in the cost per equivalent units of materials and conversion cost between February and March.

March Polishing Department data

Inventory, March 1:

| | |
|---|---|
| Direct materials (5,000 units × $4.90) ........................................ | $ 24,500 |
| Conversion (5,000 units × 30% × $13.20) ................................. | 19,800 |
| Inventory, March 1, 5,000 units, 30% completed ......................... | $ 44,300 |
| Materials from the Cutting Department, 21,000 units ...................... | 105,000 |
| Direct labor for March ................................................................. | 176,140 |
| Factory overhead for March ......................................................... | 120,000 |
| Inventory, March 31, 6,000 units, 60% completed ......................... | — |

**(1)**

| | A | B | C | D |
|---|---|---|---|---|
| 1 | Ivy Inc. | | | |
| 2 | Cost of Production Report—Polishing Department | | | |
| 3 | For the Month Ended March 31, 20-- | | | |
| 4 | | | Equivalent Units | |
| 5 | Units | Whole Units | Direct Materials | Conversion |
| 6 | | | | |
| 7 | | | | |
| 8 | | | | |
| 9 | | | | |
| 10 | | | | |
| 11 | | | | |
| 12 | | | | |
| 13 | | | | |
| 14 | | | | |
| 15 | | | | |

|     | A | B | C | D |
|-----|---|---|---|---|
| 1 | Ivy Inc. | | | |
| 2 | Cost of Production Report—Polishing Department (Concluded) | | | |
| 3 | For the Month Ended March 31, 20-- | | | |
| 4 | | Costs | | |
| 5 | Costs | Direct Materials | Conversion | Total Costs |
| 6 | | | | |
| 7 | | | | |
| 8 | | | | |
| 9 | | | | |
| 10 | | | | |
| 11 | | | | |
| 12 | | | | |
| 13 | | | | |
| 14 | | | | |
| 15 | | | | |
| 16 | | | | |
| 17 | | | | |
| 18 | | | | |
| 19 | | | | |
| 20 | | | | |
| 21 | | | | |
| 22 | | | | |
| 23 | | | | |
| 24 | | | | |
| 25 | | | | |
| 26 | | | | |

(2)

|     | A | B | C | D |
|-----|---|---|---|---|
| 1 | | Inventory in Process, March 1 | March Cost of Production Report | Difference |
| 2 | | | | |
| 3 | | | | |

Analysis:

# 19 Cost Behavior and Cost-Volume-Profit Analysis

## QUIZ AND TEST HINTS

The following hints may be helpful to you in preparing for a quiz or a test over the material covered in Chapter 19.

1. Many new terms are introduced in this chapter. You can expect true/false, multiple-choice, or matching questions testing your knowledge of these terms. Review the "Key Terms" section at the end of the chapter and be sure you understand each term. Do the Matching and Fill-in-the-Blank exercises included in this Study Guide.

2. Expect some multiple-choice questions related to the behavior of costs. For example, you might be required to classify various types of costs (direct materials, for example) as variable, fixed, or mixed for the activity of units produced. You might also have to use the high-low method to separate a mixed cost into its variable and fixed costs components.

3. The major focus of this chapter is the computation of break-even sales (units) and sales (units) required to achieve a target profit. These computations are based upon the contribution margin concept. In your studying, focus on the mathematical approach to cost-volume-profit analysis. Instructors often do not require preparation of a cost-volume-profit or a profit-volume chart.

4. The special cost-volume-profit relationships (margin of safety and operating leverage) and the assumptions of cost-volume-profit analysis often appear in the form of true/false or multiple-choice questions on tests.

5. Review the "At A Glance" section at the end of the chapter. Read and review each of the Key Points and related Learning Outcomes. For each Learning Outcome that has an Example Exercise, locate the Example Exercise in the chapter and be sure that you understand the solution and can work a similar item on a test. If you have any questions about an Example Exercise, read the section of the chapter immediately preceding the Example Exercise.

## MATCHING

***Instructions:*** Match each of the statements below with its proper term. Some terms may not be used.

| | | | |
|---|---|---|---|
| **A.** | absorption costing | **K.** | margin of safety |
| **B.** | activity bases (drivers) | **L.** | mixed cost |
| **C.** | break-even point | **M.** | operating leverage |
| **D.** | contribution margin | **N.** | profit-volume chart |
| **E.** | contribution margin ratio | **O.** | relevant range |
| **F.** | cost behavior | **P.** | sales mix |
| **G.** | cost-volume-profit analysis | **Q.** | unit contribution margin |
| **H.** | cost-volume-profit chart | **R.** | variable costing |
| **I.** | fixed costs | **S.** | variable costs |
| **J.** | high-low method | | |

_____ 1. Costs that vary in total dollar amount as the level of activity changes.

_____ 2. Sales less variable cost of goods sold and variable selling and administrative expenses.

_____ 3. A measure of activity that is thought to cause a cost; used in analyzing and classifying cost behavior.

_____ 4. The percentage of each sales dollar that is available to cover the fixed costs and provide income from operations.

_____ 5. Costs that tend to remain the same in amount, regardless of variations in the level of activity.

_____ 6. The range of activity over which changes in cost are of interest to management.

_____ 7. A technique that uses the highest and lowest total cost as a basis for estimating the variable cost per unit and the fixed cost component of a mixed cost.

_____ 8. The level of business operations at which revenues and expired costs are equal.

_____ 9. The systematic examination of the relationships among costs, expenses, sales, and operating profit or loss.

_____ 10. The manner in which a cost changes in relation to its activity base (driver).

_____ 11. A chart used to assist management in understanding the relationships among costs, expenses, sales, and operating profit or loss.

_____ 12. The dollars available from each unit of sales to cover fixed costs and provide income from operations.

_____ 13. A chart used to assist management in understanding the relationship between profit and volume.

_____ 14. A cost with both variable and fixed characteristics.

___ 15. The difference between current sales revenue and the sales at the break-even point.

___ 16. The relative distribution of sales among the various products available for sale.

___ 17. A measure of the relative mix of a business's variable costs and fixed costs, computed as contribution margin divided by income from operations.

___ 18. A method of reporting variable and fixed costs that includes only the variable manufacturing costs in the cost of the product.

## FILL IN THE BLANK—PART A

*Instructions:* Answer the following questions or complete the statements by writing the appropriate words or amounts in the answer blanks.

1. Activities that are thought to cause a cost to be incurred are called

   _____ _____.

2. The range of activity over which the changes in a cost are of interest to management is referred to as the _____ _____.

3. In terms of cost behavior, direct materials and labor costs are generally classified as _____ _____.

4. Straight-line depreciation of factory equipment and insurance on factory plant are examples of _____ (variable, fixed, or mixed) costs.

5. Rental of equipment at $2,000 per month plus $1 for each machine hour used over 10,000 hours is a type of _____ (variable, fixed, or mixed) cost.

6. The high-low method is a cost estimate technique that may be used to separate _____ (variable, fixed, or mixed) costs.

7. A management accounting reporting system that includes only variable manufacturing costs in the product cost is known as variable costing or

   _____ _____.

8. _____-_____-_____ analysis is the systematic examination of the relationship among selling prices, sales and production volume, costs, expenses, and profits.

9. Sales minus variable costs divided by sales is the calculation of the

   _____ _____ _____.

10. Given a selling price per unit of $20, variable costs per unit of $10, and fixed costs of $95,000, the break-even point in sales units is _____.

11. An increase in fixed costs will cause the break-even point to

    _____.

12. Increases in the price of direct materials and the wages of factory workers will cause the break-even point to _____.

13. If fixed costs are $200,000 and the unit contribution margin is $40, the sales volume in units needed to earn a target profit of $100,000 is _____.

14. A cost-volume-profit chart is also called a(n) _____-_____ chart.

15. On a cost-volume-profit chart, units of sales are plotted along the _____ axis.

16. The _____-_____ chart is a graphic approach to cost-volume-profit analysis that focuses on profits.

17. With computers, managers can vary assumptions regarding selling prices, costs, and volume and can see immediately the effects on the break-even point. This is known as _____ _____ _____.

18. The relative distribution of sales among the various products sold by a business is called the _____ _____.

19. The difference between the current sales revenue and the sales at the break-even point is called the _____ _____ _____.

20. _____ _____ is computed by dividing the contribution margin by the operating income.

## FILL IN THE BLANK—PART B

*Instructions:* Answer the following questions or complete the statements by writing the appropriate words or amounts in the answer blanks.

1. Activities that are thought to cause a cost to be incurred are called activity bases or _____ _____.

2. _____ _____ vary in proportion to changes in the level of activity.

3. The salary of a factory supervisor is an example of a _____ (fixed/variable) cost.

4. _____ _____ remain the same in total dollar amount as the level of activity changes.

5. The rental cost of a piece of office equipment is $2,000 per month plus $1.00 for each machine hour used over 1,500 hours. This is an example of a(n) _____ cost.

6. Mixed costs are sometimes called semivariable or _____ costs.

7. In the high-low method, the difference in total cost divided by the difference in production equals the _____ _____ _____ _____.

8. The _____ _____ is the excess of sales revenue over variable costs.

9. The contribution margin ratio is also called the _____-_____ _____.

10. The _____ _____ ratio measures the effect on operating income of an increase or decrease in sales volume.

11. The unit contribution margin is the dollars from each unit of sales available to cover _____ _____ and provide operating profits.

12. The _____-_____ _____ is the level of operations at which a business's revenues and costs are exactly equal.

13. Increases in property tax rates will cause the break-even point to _____.

14. Decreases in the unit selling price will cause the break-even point to _____.

15. Increases in the unit selling price will cause the break-even point to _____.

16. The vertical axis of a break-even chart depicts _____ and _____.

17. Analyzing the effects of changing selling prices, costs, and volume on the break-even point and profit is called "what if" analysis or _____ _____.

18. The sales volume necessary to break even or to earn a target profit for a business selling two or more products depends upon the _____ _____.

19. If the contribution margin is $200,000 and operating income is $50,000, the operating leverage is _____.

20. An important assumption of cost-volume-profit analysis is that total sales and total costs can be represented by _____ _____.

## MULTIPLE CHOICE

*Instructions:*    Circle the best answer for each of the following questions.

1. Which of the following statements describes fixed costs?

    a. costs that remain constant on a per unit basis as the activity base changes

    b. costs that vary in total in direct proportion to changes in the activity base

    c. costs that remain constant on a per unit basis, but vary in total as the activity level changes

    d. costs that remain constant in total dollar amount as the level of activity changes

2. What term is used to describe a cost which has characteristics of both a variable and fixed cost?

    a. variable cost

    b. fixed cost

    c. mixed cost

    d. sunk cost

3. If Berkson Inc.'s costs at 150,000 units of production are $240,000 (the high point of production) and $152,500 at 80,000 units of production (the low point of production), the variable cost per unit using the high-low method of cost estimation is:

    a. zero

    b. $1.25

    c. $1.60

    d. $1.91

4. Which of the following changes would have the effect of increasing the break-even point for a business?

    a. a decrease in fixed costs

    b. a decrease in unit variable cost

    c. a decrease in unit selling price

    d. none of the above

5. Which of the following costs will be classified as a fixed cost in cost-volume-profit analysis?

    a. direct materials

    b. real estate taxes

    c. direct labor

    d. supplies

6. If the contribution margin is $16 and fixed costs are $400,000, what is the break-even point in units?
   a. 25,000
   b. 250,000
   c. 400,000
   d. 6,400,000

7. If sales are $300,000 and sales at the break-even point are $250,000, what is the margin of safety?
   a. 17%
   b. 20%
   c. 83%
   d. 120%

8. If for Jones Inc. the contribution margin is $200,000 and operating income is $40,000, what is the operating leverage?
   a. 240,000
   b. 160,000
   c. 5
   d. 0.2

9. In cost-volume-profit analysis, variable costs are costs that:
   a. increase per unit with an increase in the activity level
   b. decrease per unit with a decrease in the activity level
   c. remain the same in total at different activity levels
   d. remain the same per unit at different activity levels

10. CM Inc.'s sales are 40,000 units at $12 per unit, variable costs are $8 per unit, and fixed costs are $50,000. What is CM's contribution margin ratio?
    a. 23%
    b. 33%
    c. 50%
    d. 67%

11. B-E Co.'s fixed costs are $120,000, unit selling price is $30, and unit variable cost is $18. What is B-E's break-even point in units?
    a. 4,000
    b. 6,667
    c. 10,000
    d. none of the above

12. Which of the following is a primary assumption of cost-volume-profit analysis?
   a. within the relevant range, the efficiency of operations does not change
   b. costs can be accurately divided into fixed and variable components
   c. sales mix is constant
   d. all of the above

## TRUE/FALSE

*Instructions:*   Indicate whether each of the following statements is true or false by placing a check mark in the appropriate column.

|  | True | False |
|---|---|---|
| 1. Most operating decisions by management focus on a range of activity, known as the relevant range, within which management plans to operate. | ____ | ____ |
| 2. Mixed costs, sometimes referred to as semivariable or semifixed costs, are costs that are mostly variable. | ____ | ____ |
| 3. The high-low method can be used to estimate the fixed cost and variable cost components of a mixed cost. | ____ | ____ |
| 4. Using the high-low method, the fixed costs will differ at the highest and lowest levels of activity. | ____ | ____ |
| 5. The point in the operations of a business at which revenues and expired costs are equal is called the break-even point. | ____ | ____ |
| 6. The data required to compute the break-even point are (1) total estimated fixed costs for a future period and (2) the unit contribution margin. | ____ | ____ |
| 7. Decreases in the unit selling price will decrease the break-even point. | ____ | ____ |
| 8. Decreases in fixed costs will increase the break-even point. | ____ | ____ |
| 9. The operating leverage is determined by dividing the income from operations by the sales dollars at break-even. | ____ | ____ |
| 10. A primary assumption of cost-volume-profit analysis is that the quantity of units in the beginning inventory is equal to the quantity of units in the ending inventory. | ____ | ____ |

## EXERCISE 19-1

Data for the highest and lowest levels of production for Evans Company are as follows:

|  | Total Costs | Total Units Produced |
|---|---|---|
| Highest level ................. | $550,000 | 50,000 units |
| Lowest level ................. | $250,000 | 20,000 |

### Instructions:

**(1)** Determine the differences between total costs and total units produced at the highest and lowest levels of production.

**(2)** Using the high-low method of cost estimation, estimate the variable cost per unit and the fixed cost for Evans Company.

**(3)** Based on (2), estimate the total costs for 80,000 units of production.

# EXERCISE 19-2

*Instructions:* Name the following chart and identify the items represented by the letters *a* through *f*.

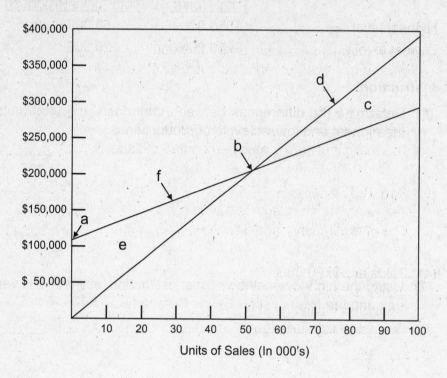

Units of Sales (In 000's)

**Chart:** _____

(a) _____

(b) _____

(c) _____

(d) _____

(e) _____

(f) _____

## EXERCISE 19-3

*Instructions:*  In each of the following cases, use the appropriate formula (margin of safety or operating leverage ratio) to determine the answer.

**(1)**  Sales are $2,000,000.
Break-even sales would be $1,700,000.
The margin of safety as a percentage of sales is ......    _____ %

**(2)**  Sales are $150,000.
Break-even sales would be $100,000.
The margin of safety as a percentage of sales is ......    _____ %

**(3)**  Operating income is $175,000.
The contribution margin is $300,000.
The operating leverage is ..........................................    _____

**(4)**  Sales are $700,000.
Variable costs are $300,000.
Operating income is $200,000.
The operating leverage is ..........................................    _____

## EXERCISE 19-4

The Timberland Company has fixed costs of $213,380. The unit selling price, variable cost per unit, and contribution margin per unit for the company's two products are provided below.

| Product | Selling Price per Unit | Variable Cost per Unit | Contribution Margin per Unit |
|---------|------------------------|------------------------|------------------------------|
| K-100 | $65 | $45 | $20 |
| V-200 | $90 | $64 | $26 |

The sales mix for products K-100 and V-200 is 55% and 45%, respectively.

**Instructions:** Determine Timberland Company's break-even in units of K-100 and V-200.

## PROBLEM 19-1

Larson Co. produces telephone answering machines. At March 1, Larson estimates fixed costs related to production to be $700,000. The unit selling price,
unit variable cost, and unit contribution margin for Larson Co. are as follows:

Unit selling price ........................    $75
Unit variable cost .......................     25
Unit contribution margin ............    $50

***Instructions:***  Perform the following calculations assuming the facts given above,
unless otherwise indicated. (Round to the nearest dollar.)

**(1)** Calculate the break-even point in units for Larson Co.

**(2)** Assume Larson Co. is contemplating paying $2,000 more to each of five
factory supervisors. What would the new break-even point be if such a plan
were put into action?

**(3)** What would the break-even point be if the cost of direct materials increased
by $1.00 per unit?

**(4)** What would the break-even point be if the selling price increased to $77 per
telephone answering machine?

**(5)** What is the sales volume necessary to earn a target profit of $300,000?

## PROBLEM 19-2

Data related to the expected sales of products A and B for Galla Inc. for the current year, which is typical of recent years, are as follows.

| Product | Selling Price per Unit | Variable Cost per Unit | Sales Mix |
|---|---|---|---|
| A | $180 | $140 | 80% |
| B | $280 | $190 | 20% |

The estimated fixed costs for the current year are $400,000.

*Instructions:*

(1) Determine the estimated sales in units and dollars to reach the break-even point for the current year.

(2) Prove the validity of the answer in (1) by completing the following condensed income statement.

|  | Product A | Product B | Total |
|---|---|---|---|
| Sales: | | | |
| _____ units × $180 .......... | _____ | _____ | _____ |
| _____ units × $280 .......... | _____ | _____ | _____ |
| Total sales ........................... | _____ | _____ | _____ |
| Variable costs: | | | |
| _____ units × $140 .......... | _____ | _____ | _____ |
| _____ units × $190 .......... | _____ | _____ | _____ |
| Total variable costs ............... | _____ | _____ | _____ |
| Contribution margin ......................................................... | | | _____ |
| Fixed costs ....................................................................... | | | _____ |
| Operating profit ................................................................ | | | _____ |

# 20 Variable Costing for Management Analysis

## QUIZ AND TEST HINTS

The following hints may be helpful to you in preparing for a quiz or a test over the material covered in Chapter 20.

1. Instructors frequently test your understanding of new terms using true/false and multiple-choice questions. Review the "Key Terms" section at the end of the chapter and be sure you understand each term. Do the Matching and Fill-in-the-Blank exercises included in this Study Guide.

2. You will likely see some multiple-choice questions requiring you to calculate the difference between absorption and variable costing income when units manufactured exceed or are less than units sold.

3. Common multiple-choice questions ask you to identify when variable costing income will be less than, equal to, or greater than absorption costing income.

4. You should be able to prepare income statements under both the absorption and variable costing formats.

5. You may be asked to prepare contribution margin statements for products, territories, or salespersons.

6. You may be required to prepare segment contribution margin income statements and contribution margin analysis for a service firm. Often, service firms will have costs with more than one activity base.

7. Review the "At A Glance" section at the end of the chapter. Read and review each of the Key Points and related Learning Outcomes. For each Learning Outcome that has an Example Exercise, locate the Example Exercise in the chapter and be sure that you understand the solution and can work a similar item on a test. If you have any questions about an Example Exercise, read the section of the chapter immediately preceding the Example Exercise.

## MATCHING

**Instructions:**    Match each of the statements below with its proper term. Some terms may not be used.

A.    absorption costing
B.    contribution margin
C.    contribution margin analysis
D.    controllable cost
E.    conversion cost
F.    manufacturing margin
G.    market segment

H.    noncontrollable cost
I.    unit cost (price) factor
J.    quantity factor
K.    sales mix
L.    units manufactured exceed units sold
M.    variable costing

_____    1.    The concept that considers the cost of products manufactured to be composed only of those manufacturing costs that increase or decrease as the volume of production rises or falls (direct materials, direct labor, and variable factory overhead).

_____    2.    The concept that considers the cost of manufactured products to be composed of direct materials, direct labor, and factory overhead.

_____    3.    Sales less variable cost of goods sold and variable selling and administrative expenses.

_____    4.    Sales less variable cost of goods sold.

_____    5.    Variable costing income is less than absorption costing income.

_____    6.    For a specific level of management, a cost that cannot be directly controlled.

_____    7.    A portion of business, such as products, customers, and regions, that is assigned to a manager for profit responsibility.

_____    8.    For a specific level of management, a cost that can be directly controlled.

_____    9.    The relative distribution of sales among the various products available for sale.

_____    10.    The systematic examination of the differences between planned and actual contribution margin.

_____    11.    The effect of a difference in unit sales price or unit cost from plan.

_____    12.    The effect of a difference in the number of units sold from plan.

## FILL IN THE BLANK—PART A

*Instructions:*  Answer the following questions or complete the statements by writing the appropriate words or amounts in the answer blanks.

1.  Generally accepted accounting principles require use of the _____ (absorption or variable) concept in determining the cost of goods sold.

2.  In the variable costing income statement, deducting variable cost of goods sold from sales yields the _____ _____.

3.  The income from operations under absorption costing will be _____ (equal to, greater than, or less than) the income from operations under variable costing when the units sold exceed the units produced.

4.  Unlike absorption costing, the variable costing concept treats _____ _____ _____ as a period expense.

5.  If the finished goods inventory was 3,000 units after the first month of operations and the fixed factory overhead was $6 per unit, then the income from operations under absorption costing is _____ (amount) _____ (less than or greater than) the income from operations under variable costing.

6.  The production volume was 10,000 units, while the sales volume was 12,000 units. The sales price was $40 per unit. The variable cost of goods sold was $28 per unit, and the variable selling and administrative expenses were $7 per unit. The contribution margin shown on the variable costing income statement is _____.

7.  For a specific level of management, _____ _____ are costs that can be influenced by management at that level.

8.  The _____ _____ refers to the relative distribution of sales among the various products sold.

9–10.  Baskins and Taylor are two salespersons that sell Products A and B. The contribution margin of Product A is $40 per unit, while for Product B it is $70 per unit. The total sales volume for both products for each salesperson is as follows:

|  | Product A | Product B |
|---|---|---|
| Baskins ........................... | 12,000 units | 10,000 units |
| Taylor ............................. | 8,000 | 15,000 |

9.  The contribution margin for Product A is _____.

10.  The contribution margin for Taylor is _____.

**11–12.** At the end of the first year of operations, 3,500 units remained in finished goods inventory. The unit manufacturing costs during the year were as follows:

|  | Unit Costs |
| --- | --- |
| Direct materials | $22 |
| Direct labor | 20 |
| Variable factory overhead | 10 |
| Fixed factory overhead | 4 |

**11.** The cost of the finished goods inventory reported on the balance sheet under the variable costing income statement is _____.

**12.** The cost of the finished goods inventory reported on the balance sheet under the absorption costing income statement is _____.

**13–16.** A business operated at 100% of capacity during its first month of operations with the following results:

| | | |
| --- | --- | --- |
| Sales (22,500 units) | | $1,125,000 |
| Manufacturing costs (25,000 units): | | |
| Direct materials | $300,000 | |
| Direct labor | 250,000 | |
| Variable factory overhead | 200,000 | |
| Fixed factory overhead | 150,000 | 900,000 |
| Selling and administrative expenses: | | |
| Variable | $146,250 | |
| Fixed | 67,500 | 213,750 |

**13.** The amount of the manufacturing margin that would be reported on the variable costing income statement is _____.

**14.** The amount of income from operations that would be reported on the absorption costing income statement is _____.

**15.** The amount of contribution margin that would be reported on the variable costing income statement is _____.

**16.** The amount of income from operations that would be reported on the variable costing income statement is _____.

**17.** In contribution margin analysis, the factor that is responsible for an increase in the amount of sales due to an increase in price is termed the _____ _____.

**18–19.** During the current year, 20,000 units were sold at a variable cost of goods sold of $320,000. The sales were planned for 21,500 units at a variable cost of goods sold of $333,250.

**18.** The amount of difference between the actual and planned variable cost of goods sold due to the quantity factor is _____ (designate amount and direction).

19. The amount of difference between the actual and planned variable cost of goods sold due to the unit cost factor is _____ (designate amount and direction).

20. If the per unit variable selling and administrative expenses were planned to be $2.25 per unit, but were actually $2.00 per unit, then the unit cost factor would result in a(n) _____ (increase or decrease) in contribution margin between planned and actual.

21. If 67,000 miles were planned by a trucking company for the period, but 64,000 miles were actually run at a cost of $1.40 per mile, then the quantity factor would result in a _____ (amount) _____ (increase or decrease) in contribution margin between planned and actual.

## FILL IN THE BLANK—PART B

***Instructions:*** Answer the following questions or complete the statements by writing the appropriate words or amounts in the answer blanks.

1. The term applied to the conventional concept that includes both fixed and variable manufacturing costs as part of the cost of products manufactured is _____ _____.

2. In the variable costing income statement, deducting variable operating expenses from manufacturing margin yields the _____ _____.

3. In the absorption costing income statement, deducting the cost of goods sold from sales yields the _____ _____.

4. In the variable costing income statement, deducting _____ _____ _____ _____ _____ from sales yields the manufacturing margin.

5. The _____ (absorption or variable) costing concept will yield a higher operating income for a period when the number of units manufactured exceeds the units sold.

6. Unlike variable costing, absorption costing treats fixed factory overhead as a(n) _____ cost.

7. The _____ (absorption or variable) costing concept is useful to management in analyzing short-run pricing plans.

8. The _____ (absorption or variable) costing concept is useful to management in analyzing long-run production plans.

9. Direct labor would be _____ (included or excluded) in determining the cost of product under the variable costing concept.

10. Straight-line depreciation on the factory building would be _____ (included or excluded) in determining the cost of product under the variable costing concept.

**11–14.** A business operated at 100% of capacity during its first month of operations with the following results:

| | | |
|---|---|---|
| Sales (14,000 units) ......................... | | $840,000 |
| Manufacturing costs (16,000 units): | | |
| Direct materials ............................. | $256,000 | |
| Direct labor ..................................... | 224,000 | |
| Variable factory overhead .............. | 128,000 | |
| Fixed factory overhead .................. | 80,000 | 688,000 |
| Selling and administrative expenses: | | |
| Variable ......................................... | $119,000 | |
| Fixed ............................................. | 56,000 | 175,000 |

**11.** The amount of contribution margin that would be reported on the variable costing income statement is _____.

**12.** The amount of the manufacturing margin that would be reported on the variable costing income statement is _____.

**13.** The amount of income from operations that would be reported on the absorption costing income statement is _____.

**14.** The amount of income from operations that would be reported on the variable costing income statement is _____.

**15–16.** At the end of the first year of operations, 5,000 units remained in finished goods inventory. The unit manufacturing costs during the year were as follows:

| | Unit Costs |
|---|---|
| Direct materials ............................. | $45 |
| Direct labor ..................................... | 26 |
| Variable factory overhead .............. | 12 |
| Fixed factory overhead .................. | 8 |

**15.** The cost of the finished goods inventory reported on the balance sheet under the variable costing income statement is _____.

**16.** The cost of the finished goods inventory reported on the balance sheet under the absorption costing income statement is _____.

**17.** In contribution margin analysis, the factor that is responsible for an increase in the amount of sales due to an increase in unit volume is termed the _____ _____.

**18–19.** During the current year, 12,500 units were sold at a variable cost of goods sold of $187,500. The sales were planned for 12,000 units at a variable cost of goods sold of $192,000.

**18.** The amount of difference between the actual and planned variable cost of goods sold due to the quantity factor is _____ (designate amount and direction).

19. The amount of difference between the actual and planned variable cost of goods sold due to the unit cost factor is _____ (designate amount and direction).

20. If the instructional cost per student credit hour were planned at $140 per credit hour, but the actual cost was $155 per credit hour for 34,500 actual student credit hours, then the unit cost factor would result in a _____ (amount) _____ (increase or decrease) in contribution margin between planned and actual.


## MULTIPLE CHOICE

*Instructions:*   Circle the best answer for each of the following questions.

1. The manufacturing margin under variable costing is determined by deducting:
    a. equipment depreciation
    b. selling commissions
    c. direct materials
    d. plant manager's salary

2. Which of the following cost elements is included in the cost of goods manufactured under absorption costing but not under variable costing?
    a. direct materials
    b. direct labor
    c. fixed factory overhead
    d. variable factory overhead

3. When units manufactured exceed units sold, the income from operations under absorption costing will be _____ the income from operations under variable costing.
    a. greater than
    b. less than
    c. equal to
    d. either greater than or less than

4. Which of the following would not be deducted in determining the contribution margin under variable costing?
    a. direct labor
    b. sales office depreciation
    c. sales commissions
    d. variable factory overhead

**5–6.** The contribution margin per unit for Products X and Y are $32 and $65 per unit, respectively. Both products are sold in the Northern and Southern territories in the following volumes:

|  | Product X | Product Y |
|---|---|---|
| Northern ......................... | 20,000 units | 30,000 units |
| Southern ......................... | 15,000 | 11,000 |

**5.** The total contribution margin for Product X is:
   **a.** $640,000
   **b.** $1,120,000
   **c.** $1,631,380
   **d.** $2,275,000

**6.** The total contribution margin for the Southern territory is:
   **a.** $832,000
   **b.** $1,195,000
   **c.** $1,615,000
   **d.** $3,785,000

**7.** Which of the following would not be an appropriate use of variable costing?
   **a.** pricing products
   **b.** controlling company-level costs
   **c.** analyzing market segments
   **d.** planning production

**8.** Which of the following is not an example of a market segment?
   **a.** production department
   **b.** territory
   **c.** product
   **d.** customer

**9–10.** The planned sales were 16,000 units at a price of $105 per unit. The actual sales were 15,400 units at a price of $112 per unit.

**9.** The quantity factor is a:
   **a.** $63,000 decrease
   **b.** $63,000 increase
   **c.** $67,200 decrease
   **d.** $67,200 increase

**10.** The price factor is a:
   **a.** $107,800 decrease
   **b.** $107,800 increase
   **c.** $112,000 increase
   **d.** $112,000 decrease

**11–12.** The planned sales were 2,500 units at a variable cost of goods sold of $85 per unit. The actual sales were 2,800 units at a variable cost of goods sold of $80 per unit.

**11.** The quantity factor is a _____ in contribution margin.

    **a.** $24,000 increase

    **b.** $24,000 decrease

    **c.** $25,500 increase

    **d.** $25,500 decrease

**12.** The unit cost factor is a _____ in contribution margin.

    **a.** $12,500 increase

    **b.** $12,500 decrease

    **c.** $14,000 increase

    **d.** $14,000 decrease

**13.** If Salesperson #1 had a contribution ratio of 60%, while Salesperson #2 had a contribution ratio of 40%, then which of the following statements is the best explanation for this result?

    **a.** Salesperson #1 had more total contribution margin than Salesperson #2.

    **b.** Salesperson #1 used less advertising expenditures than Salesperson #2.

    **c.** Salesperson #1 had a more profitable sales mix of products sold than Salesperson #2.

    **d.** Salesperson #1 had a larger sales commission as a percent of sales than Salesperson #2.

**14.** A stockbroker planned on trade execution costs of $2.40 per 100 shares of stock. The broker planned to trade 350,000 shares during the period. However, 375,000 shares were actually traded, and the actual trade execution cost was $2.50 per 100 shares of stock. How much higher was actual contribution margin than planned during the period?

    **a.** $250

    **b.** $375

    **c.** $625

    **d.** $975

# TRUE/FALSE

**Instructions:**   Indicate whether each of the following statements is true or false by placing a check mark in the appropriate column.

|   | | True | False |
|---|---|---|---|
| 1. | Absorption costing includes only variable manufacturing costs in the cost of goods manufactured. ............................ | ____ | ____ |
| 2. | Variable selling expenses are deducted in determining the contribution margin............................................. | ____ | ____ |
| 3. | Fixed factory overhead is deducted in determining the manufacturing margin. ...................................... | ____ | ____ |
| 4. | The income from operations determined under variable and absorption costing cannot be equal. ............................ | ____ | ____ |
| 5. | When units manufactured exceed units sold, the income from operations under variable costing is less than under absorption costing. ............................................. | ____ | ____ |
| 6. | The variable cost of goods sold would include factory equipment depreciation.......................................... | ____ | ____ |
| 7. | Variable costing should be used for short-term pricing decisions. .......................................................... | ____ | ____ |
| 8. | Absorption costing should rarely be used for pricing decisions. .......................................................... | ____ | ____ |
| 9. | Market segment profit analysis should focus on the contribution margin of the segment................................... | ____ | ____ |
| 10. | The quantity factor in contribution margin analysis is determined by multiplying the difference between the actual price and the planned price by the actual quantity sold............................................................... | ____ | ____ |

## EXERCISE 20-1

Power Racquet Inc. manufactures and sells sporting equipment. The company began operations on March 1 and operated at 100% of capacity during the first month. The company produced 45,000 racquets during the month, but sold 42,000 units at $45 per unit. The manufacturing costs and selling and administrative expenses were as follows:

|  | Total Cost | Number of Units | Unit Cost |
|---|---|---|---|
| Manufacturing costs: |  |  |  |
| Variable | $ 810,000 | 45,000 | $18 |
| Fixed | 360,000 | 45,000 | 8 |
| Total costs | $1,170,000 |  | $26 |
| Selling and administrative expenses: |  |  |  |
| Variable ($5 per unit sold) | $ 210,000 |  |  |
| Fixed | 160,000 |  |  |
| Total expenses | $ 370,000 |  |  |
| Total costs and expenses | $1,540,000 |  |  |

### Instructions:

**(1)** Prepare an income statement based on the absorption costing concept.

**(2)** Prepare an income statement based on the variable costing concept.

| | | |
|---|---|---|
| | | |
| | | |
| | | |
| | | |
| | | |
| | | |
| | | |
| | | |
| | | |
| | | |
| | | |
| | | |
| | | |
| | | |
| | | |

**(3)** What is the reason for the difference in the amount of income from operations reported in (1) and (2)?

## EXERCISE 20-2

On May 31, the end of the first month of operations, Jupiter Company prepared the following income statement based on the absorption costing concept:

Jupiter Company
Income Statement
For the Month Ended May 31, 20--

| | | |
|---|---:|---:|
| Sales (46,000 units) | | $650,000 |
| Cost of goods sold: | | |
|    Cost of goods manufactured | $350,000 | |
|    Less inventory, May 31 (4,000 units) | 28,000 | |
|       Cost of goods sold | | 322,000 |
| Gross profit | | $328,000 |
| Selling and administrative expenses | | 145,000 |
| Income from operations | | $183,000 |

**Instructions:** If the fixed manufacturing costs were $140,000 and the variable selling and administrative expenses were $84,000, prepare an income statement according to the variable costing concept.

## EXERCISE 20-3

Snow Glide Company manufactures and sells two styles of skis—Alpine and Nordic. These skis are sold in two regions—Eastern and Western. Information about the two styles of skis is as follows:

|  | Alpine | Nordic |
|---|---|---|
| Sales price | $350 | $400 |
| Variable cost of goods sold per unit | 180 | 280 |
| Manufacturing margin per unit | $170 | $120 |
| Variable selling expense per unit | 100 | 100 |
| Contribution margin per unit | $ 70 | $ 20 |
| Contribution margin ratio | 20% | 5% |

The sales unit volume for the territories and products for the period is as follows:

|  | Eastern | Western |
|---|---|---|
| Alpine | 20,000 | 40,000 |
| Nordic | 30,000 | 10,000 |

### Instructions:

(1) Prepare a contribution margin report by sales territory.

|  | Eastern | Western |
|---|---|---|
|  |  |  |
|  |  |  |
|  |  |  |
|  |  |  |
|  |  |  |
|  |  |  |
|  |  |  |
|  |  |  |

(2) What advice would you give to the management of Snow Glide Company?

## PROBLEM 20-1

During the first month of operations ended June 30, QuickKey Company manufactured 24,000 computer keyboards, of which 22,500 were sold. Operating data for the month are summarized as follows:

| | | |
|---|---|---|
| Sales .................................................................. | | $1,912,500 |
| Manufacturing costs: | | |
|     Direct materials ......................................... | $612,000 | |
|     Direct labor ............................................... | 460,800 | |
|     Variable manufacturing cost ...................... | 192,000 | |
|     Fixed manufacturing cost ........................... | 132,000 | $1,396,800 |
| Selling and administrative expenses: | | |
|     Variable ..................................................... | $270,000 | |
|     Fixed ......................................................... | 123,750 | $ 393,750 |

### Instructions:

(1) Prepare an income statement based on the absorption costing concept.

**(2)** Prepare an income statement based on the variable costing concept.

|  |  |  |
|---|---|---|
|  |  |  |
|  |  |  |
|  |  |  |
|  |  |  |
|  |  |  |
|  |  |  |
|  |  |  |
|  |  |  |
|  |  |  |
|  |  |  |
|  |  |  |
|  |  |  |
|  |  |  |
|  |  |  |
|  |  |  |
|  |  |  |
|  |  |  |
|  |  |  |
|  |  |  |

**(3)** Explain the reason for the difference in the amount of income from operations reported in (1) and (2).

## PROBLEM 20-2

The following data for Ho Company are available for the year ended December 31, 2010:

| | Actual | Planned | Difference—Increase or (Decrease) |
|---|---|---|---|
| Sales ....................................................... | $900,000 | $814,000 | $86,000 |
| Less: | | | |
|    Variable cost of goods sold ............. | $382,500 | $369,600 | $12,900 |
|    Variable selling and administrative expenses ........................................ | 238,500 | 246,400 | (7,900) |
|       Total ........................................... | $621,000 | $616,000 | $ 5,000 |
| Contribution margin .............................. | $279,000 | $198,000 | $81,000 |
| Number of units sold ............................. | 45,000 | 44,000 | |
| Per unit: | | | |
|    Sales price ........................................ | $20.00 | $18.50 | |
|    Variable cost of goods sold ............. | $8.50 | $8.40 | |
|    Variable selling and administrative expenses ........................................ | $5.30 | $5.60 | |

**Instructions:**   Prepare a contribution margin analysis of the sales and variable costs for Ho Company for the year ended December 31, 2010. Include in your analysis both quantity and unit price/cost factors.

## PROBLEM 20-3

The Sleepy Hollow Hotel Company operates hotels in three regions. The following information was determined from company records for the most recent period ending December 31:

Unit Cost and Revenue Information:

| | |
|---|---|
| Registration and checkout cost per guest ................... | $7 |
| Housekeeping cost per room night ............................. | $18 |
| Revenue per room night ........................................... | $92 |

Regional Information:

| | East | West | South | Total |
|---|---|---|---|---|
| Number of guests .......................... | 3,000 | 5,000 | 4,000 | 12,000 |
| Number of room nights ................. | 3,600 | 15,000 | 6,000 | 24,600 |

Planned Information:

| | |
|---|---|
| Registration and checkout cost per guest ................... | $5 |
| Housekeeping cost per room night ............................. | $19 |
| Revenue per room night ............................................ | $90 |
| Number of guests ...................................................... | 14,000 |
| Number of room nights .............................................. | 20,000 |

*Instructions:*

**(1)** Prepare a contribution margin report by region.

| | EAST | WEST | SOUTH | TOTAL |
|---|---|---|---|---|
| | | | | |
| | | | | |
| | | | | |
| | | | | |
| | | | | |
| | | | | |
| | | | | |
| | | | | |
| | | | | |
| | | | | |
| | | | | |

**(2)** Prepare a contribution margin analysis of the revenue and variable costs for Sleepy Hollow Hotel Company for the period. Include in your analysis both quantity and unit price/cost factors.

| | | |
|---|---|---|
| | | |
| | | |
| | | |
| | | |
| | | |
| | | |
| | | |
| | | |
| | | |
| | | |
| | | |
| | | |
| | | |
| | | |
| | | |
| | | |
| | | |
| | | |
| | | |
| | | |

# 21

# Budgeting

## QUIZ AND TEST HINTS

The following hints may be helpful to you in preparing for a quiz or a test over the material covered in Chapter 21.

1. Many new terms are introduced in this chapter. You can expect true/false, multiple-choice, or matching questions testing your knowledge of these terms. Review the "Key Terms" section at the end of the chapter and be sure you understand each term. Do the Matching and Fill-in-the-Blank exercises included in this Study Guide.

2. A major emphasis of this chapter is budgeting for manufacturing operations. You should be familiar with all the budgets illustrated in the chapter. The order in which the budgets are normally prepared is the same as that presented in the chapter. For example, the sales budget is normally presented first, followed by the production budget, and so on. You may be required to prepare one of these budgets on a test.

3. The cash budget, or elements thereof, such as the budgeted cash receipts or cash disbursements, will often be the subject of an exam question.

4. You can also expect to see some multiple-choice questions that require the computation of the amount of materials to be purchased, units to be produced, cash receipts for a month, and so on, as part of the budgeting process.

5. Review the "At A Glance" section at the end of the chapter. Read and review each of the Key Points and related Learning Outcomes. For each Learning Outcome that has an Example Exercise, locate the Example Exercise in the chapter and be sure that you understand the solution and can work a similar item on a test. If you have any questions about an Example Exercise, read the section of the chapter immediately preceding the Example Exercise.

## MATCHING

***Instructions:*** Match each of the statements below with its proper term. Some terms may not be used.

A. budget
B. budgetary slack
C. capital expenditures budget
D. cash budget
E. continuous budgeting
F. cost of goods sold budget
G. direct labor cost budget
H. direct materials purchases budget

I. flexible budget
J. goal conflict
K. master budget
L. production budget
M. responsibility center
N. sales budget
O. static budget
P. zero-based budgeting

_____ 1. The comprehensive budget plan linking all the individual budgets related to sales, cost of goods sold, operating expenses, projects, capital expenditures, and cash.

_____ 2. A method of budgeting that provides for maintaining a twelve-month projection into the future.

_____ 3. A concept of budgeting that requires all levels of management to start from zero and estimate budget data as if there had been no previous activities in their units.

_____ 4. An accounting device used to plan and control resources of operational departments and divisions.

_____ 5. A budget that uses the production budget as a starting point for planning materials requirements.

_____ 6. The budget summarizing future plans for acquiring plant facilities and equipment.

_____ 7. A budget of the estimated direct materials, direct labor, and factory overhead consumed by sold products.

_____ 8. A budget of estimated unit production.

_____ 9. A budget that does not adjust to changes in activity levels.

_____ 10. A budget that adjusts for varying rates of activity.

_____ 11. A budget of estimated cash receipts and payments.

_____ 12. An organizational unit for which a manager is assigned responsibility over costs, revenues, or assets.

_____ 13. Excess resources set within a budget to provide for uncertain events.

_____ 14. A budget that uses a production budget as a starting point for planning direct labor requirements.

## FILL IN THE BLANK—PART A

*Instructions:*   Answer the following questions or complete the statements by writing the appropriate words or amounts in the answer blanks.

1. The document that charts a course of future action for a business by outlining the plans of the business in financial terms is the _____.

2. Establishing specific goals for future operations is part of the _____ function of management.

3. The budgetary units of an organization are called _____ _____.

4. Comparing actual results to the plan to help prevent unplanned expenditures is part of the _____ function of management.

5. A budget that establishes lower goals than may be possible is said to contain budgetary _____.

6. When individual objectives are opposed to those that are in the best interests of the business, the situation can be described as a(n) _____ _____.

7. The length of time for which the operating budget normally is prepared is a(n) _____ _____.

8. Budgets are usually monitored and summarized by the _____ Department.

9. A(n) _____ budget shows the expected results of a responsibility center for only one activity level.

10. When constructing a flexible budget, the planner must begin by identifying _____ _____ _____.

11. Manufacturing operations require a series of budgets that are linked together in a(n) _____ _____.

12–13. The budget process is started by preparing a sales budget. For each product, the sales budget normally indicates the:

12. _____ _____ _____ _____, and

13. _____ _____ _____ _____.

14. The following data are available from the production budget of O'Connor Inc. for Product X:

Expected units of sales ................................. 615,000
Estimated units in beginning inventory .......... 73,500
Total units to be produced ........................... 705,500

The desired units in ending inventory are _____.

15. The _____ budget is the starting point for determining the estimated quantities of direct materials to be purchased.

16. The budgets that are used by managers to plan financing, investing, and cash objectives are the _____ _____

    _____ .

17. The _____ budget presents the expected receipts (inflow) and payments (outflow) of cash for a period of time.

18. The _____ _____ budget summarizes plans for acquiring fixed assets.

19–20. The Townsend Co. production budget for Product X is 300,000 units. Product X is manufactured in two departments. Direct labor in Department 1 is 0.2 hour per unit at an hourly pay rate of $17. Department 2 direct labor requirements for Product X are 0.08 hour per unit at an hourly pay rate of $20.

19. Total hours required for production of Product X are _____.

20. Total direct labor cost is _____.

## FILL IN THE BLANK—PART B

*Instructions:* Answer the following questions or complete the statements by writing the appropriate words or amounts in the answer blanks.

1. Executing actions to meet the goals of the business is the _____ function of management.

2. Giving information to employees about their performance relative to the goals they helped establish is called _____.

3. The budget becomes less effective as a tool for planning or controlling operations if employees view budget goals as unachievable. This occurs when the budget is set too _____.

4. When budgets establish lower goals than may be possible, they are said to be "padded" or to contain _____ _____.

5. The manager of the transportation department was directed to stay within the department budget. To accomplish this goal, the manager stopped shipping to customers for an entire month. This manager's behavior is said to exhibit _____ _____.

6. A variation of fiscal-year budgeting that seeks to maintain a twelve-month projection into the future is called _____

    _____.

7. _____-_____ budgeting requires managers to estimate sales, production, and other operating data as though operations are being started for the first time.

8. XYZ Motor Co. establishes its budget at only one level of activity. This type of budget is called a(n) _____ _____.

9. PDQ Construction Co. prepares its budgets based on 8,000, 9,000, and 10,000 units of production. This type of budget is known as a(n)

   _____ _____.

10. _____ budgeting systems speed up and reduce the cost of preparing budgets.

11. The budget process begins by estimating _____.

12. The production budgets are used to prepare the direct materials purchases, direct labor cost, and _____ _____ _____ budgets.

13. The direct materials purchases, direct labor cost, and factory overhead cost budgets are used to develop the _____ \_\_\_\_\_ _____ _____ budget.

14. Two major budgets comprising the budgeted balance sheet are the cash budget and the _____ _____ budget.

15. The starting point often used in estimating the quantity of sales for each product in the sales budget is _____ _____

   _____.

16. The number of units to be manufactured to meet budgeted sales and inventory needs is set forth in the _____ budget.

17. The _____ _____ _____ budget is prepared based on the production budget and the estimated labor requirements for each unit of product.

18. The _____ _____ _____ allows management to assess the effects of the individual budgets on profits for the year.

19–20. Goldman Inc. uses a flexible budgeting system to plan for its manufacturing operations. The static budget for 9,000 units of production provides for direct labor at $5 per unit and variable electric at $0.60 per unit. Fixed costs are electric power, $1,000, and supervisor salaries of $17,500.

19. Variable costs for 10,000 units of production are _____.

20. Fixed costs for 10,000 units of production are _____.

## MULTIPLE CHOICE

*Instructions:*   Circle the best answer for each of the following questions.

1. Which of the following budgets provides the starting point for preparing the direct labor cost budget?
   a. direct materials purchases budget
   b. cash budget
   c. production budget
   d. cost of goods sold budget

2. The budget which provides data on the quantities of direct materials purchases necessary to meet production needs is the:
   a. direct materials purchases budget
   b. sales budget
   c. production budget
   d. direct labor cost budget

3. This budget summarizes future plans for the acquisition of plant facilities and equipment.
   a. budgeted balance sheet
   b. production budget
   c. cash budget
   d. capital expenditures budget

4. A series of budgeted amounts for varying levels of activity is called a:
   a. variable budget
   b. continuous budget
   c. flexible budget
   d. zero-based budget

5. Which of the following budgets is used most frequently for administrative functions?
   a. phased budget
   b. zero-based budget
   c. static budget
   d. flexible budget

6. Assume 80% of sales are collected in the month of sale, with the remainder collected the following month. Sales for October and November were $640,000 and $860,000, respectively. What are the cash receipts from accounts receivable collections for November?
   a. $684,000
   b. $816,000
   c. $812,000
   d. $860,000

7. A method of budgeting which requires managers to estimate sales, production, and other operating data as though operations were being started for the first time is called:

   a. zero-based budgeting

   b. master budgeting

   c. flexible budgeting

   d. continuous budgeting

8. A method of budgeting which maintains a twelve-month projection into the future is called:

   a. annual budgeting

   b. continuous budgeting

   c. perpetual budgeting

   d. dynamic budgeting

9. An organizational unit with a manager who has authority and responsibility for the unit's performance is called a(n):

   a. economic unit

   b. profit center

   c. budgetary center

   d. responsibility center

10. Assume estimated sales for the coming year is 280,000 units. The estimated inventory at the beginning of the year is 25,000 units, and the desired inventory at the end of the year is 35,000 units. The total production indicated in the production budget is:

    a. 290,000 units

    b. 270,000 units

    c. 305,000 units

    d. 315,000 units

11. The direct materials purchases budget totals $1,200,000, while the direct labor cost budget totals $650,000. The factory overhead is budgeted at $900,000. The budgeted inventory information is as follows:

    |                | Beginning Inventory | Ending Inventory |
    |----------------|---------------------|------------------|
    | Materials      | $45,000             | $40,000          |
    | Finished goods | $80,000             | $95,000          |

    What is the cost of goods sold budgeted for the period?

    a. $2,730,000

    b. $2,740,000

    c. $2,750,000

    d. $2,760,000

12. Manufacturing costs are estimated to be $360,000 and $450,000 for July and August, respectively. These amounts include $30,000 of monthly depreciation plant and equipment expense. Cash payments are paid such that 60% are paid in the month incurred and 40% are paid in the following month. What are the budgeted cash payments for August?

    a. $252,000

    b. $366,000

    c. $384,000

    d. $414,000

## TRUE/FALSE

*Instructions:* Indicate whether each of the following statements is true or false by placing a check mark in the appropriate column.

|  | True | False |
|---|---|---|
| 1. A zero-based budget is actually a series of budgets for varying rates of activity.......... | ____ | ____ |
| 2. A budgeting method which provides for maintenance of a twelve-month projection into the future is called continuous budgeting. ............ | ____ | ____ |
| 3. Computers are seldom used in the budget process, although computers can reduce the cost of budget preparation. ............ | ____ | ____ |
| 4. The number of units of each commodity expected to be manufactured to meet budgeted sales and inventory requirements is set forth in the production budget............ | ____ | ____ |
| 5. A schedule of collections from sales is useful for developing a cash budget............ | ____ | ____ |
| 6. The amount of the expenditures for fixed assets such as machinery and equipment usually remains fairly constant from year to year............ | ____ | ____ |
| 7. Minimum cash balances are maintained to serve as a safety buffer for variations in estimates and for unexpected emergencies............ | ____ | ____ |
| 8. The budgeted balance sheet brings together the projection of all profit-making phases of operations. ............ | ____ | ____ |
| 9. The first budget usually prepared is the cash budget. ......... | ____ | ____ |
| 10. The sales budget normally indicates for each product the quantity of estimated sales and the expected unit selling price. ............ | ____ | ____ |

## EXERCISE 21-1

Texier Inc. manufactures two products, C and Q. It is estimated that the May 1 inventory will consist of 8,000 units of C and 21,000 units of Q. Estimated sales for May by sales territory are as follows:

East:      Product C—60,000 units at $15 per unit
           Product Q—75,000 units at $8 per unit

West:      Product C—80,000 units at $20 per unit
           Product Q—50,000 units at $10 per unit

An ending inventory of 20% of May sales is desired.

*Instructions:* Complete the following sales and production budgets for the month of May.

| | A | B | C | D |
|---|---|---|---|---|
| 1 | Texier Inc. | | | |
| 2 | Sales Budget | | | |
| 3 | For the Month of May, 20-- | | | |
| 4 | Product and Area | Unit Sales Volume | Unit Selling Price | Total Sales |
| 5 | Product C: | | | |
| 6 | East area | | | |
| 7 | West area | | | |
| 8 | Total | | | |
| 9 | Product Q: | | | |
| 10 | East area | | | |
| 11 | West area | | | |
| 12 | Total | | | |
| 13 | Total revenue from sales | | | |

| | A | B | C |
|---|---|---|---|
| 1 | Texier Inc. | | |
| 2 | Production Budget | | |
| 3 | For the Month of May, 20-- | | |
| 4 | | Units | |
| 5 | | Product C | Product Q |
| 6 | Sales | | |
| 7 | Plus desired inventory, May 31 | | |
| 8 | Total | | |
| 9 | Less estimated inventory, May 1 | | |
| 10 | Total production | | |

# EXERCISE 21-2

*Instructions:* Complete the following factory overhead cost budget for Nathalie Inc. for the month of January. The items listed as variable costs are assumed to vary directly with the units of product. The items listed as fixed costs are assumed to remain constant regardless of units produced.

| | A | B | C | D |
|---|---|---|---|---|
| 1 | Nathalie Inc. | | | |
| 2 | Factory Overhead Cost Budget | | | |
| 3 | For the Month of January, 20-- | | | |
| 4 | Units of product | 30,000 | 60,000 | 90,000 |
| 5 | Variable cost: | | | |
| 6 | Indirect factory wages ($.80 per unit) | $24,000 | | |
| 7 | Indirect materials ($.45 per unit) | 13,500 | | |
| 8 | Electric power ($.60 per unit) | 18,000 | | |
| 9 | Total variable cost | $55,500 | | |
| 10 | Fixed cost: | | | |
| 11 | Supervisory salaries | $30,000 | | |
| 12 | Depreciation of plant and equipment | 18,000 | | |
| 13 | Property taxes | 12,000 | | |
| 14 | Insurance | 7,500 | | |
| 15 | Electric power | 4,500 | | |
| 16 | Total fixed cost | $72,000 | | |
| 17 | Total factory overhead cost | $127,500 | | |

## EXERCISE 21-3

The Gyro Company budgeted sales of 500,000 units of Product A. Each unit of Product A requires 0.5 pounds of Material XX and 1.2 pounds of Material ZZ. Estimated and desired inventory information is as follows:

| | Estimated Beginning Inventory | Desired Ending Inventory |
|---|---|---|
| Product A ........................ | 12,000 | 10,000 |
| Material XX .................... | 8,000 | 14,000 |
| Material ZZ .................... | 20,000 | 25,000 |

### Instructions:

**(1)** Prepare a production budget.

| | A | B |
|---|---|---|
| 1 | Gyro Company | |
| 2 | Production Budget | |
| 3 | | Product A |
| 4 | | |
| 5 | | |
| 6 | | |
| 7 | | |
| 8 | | |

**(2)** Prepare a direct materials purchases budget, assuming a price per pound of $4 and $6 for Materials XX and ZZ, respectively.

| | A | B | C |
|---|---|---|---|
| 1 | Gyro Company | | |
| 2 | Direct Materials Purchases Budget | | |
| 3 | | Material XX | Material ZZ |
| 4 | | | |
| 5 | | | |
| 6 | | | |
| 7 | | | |
| 8 | | | |
| 9 | | | |
| 10 | | | |
| 11 | | | |
| 12 | | | |
| 13 | | | |

## EXERCISE 21-4

The Gyro Company from Exercise 21-3 budgeted sales of 500,000 units of Product A. Each unit of Product A requires 0.40 hours of Assembly Department labor at a cost of $12 per hour and 0.25 hours of Packing Department labor at a cost of $9 per hour. Estimated and desired inventory information is as follows:

|  | Estimated Beginning Inventory | Desired Ending Inventory |
|---|---|---|
| Product A ........................ | 12,000 | 10,000 |

**Instructions:**   Prepare a direct labor cost budget for Gyro Company.

| | A | B | C | D |
|---|---|---|---|---|
| 1 | Gyro Company | | | |
| 2 | Direct Labor Cost Budget | | | |
| 3 | | Assembly Dept. | Packing Dept. | Total |
| 4 | | | | |
| 5 | | | | |
| 6 | | | | |
| 7 | | | | |
| 8 | | | | |
| 9 | | | | |
| 10 | | | | |

## PROBLEM 21-1

The treasurer of Amant Inc. has accumulated the following budget information for the next two months:

| | March | April |
|---|---|---|
| Sales .................................................. | $240,000 | $200,000 |
| Merchandise costs ........................ | 150,000 | 120,000 |
| Operating expenses ...................... | 60,000 | 40,000 |
| Capital expenditures ...................... | — | 125,000 |

The company expects to sell about 40% of its merchandise for cash. Of sales on account, 80% are expected to be collected in full in the month of the sale and the remainder in the month following the sale. One-third of the merchandise costs are expected to be paid in the month in which they are incurred and the other two-thirds in the following month. Depreciation, insurance, and property taxes represent $20,000 of the probable monthly operating expenses. Insurance is paid in December and a $5,000 installment on property taxes is expected to be paid in March. Of the remainder of the operating expenses, 60% are expected to be paid in the month in which they are incurred and the balance in the following month. Capital expenditures of $125,000 are expected to be paid in April.

Current assets as of March 1 are composed of cash of $24,000 and accounts receivable of $45,000. Current liabilities as of March 1 are composed of accounts payable of $90,000 ($80,000 for merchandise purchases and $10,000 for operating expenses). Management desires to maintain a minimum cash balance of $50,000 at the end of March and April.

***Instructions:*** Prepare a monthly cash budget for March and April.

| | A | B | C |
|---|---|---|---|
| 1 | Amant Inc. | | |
| 2 | Cash Budget | | |
| 3 | For Two Months Ending April 30, 20-- | | |
| 4 | | March | April |
| 5 | | | |
| 6 | | | |
| 7 | | | |
| 8 | | | |
| 9 | | | |
| 10 | | | |
| 11 | | | |
| 12 | | | |
| 13 | | | |
| 14 | | | |
| 15 | | | |
| 16 | | | |
| 17 | | | |
| 18 | | | |
| 19 | | | |

# PROBLEM 21-2

The Fernandez Furniture Company produces two products, Product A and Product B. The management wishes to budget the sales, production, direct material, and direct labor for the upcoming year. In order to meet this request you have obtained information from various managers throughout the organization. The sales budget was provided by the Sales Department as follows:

| Product | Unit Sales Volume | Unit Sales Price | Total Sales |
|---------|------------------|------------------|-------------|
| Product A .............. | 168,000 | $4.20 | $ 705,600 |
| Product B .............. | 324,000 | $8.80 | 2,851,200 |
| Total ......................................................................... | | | $3,556,800 |

Information about the inventories for Product A and Product B was obtained by the production manager:

| | Product A | Product B |
|---|-----------|-----------|
| Estimated units in beginning inventory ........... | 12,000 | 24,000 |
| Desired units in ending inventory ................... | 8,000 | 36,000 |

The materials manager provided information about the materials used in production. There are three different materials used to manufacture Fernandez products: Material X, Material Y, and Material Z. The standard number of pounds required for each unit of Product A and B was determined from the bill of materials:

| Standard material pounds per unit | Product A | Product B |
|-----------------------------------|-----------|-----------|
| Material X ................................................. | 0.6 pounds | 1.8 pounds |
| Material Y ................................................. | | 3.4 pounds |
| Material Z ................................................. | 1.2 pounds | |

The purchasing manager provided the standard price per pound for each of the materials:

| Material | Price per Pound |
|----------|-----------------|
| Material X .................................... | $0.40 |
| Material Y .................................... | $0.50 |
| Material Z .................................... | $0.60 |

The materials manager was responsible for the materials inventories and provided the following inventory information:

| | Product | | |
|---|---|---|---|
| | Material X | Material Y | Material Z |
| Estimated units in beginning inventory ..... | 16,000 | 5,600 | 12,400 |
| Desired units in ending inventory ............. | 14,500 | 8,700 | 9,800 |

Products A and B are manufactured in two departments, 1 and 2. The industrial engineers provided standard direct labor information from the routing files.

| Standard hours per unit | Dept. 1 | Dept. 2 |
|---|---|---|
| Product A ................................................. | 0.20 hours | 0.15 hours |
| Product B ................................................. | 0.05 hours | 0.10 hours |

The labor rates in each department were provided by the department supervisor for each department.

| | Dept. 1 | Dept. 2 |
|---|---|---|
| Labor cost per hour ................................. | $14.00 | $18.00 |

**Instructions:**   Construct the following budgets for Fernandez Furniture Company:

**(1)**  Production budget

**(2)**  Direct materials purchases budget

**(3)**  Direct labor cost budget

**(1)**

| | A | B | C |
|---|---|---|---|
| 1 | Fernandez Furniture Company | | |
| 2 | Production Budget | | |
| 3 | | Product A | Product B |
| 4 | | | |
| 5 | | | |
| 6 | | | |
| 7 | | | |

**(2)**

| | A | B | C | D | E |
|---|---|---|---|---|---|
| 1 | Fernandez Furniture Company | | | | |
| 2 | Direct Materials Purchases Budget | | | | |
| 3 | | Material X | Material Y | Material Z | Total |
| 4 | | | | | |
| 5 | | | | | |
| 6 | | | | | |
| 7 | | | | | |
| 8 | | | | | |
| 9 | | | | | |
| 10 | | | | | |
| 11 | | | | | |
| 12 | | | | | |

**(3)**

| | A | B | C | D |
|---|---|---|---|---|
| 1 | Fernandez Furniture Company | | | |
| 2 | Direct Labor Cost Budget | | | |
| 3 | | Department 1 | Department 2 | Total |
| 4 | | | | |
| 5 | | | | |
| 6 | | | | |
| 7 | | | | |
| 8 | | | | |

# 22 Performance Evaluation Using Variances from Standard Costs

## QUIZ AND TEST HINTS

The following hints may be helpful to you in preparing for a quiz or a test over the material covered in Chapter 22.

1. Many new terms are introduced in this chapter. You can expect true/false, multiple-choice, or matching questions testing your knowledge of these terms. Review the "Key Terms" section at the end of the chapter and be sure you understand each term. Do the Matching and Fill-in-the-Blank exercises included in this Study Guide.

2. The major emphasis of this chapter is standard costing. You should be able to compute the six variances illustrated in the chapter. Be prepared to use the formulas for calculating the six variances illustrated in this chapter. The Illustrative Problem at the end of the chapter is a good study aid for the computation of variances.

3. You also should be able to perform variance analysis based on a flexible budget.

4. Depending upon whether your instructor emphasized standards in the accounts in lecture or through homework, you may be required to prepare journal entries for incorporating standards in the accounts. If your instructor did not cover this topic in class, then do not spend much time studying this section of the chapter.

5. Review the "At A Glance" section at the end of the chapter. Read and review each of the Key Points and related Learning Outcomes. For each Learning Outcome that has an Example Exercise, locate the Example Exercise in the chapter and be sure that you understand the solution and can work a similar item on a test. If you have any questions about an Example Exercise, read the section of the chapter immediately preceding the Example Exercise.

## MATCHING

*Instructions:* Match each of the statements below with its proper term. Some terms may not be used.

A.  budget performance report
B.  budgeted variable factory overhead
C.  controllable variance
D.  cost variance
E.  currently attainable standards
F.  direct labor rate variance
G.  direct labor time variance
H.  direct materials price variance
I.  direct materials quantity variance
J.  factory overhead cost variance report

K.  favorable cost variance
L.  ideal standards
M.  non-financial performance measures
N.  process
O.  standards
P.  standard cost
Q.  standard cost systems
R.  total manufacturing cost variance
S.  unfavorable cost variance
T.  volume variance

_____  1.  Standards that represent levels of operation that can be obtained with reasonable effort.

_____  2.  The cost associated with the difference between the standard quantity and the actual quantity of direct materials used in producing a commodity.

_____  3.  A report comparing actual results with budget figures.

_____  4.  Standards that represent levels of performance that can be achieved only under perfect operating conditions.

_____  5.  An estimate of the cost of direct materials, direct labor, and factory overhead required by a product.

_____  6.  The difference between the budgeted fixed overhead at 100% of normal capacity and the standard fixed overhead for the actual production achieved during the period.

_____  7.  The cost associated with the difference between the standard hours and the actual hours of direct labor spent producing a commodity.

_____  8.  The difference between the actual amount of variable factory overhead cost incurred and the amount of variable factory overhead budgeted for actual production.

_____  9.  The cost associated with the difference between the standard price and the actual price of direct materials used in producing a commodity.

_____  10.  The difference between the actual cost and the standard cost.

_____  11.  The cost associated with the difference between the standard rate and the actual rate paid for direct labor used in producing a commodity.

_____  12.  Accounting systems that use standards for each manufacturing cost entering into the finished product.

____ 13. A performance measure expressed in units other than dollars.

____ 14. Occurs when the actual cost is less than the standard cost.

____ 15. A sequence of activities for performing a task.

____ 16. The standard variable factory overhead for the actual units produced.

____ 17. Occurs when the actual cost exceeds the standard cost.

____ 18. The difference between total standard costs and total actual cost for the units produced.

____ 19. A report used by management to control factory overhead costs and variances.

____ 20. Performance goals.

## FILL IN THE BLANK—PART A

*Instructions:* Answer the following questions or complete the statements by writing the appropriate words or amounts in the answer blanks.

1. Accounting systems that use standards for each element of manufacturing cost entering into the finished product are called _____

   _____ _____.

2. When actual costs are compared with standard costs, only variances are reported for cost control. This reporting philosophy is known as the

   _____ _____ _____.

3. Standards that allow for no idle time, no machine breakdowns, and no materials spoilage are called _____ standards.

4. _____ _____ standards can be attained with reasonable effort and allow for normal production difficulties and mistakes.

5. Standards for direct materials, direct labor, and factory overhead are separated into two components: a price standard and a(n) _____ standard.

6. The _____ department is responsible for the direct materials price per square yard.

7. The difference between the actual cost and the standard cost at the actual volume is called a(n) _____ _____.

8. The sum of the direct materials cost variance, direct labor cost variance, and factory overhead cost variance is the _____ _____ cost variance.

9. The difference between the actual quantity used and the standard quantity at actual production, multiplied by the standard price per unit is the

   _____ _____ _____ _____.

10. If the actual quantity of materials used was 7,000 units at an actual price of $5 per unit and the standard quantity was 6,800 units at a standard price of $5.10 per unit, the materials price variance is _____.

11. The difference between the actual hours worked and the standard hours at actual production, multiplied by the standard rate per hour results in the _____ _____ _____ _____.

12. If the actual hours worked are 3,000 at an actual rate per hour of $12 and the standard hours are 3,100 at $11 per hour, the total direct labor cost variance is _____.

13. The _____ variance measures the efficiency of using variable overhead resources.

14. If actual variable factory overhead is $11,400, actual fixed factory overhead is $13,000, and budgeted variable factory overhead for the actual amount produced is $14,400, the controllable variance is _____.

15. The difference between the budgeted fixed overhead at 100% of normal capacity and the standard fixed overhead for actual production achieved is called the _____ _____.

16. The difference between the actual factory overhead and the total overhead applied to production is the _____ _____ _____ _____ variance.

17. The factory overhead cost variance can be verified for each variable factory overhead cost and fixed factory overhead cost element in the _____ _____ _____ _____ _____.

18. A favorable direct materials quantity variance is recorded by crediting _____ _____ _____ _____.

19. At the end of the fiscal year, minor standard cost variances are usually transferred to the _____ _____ _____ _____ account.

20. A way to bring broader perspectives, such as quality of work, to evaluating performance is to supplement financial performance measures with _____ _____ measures.

21. Nonfinancial measures can be either a(n) _____ or _____ of an activity or process.

22. A(n) _____ is a sequence of linked activities for performing a task.

23. When the actual cost exceeds the standard cost the variance is said to be _____.

# FILL IN THE BLANK—PART B

*Instructions:* Answer the following questions or complete the statements by writing the appropriate words or amounts in the answer blanks.

1. A management accounting system that enables management to determine how much a product should cost, how much it does cost, and the causes of any difference is called a(n) _____ _____ _____.

2. Standard setting normally requires the joint efforts of accountants, managers, and _____.

3. Standards that can only be achieved under perfect operating conditions are called _____ _____.

4. Duva Co. assumes normal production difficulties in its standard setting process. These standards are known as _____ _____ standards.

5. The control function of the management process requires actual performance to be compared against the budget. This is known as

   _____ _____ _____.

6. The actual costs, standard amounts for the actual level of production achieved, and the differences between the two amounts are summarized in the _____ _____ report.

7. When actual cost exceeds budgeted cost at actual volumes, the result is a(n) _____ (favorable/unfavorable) variance.

8. The difference between the actual price per unit and the standard price per unit, multiplied by the actual quantity of materials is the _____

   _____ _____ _____.

9. Excessive amounts of direct materials were used by the Hawk Shirt Manufacturing Co. because equipment used in production was not properly maintained and operated. The variance that resulted was a(n) _____

   _____ _____ _____.

10. The actual price of direct materials used to manufacture Product B was $0.03 per unit. The standard materials price was established at $0.02. The department responsible for the variance is the _____

    _____.

11. If the actual quantity of materials used was 7,000 units at an actual price of $5 per unit and the standard quantity was 6,800 units at a standard price of $5.10 per unit, the total materials cost variance is _____.

12. The difference between the actual rate per hour and the standard rate per hour, multiplied by the actual hours worked is the _____

    _____ _____ _____.

13. If the actual hours worked are 3,000 at an actual rate per hour of $12 and the standard hours are 3,100 at $11 per hour, the direct labor time variance is _____.

14. Controlling direct labor cost is normally the responsibility of the
_____ _____.

15. The impact of changing production on fixed and variable factory overhead costs can be determined by using a(n) _____ budget.

16. The difference between the actual variable overhead incurred and the budgeted variable overhead for actual production is the variable factory overhead _____ _____.

17. The efficiency of using variable overhead resources is measured by the _____ _____.

18. If budgeted fixed overhead is $12,000, standard fixed overhead for the actual production achieved is $13,000, and actual variable overhead is $13,700, the volume variance is _____.

19. An unfavorable direct materials price variance is recorded by debiting _____ _____ _____ _____.

20. Measuring both financial and _____ performance helps employees consider multiple performance objectives.

21. A chain of nonfinancial inputs and outputs can be _____ across a set of connected activities.

22. The total _____ _____ _____ is the difference between total standard costs and total actual cost for the units produced.

## MULTIPLE CHOICE

*Instructions:*  Circle the best answer for each of the following questions.

1. Standard costs serve as a device for measuring:
   a. efficiency
   b. nonfinancial performance
   c. volume
   d. quantity

2. Woodson Inc. produced 6,000 light fixtures in May of the current year. Each unit requires 0.75 standard hours. The standard labor rate is $10 per hour. Actual direct labor for May was 4,800 hours. What is the direct labor time variance?
   a. $3,000 favorable
   b. $6,000 unfavorable
   c. $3,000 unfavorable
   d. $9,000 favorable

3. The following data relate to direct materials cost for May:

   Standard costs (5,000 lbs. at $2 per lb.) .............. $10,000
   Actual costs (5,100 lbs. at $3 per lb.) .................. 15,300

   What is the direct materials quantity variance?

   a. $200 favorable
   b. $200 unfavorable
   c. $300 favorable
   d. $300 unfavorable

4. Lloyd Company produces music boxes. The standard factory overhead cost at 100% of normal capacity is $100,000 (20,000 hours at $5: $3 variable, $2 fixed). If 700 hours were unused, the fixed factory overhead volume variance would be:

   a. $700 favorable
   b. $1,400 favorable
   c. $2,100 unfavorable
   d. $1,400 unfavorable

5. The Hill Company produced 5,000 units of X. The standard time per unit is 0.25 hours. The actual hours used to produce 5,000 units of X were 1,350 hours. The standard labor rate is $12 per hour. The actual labor cost was $18,900. What is the total direct labor cost variance?

   a. $1,200 unfavorable
   b. $3,900 unfavorable
   c. $1,400 unfavorable
   d. $2,700 unfavorable

6. The cost associated with the difference between the standard quantity and the actual quantity of direct materials used in producing a commodity is called the:

   a. direct materials quantity variance
   b. direct materials price variance
   c. direct materials volume variance
   d. controllable materials variance

7. The cost associated with the difference between the standard hours and the actual hours of direct labor spent producing a commodity is called the:

   a. direct labor quantity variance
   b. direct labor volume variance
   c. direct labor rate variance
   d. direct labor time variance

8. The difference between the budgeted fixed overhead at 100% of normal capacity and the standard fixed overhead for the actual production achieved during the period is called the:

   a. efficiency variance

   b. controllable variance

   c. volume variance

   d. total overhead variance

9. An unfavorable volume variance might be caused by which of the following factors?

   a. an uneven work flow

   b. machine breakdowns

   c. repairs leading to work stoppages

   d. all of the above

10. Which of the following is an example of a nonfinancial performance measure?

    a. number of customer complaints

    b. direct labor time variance

    c. controllable overhead variance

    d. all of the above

11. A quantity of 1,200 gallons of Material X is purchased at a price of $4.50 per gallon. The standard price is $4.00 per gallon. The journal entry for this purchase will include a:

    a. debit to Materials for $5,400

    b. debit to Direct Materials Price Variance for $600

    c. credit to Direct Materials Price Variance for $600

    d. debit to Work in Process for $4,800

12. Factory overhead is applied at a rate of $9 per labor hour, of which $6 is variable. The actual variable factory overhead is $32,000. In the current period, 2,500 units are produced at a standard time of 2 labor hours per unit. These units require 5,500 actual labor hours. What is the controllable variance?

    a. $2,000 favorable

    b. $2,000 unfavorable

    c. $1,000 favorable

    d. $1,000 unfavorable

## TRUE/FALSE

*Instructions:* Indicate whether each of the following statements is true or false by placing a check mark in the appropriate column.

|  |  | True | False |
|---|---|---|---|
| 1. | Differences between the standard costs of a department or product and the actual costs incurred are termed variances.......................................................................... | _____ | _____ |
| 2. | If the actual unit price of the materials differs from the standard price, there is a quantity variance........................ | _____ | _____ |
| 3. | If the actual direct labor hours spent producing a product differ from the standard hours, there is a direct labor time variance. ................................................................. | _____ | _____ |
| 4. | The difference between the actual factory overhead and the budgeted factory overhead for the level of production achieved is called the volume variance. ............................. | _____ | _____ |
| 5. | Factory overhead costs are more difficult to manage than are direct labor and materials costs..................................... | _____ | _____ |
| 6. | At the end of the year, the variances from standard are usually transferred to the work in process account. ............ | _____ | _____ |
| 7. | A standard level of operation that can be attained with reasonable effort is called an ideal standard. ....................... | _____ | _____ |
| 8. | A useful means of reporting standard factory overhead cost variance data is through a factory overhead cost variance report................................................................. | _____ | _____ |
| 9. | Standards should only be applied in factory settings. ......... | _____ | _____ |
| 10. | An example of nonfinancial performance measures is the number of customer complaints.......................................... | _____ | _____ |

## EXERCISE 22-1

The following data relate to the direct materials and direct labor costs for the production of 10,000 units of product:

Direct Materials
Actual:     77,000 pounds at $1.82 ............... $140,140
Standard:   75,000 pounds at $1.80 ...............  135,000

Direct Labor
Actual:     42,500 hours at $19.75 ............... $839,375
Standard:   42,000 hours at $20.00 ...............  840,000

### Instructions:

**(1)** Compute the price variance, quantity variance, and total direct materials cost variance.

Price variance:

Quantity variance:

Total direct materials cost variance:

**(2)** Compute the rate variance, time variance, and total direct labor cost variance.

Rate variance:

Time variance:

Total direct labor cost variance:

## EXERCISE 22-2

The following data relate to factory overhead cost for the production of 20,000 units of product:

Actual:        Variable factory overhead ............ $153,500
               Fixed factory overhead ...............    120,000
Standard:    30,000 hours at $8 ......................    240,000

Productive capacity of 100% was 40,000 hours, and the factory overhead cost budgeted at the level of 30,000 standard hours was $270,000.

***Instructions:***   Compute the fixed factory overhead volume variance, variable factory overhead controllable variance, and total factory overhead cost variance. The fixed factory overhead rate was $3 per hour.

Volume variance:

Controllable variance:

Total factory overhead cost variance                            $ _____

# EXERCISE 22-3

During January, Nathalie Inc. manufactured 60,000 units, and the factory overhead costs were indirect factory wages, $50,500; electric power, $39,500 (included both variable and fixed components); indirect materials, $27,600; supervisory salaries, $30,000; depreciation of plant and equipment, $18,000; property taxes, $12,000; and insurance, $7,500.

*Instructions:* Prepare a budget performance report for factory overhead for January based on the above data and the factory overhead cost budget shown below.

| | A | B | C | D | E |
|---|---|---|---|---|---|
| 1 | Nathalie Inc. | | | | |
| 2 | Budget Performance Report—Factory Overhead Cost | | | | |
| 3 | For the Month Ended January 31, 20-- | | | | |
| 4 | | Budget | Actual | Unfavorable | Favorable |
| 5 | Variable cost: | | | | |
| 6 | Indirect factory wages | $ 48,000 | | | |
| 7 | Indirect materials | 27,000 | | | |
| 8 | Electric power | 36,000 | | | |
| 9 | Total variable cost | $111,000 | | | |
| 10 | Fixed cost: | | | | |
| 11 | Supervisory salaries | $ 30,000 | | | |
| 12 | Depreciation of plant and equipment | 18,000 | | | |
| 13 | Property taxes | 12,000 | | | |
| 14 | Insurance | 7,500 | | | |
| 15 | Electric power | 4,500 | | | |
| 16 | Total fixed cost | $ 72,000 | | | |
| 17 | Total factory overhead cost | $183,000 | | | |

## EXERCISE 22-4

Each year, a regional IRS office processes thousands of individual tax returns. The standard for processing returns was broken into two types as follows:

| Type of Return | Standard Time to Complete Processing |
|---|---|
| Traditional paper return ................. | 45 min. |
| Return filed electronically .............. | 8 min. |

By filing their tax returns electronically, individuals reduce the amount of processing time required by the IRS employees.

The regional office employs 30 full-time people (40 hrs./wk.) at $16.00 per hour. For the most recent week, the office processed 1,300 traditional returns and 225 electronically filed returns.

*Instructions:*

**(1)** Compute the amount spent on labor for the week.

**(2)** Determine the flexible budget in hours for the actual volume for the week.

**(3)** Compute the time variance.

# PROBLEM 22-1

Haley Inc. has established the following standard unit costs:

| | |
|---|---:|
| Materials:  10 lbs. @ $6 per lb. ...................... | $ 60.00 |
| Labor:  3 hrs. @ $15 per hr. ...........\............... | 45.00 |
| Factory overhead:  3 hrs. @ $3.50 per hr. ...... | 10.50 |
| Total standard cost per unit ........................... | $115.50 |

The factory overhead budget includes the following data:

| | | |
|---|---:|---:|
| Percent of capacity ......................................... | 85% | 100% |
| Direct labor hours ......................................... | 76,500 | 90,000 |
| Variable costs ............................................... | $153,000 | $180,000 |
| Fixed costs .................................................... | 135,000 | 135,000 |
| Total factory overhead cost ........................... | $288,000 | $315,000 |
| Variable overhead rate per hour ..................... | | $    2.00 |
| Fixed overhead rate per hour ......................... | | 1.50 |
| Total overhead rate per hour ......................... | | $    3.50 |

Actual manufacturing costs incurred:

| | |
|---|---:|
| Materials:  250,000 lbs. @ $6.20 .......................................... | $1,550,000 |
| Labor:  77,400 hrs. @ $14.60 ............................................... | 1,130,040 |
| Factory overhead (including $135,000 fixed) ....................... | 295,000 |
| Total actual cost for 25,500 units ......................................... | $2,975,040 |
| Standard cost of 25,500 units (standard time, 76,500 hrs.) . | 2,945,250 |
| Overall variance to be analyzed (unfavorable) .................... | $    29,790 |

## Instructions:

**(1)** Determine the price variance and quantity variance for the direct materials cost. Beside the amount of each variance, write the letter F or U to indicate whether the variance is favorable or unfavorable.

### Direct Materials Cost Variances

Price variance:

Quantity variance:

Total direct materials cost variance:

*Chapter 22*    443

**(2)** Determine the rate variance and time variance for the direct labor cost. Beside the amount of each variance, write the letter F or U to indicate whether the variance is favorable or unfavorable.

Direct Labor Cost Variances

Rate variance:

Time variance:

Total direct labor cost variance:

**(3)** Determine the controllable variance and the volume variance for the factory overhead cost. Beside the amount of each variance, write the letter F or U to indicate whether the variance is favorable or unfavorable. In addition, provide an alternative analysis of factory overhead using a T account.

Factory Overhead Cost Variances

Variance

Controllable variance:

Actual variable factory overhead cost incurred .... $ _____

Budgeted variable factory overhead for actual product produced ................................................. _____

    Variance ......................................................... $ _____

Volume variance:

Budgeted hours at 100% of normal capacity ....... _____ hrs.

Standard hours for amount produced .................. _____ hrs.

Productive capacity not used .............................. _____ hrs.

Standard fixed factory overhead cost rate ........... $ _____

    Variance ......................................................... _____

Total factory overhead cost variance ....................................................... $ _____

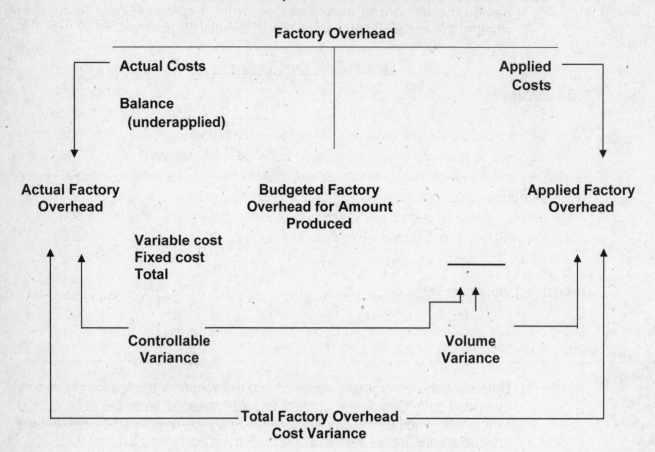

**Alternative Computation of Overhead Variances**

## PROBLEM 22-2

The following data were taken from the records of Piazza Company Inc. for January of the current year:

| | |
|---|---:|
| Administrative expenses | $ 42,000 |
| Selling expenses | 68,000 |
| Cost of goods sold (at standard) | 812,000 |
| Fixed factory overhead volume variance—unfavorable | 10,000 |
| Variable factory overhead controllable variance—favorable | 4,000 |
| Direct materials quantity variance—unfavorable | 1,500 |
| Direct materials price variance—unfavorable | 500 |
| Direct labor time variance—favorable | 3,000 |
| Direct labor rate variance—unfavorable | 1,200 |
| Sales | 995,000 |

**Instructions:** Prepare an income statement for presentation to management.

Piazza Company, Inc.

Income Statement

For the Month Ended January 31, 20--

| | FAVORABLE | UNFAVORABLE | |
|---|---|---|---|
| | | | |
| | | | |
| | | | |
| | | | |
| | | | |
| | | | |
| | | | |
| | | | |
| | | | |
| | | | |
| | | | |
| | | | |
| | | | |
| | | | |
| | | | |
| | | | |
| | | | |

# 23   Performance Evaluation for Decentralized Operations

## QUIZ AND TEST HINTS

The following hints may be helpful to you in preparing for a quiz or a test over the material covered in Chapter 23.

1. Many new terms are introduced in this chapter. You can expect true/false, multiple-choice, or matching questions testing your knowledge of these terms. Review the "Key Terms" section at the end of the chapter and be sure you understand each term. Do the Matching and Fill-in-the-Blank exercises included in this Study Guide.

2. The major focus of this chapter is responsibility accounting. Budget performance reports for cost centers have been discussed in earlier chapters, therefore, expect some multiple-choice questions on cost centers. You will probably not have to prepare a budget performance report. You can expect questions requiring you to determine the amount of service department expenses to charge to a profit center, and to calculate income from operations.

3. For investment centers, you should be able to compute rate of return on investment (including the profit margin and investment turnover) and residual income. Be prepared to use the DuPont formula. The Illustrative Problem at the end of the chapter is a good study aid for these computations.

4. This chapter also discusses transfer pricing. Most instructors use multiple-choice questions to cover this topic on tests and quizzes. Know the formulas determining the increase in income from operations for both the purchasing and supplying divisions for transfer prices that are negotiated between the variable cost and market price.

5. Review the "At A Glance" section at the end of the chapter. Read and review each of the Key Points and related Learning Outcomes. For each Learning Outcome that has an Example Exercise, locate the Example Exercise in the chapter and be sure that you understand the solution and can work a similar item on a test. If you have any questions about an Example Exercise, read the section of the chapter immediately preceding the Example Exercise.

## MATCHING

*Instructions:*   Match each of the statements below with its proper term. Some terms may not be used.

| | | | |
|---|---|---|---|
| A. | balanced scorecard | K. | market price approach |
| B. | controllable expenses | L. | negotiated price approach |
| C. | controllable revenues | M. | profit center |
| D. | cost center | N. | profit margin |
| E. | cost price approach | O. | rate of return on investment |
| F. | decentralization | P. | residual income |
| G. | DuPont formula | Q. | responsibility accounting |
| H. | income from operations | R. | service department charges |
| I. | investment center | S. | transfer price |
| J. | investment turnover | | |

_____ 1. A measure of managerial efficiency in the use of investments in assets, computed as income from operations divided by invested assets.

_____ 2. An approach to transfer pricing that uses the price at which the product or service transferred could be sold to outside buyers as the transfer price.

_____ 3. Revenues less operating expenses and service department charges for a profit or investment center.

_____ 4. The costs of services provided by an internal service department and transferred to a responsibility center.

_____ 5. An approach to transfer pricing that uses cost as the basis for setting the transfer price.

_____ 6. A decentralized unit in which the manager has the responsibility and authority to make decisions that affect not only costs and revenues but also the fixed assets available to the center.

_____ 7. Costs that can be influenced by the decisions of a manager.

_____ 8. An approach to transfer pricing that allows managers of decentralized units to agree (negotiate) among themselves as to the transfer price.

_____ 9. A component of the rate of return on investment, computed as the ratio of income from operations to sales.

_____ 10. The price charged one decentralized unit by another for the goods or services provided.

_____ 11. The separation of a business into more manageable operating units.

_____ 12. The excess of divisional income from operations over a "minimum" acceptable income from operations.

_____ 13. A decentralized unit in which the manager has the responsibility and the authority to make decisions that affect both costs and revenues (and thus profits).

___ 14. The process of measuring and reporting operating data by areas of responsibility.

___ 15. A decentralized unit in which the department or division manager has responsibility for the control of costs incurred and the authority to make decisions that affect these costs.

___ 16. A component of the rate of return on investment, computed as the ratio of sales to invested assets.

___ 17. A performance evaluation approach that incorporates multiple performance dimensions by combining financial and nonfinancial measures.

___ 18. Revenues earned by a profit center.

___ 19. A formula that multiplies the profit margin by the investment turnover.

## FILL IN THE BLANK—PART A

*Instructions:* Answer the following questions or complete the statements by writing the appropriate words or amounts in the answer blanks.

1. A business operating structure in which all major planning and operating decisions are made by top management can be described as

   _____.

2. Decentralized operating units of a business over which a manager has responsibility are referred to as _____ _____.

3. The process of measuring and reporting operating data by responsibility center is called _____ _____.

4. A responsibility center in which the manager is not required to make decisions concerning sales or the amount of fixed assets invested in the center is called a(n) _____ _____.

5. The principal difference in the responsibility accounting reports provided to higher levels of management is that these reports are _____ (more/less) summarized than for lower levels of management.

6. In a profit center, the manager has the responsibility and authority to make decisions that affect both costs and _____.

7. Costs that can be influenced by the decisions of profit center managers are said to be _____.

8. The costs of services charged to a profit center, based on its use of those services, are called _____ _____

   _____.

9. A measure of the services performed by a service department, which serves as a basis for charging profit centers, is called the

   _____ _____.

10. The payroll department processed a total of 50,000 payroll checks and had total expenses of $240,000. If H Division has 10,000 payroll checks for the period, it should be charged _____ for payroll services.

11. If sales are $400,000, cost of goods sold is $235,000, selling expenses are $70,000, and service department charges are $42,000, income from operations is _____.

12. A segment of a business in which the manager has responsibility and authority to make decisions regarding costs, revenues, and invested assets is known as a(n) _____ _____.

13. Income from operations divided by invested assets equals _____ _____ _____ _____ _____.

14. The ratio of income from operations to sales is called the _____ _____.

15–17. Income from operations is $70,000, invested assets are $280,000, and sales are $875,000.

15. The profit margin is _____.

16. The investment turnover is _____.

17. The rate of return on investment is _____.

18. The rate of return on investment is the product of the profit margin and the investment turnover, otherwise known as the _____ _____.

19. The excess of income from operations over a minimum amount of desired income from operations is termed _____ _____.

20. Transfer prices can be set as low as the variable cost per unit or as high as the _____ _____.

21. The _____ _____ approach allows the managers of decentralized units to agree among themselves as to the transfer price.

22. The _____ _____ is a set of financial and nonfinancial measures that reflect multiple performance dimensions of a business.

## FILL IN THE BLANK—PART B

*Instructions:* Answer the following questions or complete the statements by writing the appropriate words or amounts in the answer blanks.

1. Separating a business into divisions or operating units and delegating responsibility for these units to managers is called _____.

2. A manager's area of responsibility is called a(n) _____ _____.

3. Three common types of responsibility centers are cost centers, profit centers, and _____ _____.

4. Responsibility accounting for cost centers focuses on _____.

5. Responsibility accounting reports for a supervisor of the mail room would contain _____ (more/less) detailed information than the report issued to the vice-president of administration.

6. A division over which the manager has the responsibility and the authority to make decisions that affect both costs and revenues is known as a(n) _____ _____.

7. The manager of the Suit Department of Macy's can influence the amount of salaries paid to departmental personnel. These expenses are said to be _____.

8. The costs of services provided by the Payroll Department to a profit center within the same company are called _____ _____ _____.

9. Service department charges are _____ (direct/indirect) expenses to a profit center.

10. The payroll department processed a total of 50,000 payroll checks and had total expenses of $240,000. If J Division has 8,000 payroll checks for the period, it should be charged _____ for payroll services.

11. If sales are $400,000, cost of goods sold is $220,000, selling expenses are $70,000, and service department charges are $42,000, income from operations is _____.

12. Three measures used to evaluate the performance of investment center managers are income from operations, rate of return on investments, and _____ _____.

13. ROI is calculated by dividing income from operations by _____ _____.

14. The ratio of sales to invested assets is called the _____ _____.

**15–17.** Income from operations is $70,000, invested assets are $350,000, and sales are $875,000.

**15.** The profit margin is _____.

**16.** The investment turnover is _____.

**17.** The rate of return on investment is _____.

**18.** Measures of product quality, customer complaints, and warranty expenses are examples of _____

_____  _____.

**19.** Division A manufactures a radio that is used in the automobile produced in Division B. The charge to Division B for the product is called a(n)

_____  _____.

**20.** Using the _____  _____ approach, the transfer price is the price at which the product or service could be sold to outside buyers.

**21.** The balanced scorecard consists of the innovation and learning, _____, _____, and _____ _____ dimensions.

## MULTIPLE CHOICE

*Instructions:*   Circle the best answer for each of the following questions.

**1.** When the manager has responsibility and authority to make decisions that affect costs, but no responsibility or authority over revenues and assets invested in the department, the department is referred to as:

   **a.** cost center

   **b.** a profit center

   **c.** an investment center

   **d.** none of the above

**2.** If a selling division organized as a profit center has excess capacity, the most appropriate approach to setting the transfer price is:

   **a.** market price

   **b.** negotiated price

   **c.** cost price

   **d.** marginal price

3. Which of the following expressions is frequently referred to as the profit margin factor in determining the rate of return on investment?

    a. income from operations divided by invested assets

    b. sales divided by invested assets

    c. income from operations divided by sales

    d. DuPont formula

4. The manager of which of the following centers has the most authority and responsibility?

    a. cost center

    b. profit center

    c. data center

    d. investment center

5. Division F has sales of $750,000; cost of goods sold of $450,000; operating expenses of $228,000; and invested assets of $300,000. What is the rate of return on investment of Division F?

    a. 9.6%

    b. 10%

    c. 20%

    d. 24%

6. Division F has sales of $750,000; cost of goods sold of $450,000; operating expenses of $228,000; and invested assets of $300,000. What is the investment turnover of Division F?

    a. 1.7

    b. 2.5

    c. 4.2

    d. 10.4

7. The profit margin for Division Q is 15% and the investment turnover is 1.2. What is the rate of return on investment for Division Q?

    a. 12.5%

    b. 15%

    c. 18%

    d. 20%

8. Which of the following is considered an advantage of decentralization?

    a. Decentralized decision making provides excellent training for managers.

    b. Decisions made by different managers all positively affect the overall profitability of the company.

    c. Assets and costs are duplicated across operating divisions.

    d. all of the above

9. Which of the following is an example of a service department?

   a. information systems

   b. purchasing

   c. payroll

   d. all of the above

10. A good example of a nonfinancial performance measure is:

    a. residual income

    b. income from operations

    c. customer retention rate

    d. investment turnover

11. The Payroll Department has a budget of $130,000. It is estimated that the company has 100 employees paid on a weekly (52 weeks per year) basis. The Video Division has 30 employees. Payroll Department service costs are charged to divisions on the basis of payroll checks. What would be the February Payroll Department service department charge to the Video Division?

    a. $750

    b. $3,000

    c. $3,250

    d. $39,000

12. The Collection Department has an annual budget of $180,000. The Publishing Division has an outstanding balance of $500,000 of accounts receivable, representing 1,200 invoices and 300 different customers. The Collection Department collects approximately 10,000 invoices per month, of which 4,000 are related to the Publishing Division. Collection Department service costs are charged to divisions on the basis of invoices. What would be the monthly Collection Department service department charge to the Publishing Division?

    a. $1,800

    b. $6,000

    c. $7,800

    d. $72,000

## TRUE/FALSE

**Instructions:**   Indicate whether each of the following statements is true or false by placing a check mark in the appropriate column.

|  |  | **True** | **False** |
|---|---|---|---|
| 1. | A primary disadvantage of decentralized operations is that decisions made by one manager may negatively affect the profitability of the entire company. ........................................ | ____ | ____ |
| 2. | In an investment center, the manager has responsibility and authority to make decisions that affect not only costs and revenues, but also the assets available to the center... | ____ | ____ |
| 3. | Responsibility accounting reports for cost centers contain the same amount of detail, regardless of the level of operations to which the report is addressed. .......... | ____ | ____ |
| 4. | The primary responsibility accounting report for a cost center is the income statement. ........................................... | ____ | ____ |
| 5. | Three measures of investment center performance are rate of return on investment, residual income, and income from operations. ........................................................ | ____ | ____ |
| 6. | Rate of return on investment as a measure of investment center performance reflects not only the revenues and costs of the division, but also the amount of invested assets........................................................................ | ____ | ____ |
| 7. | The rate of return on investment is computed by dividing sales by invested assets. ............................................... | ____ | ____ |
| 8. | If the rate of return on investment is 18% and the investment turnover is 3, the profit margin is 9%. ......................... | ____ | ____ |
| 9. | If the divisional profit margin decreases and the investment turnover remains unchanged, the rate of return on investment will decrease............................................... | ____ | ____ |
| 10. | The market approach to transfer pricing should be used when the transferring division has excess capacity............. | ____ | ____ |

## EXERCISE 23-1

Condensed income statements for Divisions M and N of Perlita Inc. and the amount invested in each division are as follows:

|  | Division M | | Division N |
|---|---|---|---|
| Sales ............................................. | $ 500,000 | (c) $ | |
| Cost of goods sold ........................ | (a) _____ | | 275,000 |
| Gross profit .................................... | $ 220,000 | | $ 245,000 |
| Operating expenses and service department charges ................... | 100,000 | (d) | _____ |
| Income from operations ................ | (b) $ _____ | | $ 110,000 |
| Invested assets ............................. | $ 750,000 | | $ 500,000 |

### Instructions:

(1) Insert the amounts of the missing items (a)–(d) in the condensed divisional income statements above.

(2) Determine the rate of return on investment for each division.

Division M:

Division N:

(3) On the basis of income from operations, which division is more profitable?

(4) On the basis of rate of return on investment, which division is more profitable?

## EXERCISE 23-2

Based on the data in Exercise 23-1, assume that Perlita Inc. has established a minimum rate of return for invested assets at 12%.

### Instructions:

**(1)** Determine the residual income for each division of Perlita.

Division M:

Division N:

**(2)** On the basis of residual income, which division is more profitable?

## EXERCISE 23-3

One item is omitted from each of the following computations of the rate of return on investment using the DuPont formula:

| Rate of Return on Investment | = | Profit Margin | × | Investment Turnover |
|:---:|:---:|:---:|:---:|:---:|
| 16% | | 10% | | (a) _____ |
| 17.5% | | (b) _____ | | 1.4 |
| (c) _____ | | 21% | | 0.9 |
| 21.6% | | (d) _____ | | 1.2 |
| 24% | | 16% | | (e) _____ |

*Instructions:*   Determine the missing items.

# EXERCISE 23-4

The materials used by the Estes Division of the Western Company are currently purchased from outside suppliers at $50 per unit. These same materials are produced by the Sierra Division. The Sierra Division can produce the materials needed by the Estes Division at a variable cost of $32 per unit. The division is currently producing 65,000 units, but has a capacity to produce 85,000 units. The two divisions have recently negotiated a transfer price of $44 per unit for 16,000 units.

*Instructions:* Determine the increase in each division's income from operations as a result of this transfer.

Estes (Purchasing) Division:

Sierra (Supplying) Division:

## PROBLEM 23-1

The budget for Department F of Plant 7 for the current month ended July 31 is as follows:

| | |
|---|---:|
| Factory wages | $65,000 |
| Materials | 39,500 |
| Supervisory salaries | 15,000 |
| Power and light | 8,900 |
| Depreciation of plant and equipment | 7,500 |
| Maintenance | 4,300 |
| Insurance and property taxes | 2,000 |

During July, the costs incurred in Department F of Plant 7 were factory wages, $73,600; materials, $37,700; supervisory salaries, $15,000; power and light, $9,600; depreciation of plant and equipment, $7,500; maintenance, $3,900; and insurance and property taxes, $2,000.

**Instructions:**   Prepare a budget performance report for the supervisor of Department F, Plant 7, for the month of July, using the following form:

*Budget Performance Report—Supervisor, Department F, Plant 7*

*For the Month Ended July 31, 20--*

| | BUDGET | ACTUAL | OVER | UNDER |
|---|---|---|---|---|
| | | | | |
| | | | | |
| | | | | |
| | | | | |
| | | | | |
| | | | | |
| | | | | |
| | | | | |
| | | | | |
| | | | | |
| | | | | |
| | | | | |
| | | | | |
| | | | | |
| | | | | |
| | | | | |
| | | | | |
| | | | | |

## PROBLEM 23-2

*Instructions:*  Using the following information, complete the income statement for Divisions J and K of Firefly Co. on the following page.

(1) Division J sales ................................. $280,000
    Division K sales ...............................   420,000

(2) Cost of J sales ...............................   122,500
    Cost of K sales ...............................   227,500

(3) Division J operating expenses ........    48,000
    Division K operating expenses .......    72,000

The following service department expenses should be charged to the two divisions on the following bases:

(4)

| Corporate Service Department | Amount | Basis for Charging |
|---|---|---|
| Payroll accounting ................... | $60,000 | Number of payroll checks |
| Central purchasing ................ | 88,000 | Number of requisitions |
| Brochures .............................. | 50,000 | Number of brochure pages |

| | Number of Payroll Checks | Number of Requisitions | Number of Brochure Pages |
|---|---|---|---|
| Division J ...................... | 400 | 2,200 | 500 |
| Division K .................... | 600 | 1,800 | 300 |
| Total .......................... | 1,000 | 4,000 | 800 |

*Firefly Co.*

*Income Statement—Divisions J and K*

*For the Year Ended May 31, 20--*

| | DIVISION J | DIVISION K | TOTAL |
|---|---|---|---|
| Net sales | | | |
| Cost of goods sold | | | |
| Gross profit | | | |
| Operating expenses | | | |
| Income from operations before service department charges | | | |
| Less service department charges: | | | |
| Payroll accounting | | | |
| Purchasing | | | |
| Brochure advertising | | | |
| Total service department charges | | | |
| Income from operations | | | |
| | | | |

Supporting Schedules:

| | NUMBER OF PAYROLL CHECKS | NUMBER OF REQUISITIONS | NUMBER OF BROCHURE PAGES |
|---|---|---|---|
| | | | |
| | | | |
| | | | |
| | | | |
| | | | |
| | | | |
| | | | |
| | | | |
| | | | |
| | | | |
| | | | |
| | | | |
| | | | |
| | | | |
| | | | |
| | | | |
| | | | |
| | | | |
| | | | |

## PROBLEM 23-3

TP Co. has two manufacturing divisions, X and Y. Division X currently purchases 10,000 units of materials from an outside supplier at $30 per unit. The same materials are produced by Division Y at a variable cost of $22 per unit. Division Y is operating at full capacity of 40,000 units and can sell all it produces either to outside buyers at $30 or to Division X.

### Instructions:

(1) Assume that Division Y sells 10,000 units of its product to Division X rather than to outside buyers. If the sale is made at a market price of $30, what will be the effect on:

    (a) Division X's income from operations?

        _____ increase by $_____

        _____ decrease by $_____

        _____ no effect

    (b) Division Y's income from operations?

        _____ increase by $_____

        _____ decrease by $_____

        _____ no effect

(2) Assume that Division Y sells 40,000 units of product at $30 to outside buyers and still has excess capacity of 10,000 units. If 10,000 units of product are sold to Division X at a negotiated transfer price of $27, what will be the effect on:

    (a) Division X's income from operations?

        _____ increase by $_____

        _____ decrease by $_____

        _____ no effect

    (b) Division Y's income from operations?

        _____ increase by $_____

        _____ decrease by $_____

        _____ no effect

**(3)** Assume the same facts as in (2), but use a negotiated transfer price of $20. What will be the effect on:

**(a)** Division X's income from operations?

_____ increase by $_____

_____ decrease by $_____

_____ no effect

**(b)** Division Y's income from operations?

_____ increase by $_____

_____ decrease by $_____

_____ no effect

# 24    Differential Analysis and Product Pricing

## QUIZ AND TEST HINTS

The following hints may be helpful to you in preparing for a quiz or a test over the material covered in Chapter 24.

1. Many new terms are introduced in this chapter. You can expect true/false, multiple-choice, or matching questions testing your knowledge of these terms. Review the "Key Terms" section at the end of the chapter and be sure you understand each term. Do the Matching and Fill-in-the-Blank exercises included in this Study Guide.

2. You can expect short problems testing your ability to perform differential analysis for one or more of the six types of differential analysis illustrations presented in the chapter. Part 5 of the Illustrative Problem at the end of the chapter is a useful study aid for differential analysis of accepting additional business at a special price.

3. You also are likely to see a short problem applying the cost-plus approach to setting product prices. Remember that there are three versions of the cost-plus approach: total cost, product cost, and variable cost. You may find the Illustrative Problem to be a useful study aid.

4. If your instructor emphasized product pricing under production bottlenecks, you might also see a short problem in that area. At least be able to compute the contribution margin per bottleneck hour and describe how this information is used to adjust the product price.

5. Review the "At A Glance" section at the end of the chapter. Read and review each of the Key Points and related Learning Outcomes. For each Learning Outcome that has an Example Exercise, locate the Example Exercise in the chapter and be sure that you understand the solution and can work a similar item on a test. If you have any questions about an Example Exercise, read the section of the chapter immediately preceding the Example Exercise.

## MATCHING

*Instructions:* Match each of the statements below with its proper term. Some terms may not be used.

A.  activity-based costing
B.  differential analysis
C.  differential cost
D.  differential revenue
E.  markup
F.  opportunity cost
G.  product cost concept

H.  production bottleneck
I.  sunk cost
J.  target costing
K.  theory of constraints (TOC)
L.  total cost concept
M.  variable cost concept

_____  1.  The amount of income forgone from an alternative use of cash or its equivalent.

_____  2.  A condition that occurs when product demand exceeds production capacity.

_____  3.  A concept used in applying the cost-plus approach to product pricing in which all the costs of manufacturing the product plus the selling and administrative expenses are included in the cost amount to which the markup is added.

_____  4.  A cost that is not affected by subsequent decisions.

_____  5.  The area of accounting concerned with the effect of alternative courses of action on revenues and costs.

_____  6.  A concept used in applying the cost-plus approach to product pricing in which only the variable costs are included in the cost amount to which the markup is added.

_____  7.  The amount of increase or decrease in revenue expected from a particular course of action as compared with an alternative.

_____  8.  A cost allocation method that identifies activities causing the incurrence of costs and allocates these costs to products (or other cost objects), based upon activity drivers (bases).

_____  9.  The amount of increase or decrease in cost expected from a particular course of action compared with an alternative.

_____  10.  A manufacturing strategy that attempts to remove the influence of bottlenecks (constraints) on a process.

_____  11.  A concept used in applying the cost-plus approach to product pricing in which only the costs of manufacturing the product, termed the product cost, are included in the cost amount to which the markup is added.

_____  12.  A concept used to design and manufacture a product at a cost that will deliver a desired profit for a given market-determined price.

_____  13.  An amount that is added to a "cost" amount to determine product price.

# FILL IN THE BLANK—PART A

*Instructions:* Answer the following questions or complete the statements by writing the appropriate words or amounts in the answer blanks.

1. The amount of increase or decrease in revenue expected from a course of action as compared with an alternative is called _____ _____.

2. The amount of increase or decrease in cost that is expected from a course of action as compared with an alternative is called the _____ _____.

3. In the lease or sell decision regarding a piece of equipment, the book value of the equipment would be considered a(n) _____ _____.

4. In using differential analysis, two additional factors that often need to be considered besides the basic differential revenue and costs are (1) differential revenue from investing the funds generated by the alternatives, and (2) any _____ _____ _____.

5. Product A has a loss from operations of $18,000 and allocated fixed costs of $25,000. The income from operations from all products is $75,000 and total fixed costs are $30,000. The estimated income from operations if Product A is discontinued would be _____.

6. Part Z can be purchased for $30 per unit or manufactured internally for $8 of direct materials, $9 of direct labor, and $15 of factory overhead ($7 of which is fixed). The cost savings from manufacturing Part Z internally would be _____.

7. The amount of income that is forgone from an alternative use of cash is called _____ _____.

8. McKeon Gas Co. is deciding whether to sell one of its products at an intermediate stage of development or process it further. The decision will rest on differential revenues and the differential costs of _____ _____.

9. H. Hoch and Co. is considering doing additional business at a special price. If Hoch is operating below full capacity, the differential costs of the additional production are the _____ manufacturing costs.

10. In deciding whether to accept business at a price lower than the normal price, the minimum short-run price should be set high enough to cover all _____ _____.

11–12. The two market methods of setting the normal selling price are:

11. _____-_____.

12. _____-_____.

13. The markup percentage for the total cost concept is determined by dividing desired profit by _____ _____.

14. The markup percentage for the variable cost concept is determined by dividing desired profit plus _____ _____ _____ by total variable costs.

15–17. Product M has total cost per unit of $60, including $20 per unit of selling and administrative costs. Total variable cost is $36 per unit, and desired profit is $6 per unit.

15. The markup percentage based on total cost is _____.

16. The markup percentage based on product cost is _____.

17. The markup percentage based on variable cost is _____.

18. The difference between the existing product cost and the target cost is termed the _____.

19. A method of more accurately measuring costs of producing and selling product and focusing on identifying and tracing activities to specific products is known as _____-_____ _____.

20. When the demand for the company's product exceeds its ability to produce the product, the resultant difficulty is referred to as a(n) _____ _____.

21. The manufacturing strategy that focuses on reducing the influence of bottlenecks on a process is the _____ _____ _____.

## FILL IN THE BLANK—PART B

*Instructions:* Answer the following questions or complete the statements by writing the appropriate words or amounts in the answer blanks.

1. A method of decision making that focuses on the effect of alternative courses of action on the relevant revenues and costs is _____ _____.

2. Costs that have been incurred in the past that are not relevant to the decision are called _____ _____.

3. The difference between the differential revenue and differential costs is called the _____ _____.

4. The relevant financial factors to be considered in a lease or sell decision are differential costs and _____ _____.

5. Product B has a loss from operations of $12,000 and allocated fixed costs of $8,000. The income from operations from all products is $75,000 and total fixed costs are $30,000. The estimated income from operations if Product B is discontinued would be _____.

6. Make or buy options often arise when a manufacturer has excess _____.

7. A net cash outlay of $225,000 for a new piece of equipment could alternatively be invested to earn 10%. The $22,500 forgone by not investing the funds is called a(n) _____ _____.

8. Product K is produced for $4 per gallon and can be sold without additional processing for $5 per gallon. Product K can be processed further into Product G at a cost of $2 per gallon ($0.80 fixed). Product G can be sold for $6.50 per gallon. The differential income per gallon from processing Product K into Product G is _____.

9. The law that prohibits price discrimination within the United States, unless differences in prices can be justified by different costs of serving different customers, is the _____-_____

_____.

10–12. The three cost concepts used in applying the cost-plus approach to setting normal product prices are:

10. _____ _____.

11. _____ _____.

12. _____ _____.

13. Under the _____ _____ concept, all costs of manufacturing a product plus the selling and administrative expenses are included in the cost amount to which the markup is added.

14. Contractors who sell products to government agencies often use the _____ _____ concept of applying the cost-plus approach to product pricing.

15. The markup percentage for the product cost concept is determined by dividing desired profit plus total selling and administrative expenses by _____ _____ _____.

16–18. Product N has total cost per unit of $40, including $15 per unit of selling and administrative costs. Total variable cost is $30 per unit, and desired profit is $5 per unit.

16. The markup percentage based on total cost is _____.

17. The markup percentage based on product cost is _____.

18. The markup percentage based on variable cost is _____.

19. A cost reduction concept, pioneered by the Japanese, that assumes that the selling price is set by the marketplace is _____

_____.

20. The term used to describe a situation when the demand for a company's product exceeds the ability of the company to produce it is

_____ _____.

## MULTIPLE CHOICE

*Instructions:*   Circle the best answer for each of the following questions.

1. The area of accounting concerned with the effect of alternative courses of action on revenues and costs is called:

    a. gross profit analysis

    b. capital investment analysis

    c. differential analysis

    d. cost-volume-profit analysis

2. A business received an offer from an exporter for 10,000 units of product at $18 per unit. The acceptance of the offer will not affect normal production or the domestic sales price. The following data are available:

    Domestic sales price ......................... $25
    Unit manufacturing costs:
        Variable ....................................    16
        Fixed ...........................................    4

    What is the amount of gain or loss from acceptance of the offer?

    a. $20,000 gain

    b. $20,000 loss

    c. $70,000 gain

    d. $70,000 loss

3. The amount of income that is forgone from the best available alternative to the proposed use of cash or its equivalent is called:

    a. sunk cost

    b. opportunity cost

    c. differential cost

    d. opportunity revenue

4. For which cost concept used in applying the cost-plus approach to product pricing are total selling and general expenses and desired profit allowed for in the determination of markup?

    a. total cost

    b. product cost

    c. variable cost

    d. none of the above

5. A business produces Product A in batches of 5,000 gallons, which can be sold for $3 per gallon. The business has been offered $5 per finished gallon to process two batches of Product A further into Product B. Product B will require additional processing costs of $7,800 per batch, and 10% of the gallons of Product A will evaporate during processing. What is the amount of gain or loss from further processing of Product A?

   a. $7,200 gain

   b. $4,400 gain

   c. $2,400 gain

   d. $600 loss

6. Which of the following cost concepts is not used in applying the cost-plus approach to setting the selling price?

   a. product cost

   b. total cost

   c. variable cost

   d. fixed cost

7. Which of the following concepts accepts a product price as given by the marketplace as the first step in determining the markup?

   a. total cost plus markup concept

   b. variable cost plus markup concept

   c. target costing

   d. product cost plus markup concept

8. The Majestic Company's casting operation is a production bottleneck. Majestic produces three products with the following per unit characteristics.

| | Product A | Product B | Product C |
|---|---|---|---|
| Sales price ............................... | $100 | $120 | $200 |
| Variable cost per unit ................. | 40 | 50 | 120 |
| Contribution margin per unit ...... | 60 | 70 | 80 |
| Fixed cost per unit .................... | 10 | 30 | 50 |
| Net profit per unit ...................... | 50 | 40 | 30 |
| Casting time ............................. | 3.5 hrs. | 3 hrs. | 4 hrs. |

   Which product is the most profitable to the company?

   a. Product A

   b. Product B

   c. Product C

   d. Products A and C

9. Which of the following is a market method of setting the selling price?

   a. competition-based

   b. total cost-based

   c. variable cost-based

   d. product cost-based

10. Management is considering replacing its blending equipment. The annual costs of operating the old equipment are $250,000. The annual costs of operating the new equipment are expected to be $220,000. The old equipment has a book value of $35,000 and can be sold for $25,000. The cost of the new equipment would be $260,000. Which of these amounts should be considered a sunk cost in deciding whether to replace the old equipment?

    a. $250,000

    b. $220,000

    c. $35,000

    d. $25,000

11. A business has been purchasing 5,000 units of a part from an outside supplier for $40 per unit. In addition to the purchase price, there are import duties of 10% of the purchase price. A proposal was received to manufacture the part internally using excess manufacturing capacity. The per-unit cost for the part was estimated as follows:

    | | |
    |---|---|
    | Direct materials | $21 |
    | Direct labor | 15 |
    | Variable factory overhead | 5 |
    | Fixed factory overhead | 9 |
    | Total cost per unit | $50 |

    What is the differential income or loss from manufacturing the part, rather than purchasing it from the outside supplier?

    a. $15,000 income

    b. $5,000 loss

    c. $30,000 loss

    d. $50,000 loss

12. A business has three product lines: small, medium, and large speakers. The small speaker line has a loss from operations of $25,000, while the medium and large speaker lines have a combined income from operations of $100,000. The total fixed costs of $50,000 are allocated on the basis of sales volume across the three product lines. The small product line has 30% of the sales volume. What is the differential income or loss from discontinuing the small speaker product line?

    a. $10,000 income

    b. $25,000 income

    c. $10,000 loss

    d. $15,000 loss

13. A business currently sells mobile phones in the domestic market for $80. The cost of the phones includes $50 variable cost per unit and $20 fixed cost per unit. A bid is received from an overseas customer for 1,000 phones at a price of $60 per phone. An additional 10% export fee on price would be assessed to the mobile phone company for overseas sales. What would be the differential income or loss from accepting the overseas bid?

   a. $4,000 loss
   b. $14,000 loss
   c. $4,000 income
   d. $10,000 income

## TRUE/FALSE

*Instructions:*   Indicate whether each of the following statements is true or false by placing a check mark in the appropriate column.

|  | True | False |
|---|---|---|
| 1. In deciding whether to replace fixed assets, the book values of the fixed assets being replaced are sunk costs and are irrelevant. | ____ | ____ |
| 2. The amount of increase or decrease in cost that is expected from a particular course of action as compared with an alternative is called opportunity cost. | ____ | ____ |
| 3. In deciding whether to accept business at a special price, a company that is operating below full capacity will decrease its operating income if the special price does not exceed all costs. | ____ | ____ |
| 4. Discontinuing an unprofitable segment of business will usually eliminate all of the related fixed costs. | ____ | ____ |
| 5. The amount of income that would result from the best available alternative to the proposed use of cash or its equivalent is called differential cost. | ____ | ____ |
| 6. Using the total cost concept of applying the cost-plus approach to product pricing, all costs of manufacturing the product plus the selling and administrative expenses are included in the cost amount to which the markup is added. | ____ | ____ |
| 7. In differential analysis, two additional factors to be considered in making a lease or sell decision are (1) differential revenue from investing funds generated by alternatives and (2) any income tax differential. | ____ | ____ |
| 8. Using the cost-plus approach to product pricing, managers determine product prices by adding a markup to a cost amount. | ____ | ____ |

|  | True | False |
|---|---|---|

9. Contractors who sell to government agencies often use the total cost approach to product pricing. ........................... ____  ____

10. The best way to measure product profitability in a production bottleneck environment is with contribution margin per unit. ................................................................................................ ____  ____

## EXERCISE 24-1

Walden Transportation Inc. has a truck that it no longer needs. The truck can be sold for $18,000 or it can be leased for a period of 5 years at $4,000 per year. At the end of the lease, the truck is expected to be sold for a negligible amount. The truck cost $50,000 four years ago, and $35,000 depreciation has been taken on it to date. To be sold for $18,000, the truck must first be repainted at a cost of $900. If the truck is to be leased for the 5-year period, Walden must provide the licenses, which cost $220 per year. The lessee must provide insurance at an annual cost of $200, tires at an estimated annual cost of $600, and repairs that are expected to amount to $2,000 during the 5-year period.

*Instructions:*   Complete the following form to determine which alternative is more advantageous to Walden Transportation Inc. and to determine the amount of that advantage. (Ignore the fact that if the truck is leased, not all of the revenue is received at once.)

Walden Transportation Inc.
Proposal to Lease or Sell Truck

Differential revenue from alternatives:

   Revenue from lease ............................................... $ _____

   Revenue from sale .................................................. _____

     Differential revenue from lease .......................... $ _____

Differential cost of alternatives:

   License expenses during lease ............................. $ _____

   Repainting expense on sale ................................... _____

     Differential cost of leasing ............................... _____

Net differential income (loss) from lease alternative .... $ _____

## EXERCISE 24-2

Tran Inc. has been purchasing metal blades for $14 a set for use in producing food processors. The cost of manufacturing the blades is estimated at $6.75 for direct materials, $5.10 for direct labor, and $1.80 for factory overhead ($1.00 fixed and $0.80 variable). Because there is unused capacity available, there would be no increase in the total amount of fixed factory overhead costs if Tran manufactures the blades.

*Instructions:* Complete the following form to determine whether Tran Inc. should make or buy the blades.

Tran Inc.
Proposal to Manufacture Metal Blades

| | | |
|---|---|---|
| Purchase price of blades .............................................. | | $ _____ |
| Differential cost to manufacture blades: | | |
|    Direct materials ..................................................... | $ _____ | |
|    Direct labor ........................................................... | _____ | |
|    Variable factory overhead ...................................... | _____ | _____ |
| Cost savings (increase) from manufacturing blades ... | | $ _____ |

## EXERCISE 24-3

English Chairs Inc. produces a line of rocking chairs in one section of the plant, and stuffed chairs and recliner chairs in other sections. The controller has supplied the following condensed income statement for the year just ended:

English Chairs Inc.
Condensed Income Statement
For the Year Ended December 31, 20--

| | Stuffed Chairs | Recliner Chairs | Rocking Chairs | Total |
|---|---|---|---|---|
| Sales ................................................ | $500,000 | $250,000 | $350,000 | $1,100,000 |
| Cost of goods sold: | | | | |
|   Variable costs ............................ | $250,000 | $110,000 | $180,000 | $ 540,000 |
|   Fixed costs ................................. | 50,000 | 30,000 | 90,000 | 170,000 |
|     Total cost of goods sold ....... | $300,000 | $140,000 | $270,000 | $ 710,000 |
| Gross profit ...................................... | $200,000 | $110,000 | $ 80,000 | $ 390,000 |
| Operating expenses: | | | | |
|   Variable expenses ...................... | $100,000 | $ 60,000 | $ 75,000 | $ 235,000 |
|   Fixed expenses .......................... | 60,000 | 25,000 | 43,000 | 128,000 |
|     Total operating expenses ..... | $160,000 | $ 85,000 | $118,000 | $ 363,000 |
| Income (loss) from operations ......... | $ 40,000 | $ 25,000 | $ (38,000) | $ 27,000 |

*Instructions:* Complete the following form and determine whether the rocking chairs section should be continued.

English Chairs Inc.
Proposal to Discontinue Rocking Chairs
December 31, 20--

Differential revenue from sales of rocking chairs:

Revenue from sales ....................................................     $ _____

Differential cost of sales of rocking chairs:

Variable cost of goods sold .........................................     $ _____

Variable operating expenses ........................................     _____     _____

Differential income (loss) from sales of rocking chairs .......     $ _____

The rocking chairs section probably _____ be continued.


## EXERCISE 24-4

Golub Inc. has a machine which cost $250,000 five years ago and has $155,000 accumulated depreciation to date. The company can sell the machine for $83,000 and replace it with a larger one costing $370,000. The variable annual operating cost of the present machine amounts to $65,000. The variable annual operating cost of the new machine is estimated to be $30,000. It is estimated that either machine could be used for seven years from this date, December 31, 20--, and that at the end of the seven-year period neither would have a significant residual value.

*Instructions:* Complete the following schedule and determine the advisability of replacing the present machine.

Golub Inc.
Proposal to Replace Machine
December 31, 20--

Annual variable costs—present machine ......................................     $ _____

Annual variable costs—new machine ...........................................     _____

Annual differential decrease (increase) in variable costs ..............     $ _____

Number of years applicable ........................................................     _____

Total differential decrease (increase) in variable costs ..................     $ _____

Proceeds from sale of present machine ......................................     _____     $ _____

Cost of new machine ................................................................     _____

Net differential decrease (increase) in cost, seven-year total ........     $ _____

Annual net differential decrease (increase) in cost—new machine     $ _____

## PROBLEM 24-1

Smith Company recently began production of a new product, G, which required the investment of $500,000 in assets. The costs and expenses of producing and selling 50,000 units of Product G are as follows:

Variable costs:

| | |
|---|---|
| Direct materials .............................................. | $1.20 per unit |
| Direct labor .................................................. | 2.40 |
| Factory overhead .......................................... | .40 |
| Selling and administrative expenses .......... | 1.00 |
| Total .................................................. | $5.00 per unit |

Fixed costs:

| | |
|---|---|
| Factory overhead ......................................... | $35,000 |
| Selling and administrative expenses .......... | 15,000 |

Smith Company is currently establishing a selling price for Product G. The president of Smith Company has decided to use the cost-plus approach to product pricing and has indicated that Product G must earn a 12% rate of return on invested assets.

*Instructions:*

(1) Determine the amount of desired profit from the production and sale of Product G.

(2) Assuming that the total cost concept is used, determine (a) the cost amount per unit, (b) the markup percentage, and (c) the selling price of Product G.

(a)

(b)

(c)

## PROBLEM 24-2

Based upon the data in Problem 24-1, assume that Smith Company uses the product cost concept of product pricing.

***Instructions:***    Determine (1) the cost amount per unit, (2) the markup percentage, and (3) the selling price of Product G. (Round to the nearest cent.)

**(1)**

**(2)**

**(3)**

## PROBLEM 24-3

Based upon the data in Problem 24-1, assume that Smith Company uses the variable cost concept of product pricing.

***Instructions:*** Determine (1) the cost amount per unit, (2) the markup percentage, and (3) the selling price of Product G.

**(1)**

**(2)**

**(3)**

## PROBLEM 24-4

The Zelda Company produces three products, Products D, E, and F. All three products require heat treatment in a furnace operation. The furnace operation is a production bottleneck. The annual cost of the furnace operation is $180,000. Information about the three products is as follows:

|  | Product D | Product E | Product F |
|---|---|---|---|
| Sales price per unit ............................. | $750 | $600 | $400 |
| Variable cost per unit ......................... | 300 | 350 | 200 |
| Contribution margin per unit .............. | $450 | $250 | $200 |
| Fixed cost per unit ............................. | 200 | 200 | 150 |
| Profit per unit ...................................... | $250 | $ 50 | $ 50 |
|  |  |  |  |
| Furnace hours per unit ........................ | 15 | 10 | 8 |

**Instructions:** Determine the price for Products E and F that would generate the same profitability as Product D.

# 25 Capital Investment Analysis

## QUIZ AND TEST HINTS

The following hints may be helpful to you in preparing for a quiz or a test over the material covered in Chapter 25.

1. Many new terms are introduced in this chapter. You can expect true/false, multiple-choice, or matching questions testing your knowledge of these terms. Review the "Key Terms" section at the end of the chapter and be sure you understand each term. Do the Matching and Fill-in-the-Blank exercises included in this Study Guide.

2. You can expect some problems requiring you to perform capital investment analysis using each of the four methods illustrated in the chapter. Often, instructors will use multiple-choice questions to test your knowledge of the average rate of return method, cash payback method, and present value index. Short problems will be used to test your knowledge of the net present value and internal rate of return methods. The chapter illustrations and the Illustrative Problem at the end of the chapter are good study aids.

3. The remaining chapter topics are tested most often using true/false or multiple-choice questions. Review the "At A Glance" section at the end of the chapter. Read and review each of the Key Points and related Learning Outcomes. For each Learning Outcome that has an Example Exercise, locate the Example Exercise in the chapter and be sure that you understand the solution and can work a similar item on a test. If you have any questions about an Example Exercise, read the section of the chapter immediately preceding the Example Exercise.

# MATCHING

***Instructions:*** Match each of the statements below with its proper term. Some terms may not be used.

A. annuity
B. average rate of return
C. capital investment analysis
D. capital rationing
E. cash payback period
F. currency exchange rate
G. inflation

H. internal rate of return method
I. net present value method
J. present value concept
K. present value index
L. present value of an annuity
M. time value of money concept


_____ 1. A method of analysis of proposed capital investments that uses present value concepts to compute the rate of return from the net cash flows expected from the investment.

_____ 2. An index computed by dividing the total present value of the net cash flow to be received from a proposed capital investment by the amount to be invested.

_____ 3. A series of equal cash flows at fixed intervals.

_____ 4. The expected period of time that will elapse between the date of a capital expenditure and the complete recovery in cash (or equivalent) of the amount invested.

_____ 5. The concept that an amount of money invested today will earn income.

_____ 6. A method of analysis of proposed capital investments that focuses on the present value of the cash flows expected from the investments.

_____ 7. The sum of the present values of a series of equal cash flows to be received at fixed intervals.

_____ 8. The process by which management plans, evaluates, and controls long-term capital investments involving property, plant, and equipment.

_____ 9. A period when prices in general are rising and the purchasing power of money is declining.

_____ 10. Cash to be received (or paid) in the future is not the equivalent of the same amount of money received (or paid) at an earlier date.

_____ 11. The process by which management allocates available investment funds among competing capital investment proposals.

_____ 12. A method of evaluating capital investment proposals that focuses on the expected profitability of the investment.

_____ 13. The rate at which currency in another country can be exchanged for local currency.

## FILL IN THE BLANK—PART A

*Instructions:* Answer the following questions or complete the statements by writing the appropriate words or amounts in the answer blanks.

1. The process by which management plans, evaluates, and controls investments in fixed assets is called _____ _____ _____.

2. Two methods for evaluating capital investment proposals using present values are the net present value method and the _____ _____ _____ _____ method.

3. The methods that ignore present value are often useful in evaluating capital investment proposals that have relatively _____ useful lives.

4. Mist Company is considering whether or not to buy a new machine costing $400,000. The machine has a useful life of 8 years, with a residual value of $28,000, and is expected to produce average yearly revenues of $53,500. The average rate of return on this machine is _____.

5. One advantage of the _____ _____ _____ _____ method is that it emphasizes accounting income, which is often used by investors and creditors in evaluating management performance.

6. The _____ _____ period is the amount of time that will pass between the date of the investment and the complete recovery of the funds invested.

7. A new machine will cost $15,000 per year to operate and is expected to generate $65,000 in revenues. The machine is expected to last for 10 years and will cost $300,000. The cash payback period on this investment is _____.

8. Managers who are primarily concerned with liquidity will prefer to use the _____ _____ method of evaluating capital investments.

9. A series of equal net cash flows at fixed intervals is called a(n) _____.

10. The _____ _____ _____ method analyzes capital investment proposals by comparing the initial cash investment with the present value of the net cash flows.

11. A project has estimated annual net cash flows of $50,000 for 5 years and is estimated to cost $180,000. Assuming a minimum rate of return of 10%, the net present value of this project is _____.

12. A present value _____ is calculated by dividing the total present value of the net cash flow by the amount to be invested.

13. An advantage of the _____ _____ _____ method is that it considers the time value of money.

14. The present value factor for an annuity is calculated by dividing the total amount to be invested by the equal _____ _____ _____ _____ created by the investment.

15. A company is using the internal rate of return method to appraise a capital investment decision. Several proposals have been ranked according to their internal rate of return. The company should choose the proposal with the _____ (highest/lowest) rate of return.

16. Factors that complicate capital investment analysis include federal income tax, unequal lives of alternative proposals, leasing, _____, changes in price levels, and qualitative factors.

17. To evaluate capital investment alternatives with different useful lives, net present values should be adjusted so that each alternative ends at the _____ time.

18. Investments designed to affect a company's long-term ability to generate profits are called _____ investments.

19. Product quality, manufacturing flexibility, employee morale, manufacturing productivity, and manufacturing control are _____ considerations affecting capital investment analysis.

20. In capital rationing, alternative proposals are initially screened by establishing _____ standards for the cash payback and the average rate of return.

## FILL IN THE BLANK—PART B

*Instructions:* Answer the following questions or complete the statements by writing the appropriate words or amounts in the answer blanks.

1. Methods of evaluating capital investment proposals can be grouped into two categories based on whether or not they involve _____ _____.

2. Two methods for evaluating capital investment proposals that do not use present values are the average rate of return method and the _____ _____ method.

3. The _____ _____ of money concept recognizes that an amount of cash invested today will earn income and therefore has value over time.

4. The _____ _____ _____ _____ is a measure of the average income as a percent of the average investment in fixed assets.

5. The average rate of return for a project that is estimated to yield total income of $270,000 over three years, cost $680,000, and has a $40,000 residual value is _____.

6. The excess of cash flowing in (from revenues) over the cash flowing out (for expenses) is called the _____ _____ _____.

7. When annual net cash flows are not equal, the _____ _____ _____ is determined by adding the annual net cash flows until the cumulative sum equals the amount of the proposed investment.

8. Present value methods for evaluating capital investment proposals consider both the amounts and the _____ of net cash flows.

9. The sum of the present values of a series of equal net cash flows is known as the _____ _____ _____ _____ _____.

10. If the _____ _____ _____ of the cash flows expected from a proposed investment equals or exceeds the amount of the initial investment, the proposal is desirable.

11. Shine Company is using the net present value method to evaluate an investment. The investment will cost $60,000, is expected to last for 3 years, and will generate net annual cash flows of $30,000. The desired rate of return is 12%. The net present value of this investment is _____.

12. Project X costs $50,000 and has a total present value of $72,000. The present value index is _____.

13. The _____ _____ _____ _____ method uses present value concepts to compute the rate of return from the net cash flows expected from capital investment proposals.

14. You are using the internal rate of return method to evaluate an investment alternative. You can buy new equipment costing $26,500. The equipment has a useful life of 4 years and is expected to produce annual cash flows of $10,000. Assuming a 10% rate of return, the net present value of this investment is _____.

15. A new fabricating machine will cost $79,600 and will generate equal annual cash flows of $16,000. The present value factor of this machine is _____.

16. The primary advantage of the _____ _____ _____ _____ method is that the present values of the net cash flows over the entire useful life of the proposal are considered.

17. _____ allows a business to use fixed assets without spending large amounts of cash to purchase them and may be evaluated using capital investment analysis techniques.

18. A period of increasing prices, sometimes called a period of _____, can significantly affect capital investment analysis.

19. Capital _____ is the process by which management allocates funds among competing capital investment proposals.

20. Qualitative considerations in capital investment analysis are most appropriate for _____ _____.

## MULTIPLE CHOICE

*Instructions:*   Circle the best answer for each of the following questions.

1. Which of the following methods of evaluating capital investment proposals ignores present value concepts?

   a.  average rate of return method

   b.  discounted cash flow method

   c.  discounted internal rate of return method

   d.  none of the above

2. The method of evaluating capital investment proposals that determines the total present value of cash flows expected from investment proposals and compares these values with the amounts to be invested is:

   a.  average rate of return method

   b.  cash payback method

   c.  discounted internal rate of return method

   d.  net present value method

3. The method of evaluating capital investment proposals that uses present value concepts to compute the rate of return from the net cash flows expected from the proposals is:

   a.  average rate of return method

   b.  cash payback method

   c.  internal rate of return method

   d.  net present value method

4. Jones Inc. is considering the purchase of a machine that costs $360,000. The machine is expected to have a useful life of 10 years, with no salvage value, and is expected to yield an annual net cash flow of $120,000 and an annual operating income of $60,000. What is the estimated cash payback period for the machine?

   a.  2 years

   b.  3 years

   c.  5 years

   d.  6 years

5. Management is considering an $800,000 investment in a project with a 6-year life and no residual value. If the total income from the project is expected to be $600,000, the average rate of return is:

   a.  12.5%

   b.  25%

   c.  32%

   d.  44%

6. Which of the following is a qualitative consideration that may impact upon capital investment analysis?

    a. manufacturing flexibility

    b. expected net cash inflows

    c. amounts of cash to be invested

    d. timing of cash inflows

7. Genko Company has purchased a machine for $145,000. The machine is expected to generate a positive annual net cash flow of $50,000 for four consecutive years. What is the present value index, assuming a minimum rate of return of 10%?

    a. 0.942

    b. 0.915

    c. 1.093

    d. 1.379

8. The net present value method is also called the:

    a. internal rate of return method

    b. time-adjusted rate of return method

    c. average rate of discounted return method

    d. discounted cash flow method

9. A disadvantage of the cash payback method is that it:

    a. focuses on measures that are not important to bankers and other creditors

    b. emphasizes accounting income

    c. does not use present value concepts in valuing cash flows occurring in different periods

    d. cannot be used when annual net cash flows are not equal

10. Which of the following factors may have an impact on a capital investment decision?

    a. federal income taxes

    b. unequal lives of proposed investments

    c. changes in price levels

    d. all of the above

11. A business is considering the investment in a new machine that will cost $320,000 with no salvage value. The machine is expected to reduce labor costs by $70,000 per year and material scrap by $20,000 per year. The machine is expected to have a 5-year life. What is the present value of this investment, assuming a 12% interest rate?

    a. $4,450

    b. $130,000

    c. $(64,850)

    d. $(67,650)

12. A business invests $83,200 in a project that is expected to generate $20,000 in annual cash flows at the end of each of the next seven years. What is the internal rate of return on this project?

   a. 10%

   b. 12%

   c. 15%

   d. 20%

13. A machine will cost $45,000 and is expected to generate equal annual cash flows of $15,000 at the end of each of the next five years. In addition, the machine is expected to have a salvage value of $8,000 at the end of the fifth year. Determine the net present value of this investment, assuming an interest rate of 20%.

   a. $(14,850)

   b. $(135)

   c. $3,081

   d. $23,793

## TRUE/FALSE

**Instructions:** Indicate whether each of the following statements is true or false by placing a check mark in the appropriate column.

|  | True | False |
|---|---|---|
| 1. The two common present value methods used in evaluating capital investment proposals are (1) the net present value method and (2) the internal rate of return method...... | ____ | ____ |
| 2. Two methods of evaluating capital investment proposals that ignore present value are (1) the average rate of return method and (2) the cash payback period method................ | ____ | ____ |
| 3. The expected time that will pass between the date of capital investment and the complete recovery of cash (or equivalent) of the amount invested is called the present value period.......................................................................... | ____ | ____ |
| 4. The methods of evaluating capital investment proposals that ignore present value are especially useful in evaluating capital investments that have relatively long useful lives. .......................................................................... | ____ | ____ |
| 5. The net present value method, sometimes called the internal rate of return or time-adjusted rate of return method, uses present value concepts to compute the rate of return from the net cash flows expected from the capital investment proposals. ...................................................... | ____ | ____ |

                                                                  **True    False**

6. The present value index is computed by dividing the
   amount to be invested by the total present value of the
   net cash flow. ............................................................   ____    ____

7. The present value factor for an annuity of $1 is computed
   by dividing the amount to be invested by the equal annual
   net cash flow. ...........................................................   ____    ____

8. Proposals that are funded in the capital rationing process
   are included in the capital expenditures budget to aid the
   planning and financing of operations. .........................   ____    ____

9. One advantage of the average rate of return method is
   that it includes the amount of income earned over the
   entire life of the proposal. ......................................   ____    ____

10. One advantage of the cash payback method is that it
    includes cash flows occurring after the payback period. .....   ____    ____

# EXERCISE 25-1

Daily Inc. is considering the acquisition of a newly developed machine at a cost
of $620,000. This machine is expected to have a useful life of 5 years and no
residual value. Use of the new machine is expected to yield total income of
$240,000 during the 5 years of its useful life and to provide an average annual
net cash flow of $200,000. The minimum rate of return desired by Daily is 12%.
The maximum cash payback period desired by Daily is 3 years.

*Instructions:*   Using the information given, make the analyses indicated and
write your answers in the spaces provided.

(1) What average rate of return (based on the average
    investment) can Daily expect to achieve during the
    useful life of this machine? ...........................................   _____ %

(2) What is the expected cash payback period for this
    proposed expenditure? ...................................................   _____ years

(3) Based on the analysis of average rate of return,
    should the management of Daily acquire the new
    machine? ....................................................................   yes ____   no ____

(4) Based on the expected cash payback period,
    should management acquire the new machine? ...........   yes ____   no ____

## EXERCISE 25-2

Crusty Corp. is evaluating two capital investment proposals, each requiring an investment of $250,000 and each with a 6-year life and expected total net cash flows of $360,000.

Proposal 1 is expected to provide equal annual net cash flows of $60,000. Proposal 2 is expected to have the following unequal net cash flows:

| | | | | |
|---|---|---|---|---|
| Year 1 | $100,000 | | Year 4 | $45,000 |
| Year 2 | 80,000 | | Year 5 | 45,000 |
| Year 3 | 70,000 | | Year 6 | 20,000 |

***Instructions:***   Determine the cash payback period for each proposal.

Proposal 1:

Proposal 2:

# EXERCISE 25-3

Assume that Crusty Corp. is re-evaluating the two capital investment proposals described in Exercise 25-2, taking into consideration present value concepts.

***Instructions:***   Determine the net present value for each proposal using a rate of 10%.

Proposal 1:

Proposal 2:

|   | A | B | C | D |
|---|---|---|---|---|
| 1 | Year | Present Value of 1 at 10% | Net Cash Flow | Present Value of Net Cash Flow |
| 2 |  |  |  |  |
| 3 |  |  |  |  |
| 4 |  |  |  |  |
| 5 |  |  |  |  |
| 6 |  |  |  |  |
| 7 |  |  |  |  |
| 8 |  |  |  |  |
| 9 |  |  |  |  |
| 10 |  |  |  |  |
| 11 |  |  |  |  |
| 12 |  |  |  |  |

# EXERCISE 25-4

The management of Argo Inc. has decided to use the internal rate of return method to analyze a capital investment proposal that involves an investment of $358,900 and annual net cash flows of $120,000 for each of the 5 years of useful life.

## Instructions:

**(1)** Determine the present value factor for an annuity of $1 which can be used in determining the internal rate of return.

**(2)** Using the factor determined in (1) and the present value of an annuity of $1 table appearing in Chapter 25, determine the internal rate of return for the proposal.

## PROBLEM 25-1

### Instructions:

(1) Complete the following table using the net present value method to evaluate capital investment in new equipment.

| | A | B | C | D |
|---|---|---|---|---|
| 1 | Year | Present Value of 1 at 12% | Net Cash Flow | Present Value of Net Cash Flow |
| 2 | 1 | 0.893 | $ 80,000 | |
| 3 | 2 | 0.797 | 60,000 | |
| 4 | 3 | 0.712 | 60,000 | |
| 5 | 4 | 0.636 | 60,000 | |
| 6 | 5 | 0.567 | 60,000 | |
| 7 | Total | | $320,000 | |
| 8 | | | | |
| 9 | Amount to be invested in equipment | | | 180,000 |
| 10 | | | | |
| 11 | Excess of present value over amount to be invested | | | |

(2) Compute the present value index for the new equipment. (Round to two decimal places.)

(3) Based on the net present value method, should management acquire the new machine? ............................................................... yes _____   no _____

## PROBLEM 25-2

Preston Co. is evaluating two projects which have different useful lives but which have an equal investment requirement of $180,000. The estimated net cash flows from each project are as follows:

| Year | Project 1 | Project 2 |
|------|-----------|-----------|
| 1 | $55,000 | $55,000 |
| 2 | 50,000 | 55,000 |
| 3 | 45,000 | 55,000 |
| 4 | 40,000 | 55,000 |
| 5 | 40,000 | 55,000 |
| 6 | 30,000 | |
| 7 | 15,000 | |

Preston Co. has selected a rate of 10% for purposes of net present value analysis. Preston also estimates that there will be no residual value at the end of each project's useful life, but at the end of the fifth year, Project 1's residual value would be $60,000.

### Instructions:

**(1)** For each project, compute the net present value.

Project 1:

| | A | B | C | D |
|---|---|---|---|---|
| 1 | Year | Present Value of 1 at 10% | Net Cash Flow | Present Value of Net Cash Flow |
| 2 | | | | |
| 3 | | | | |
| 4 | | | | |
| 5 | | | | |
| 6 | | | | |
| 7 | | | | |
| 8 | | | | |
| 9 | | | | |
| 10 | | | | |
| 11 | | | | |
| 12 | | | | |
| 13 | | | | |

Project 2:

| | A | B | C | D |
|---|---|---|---|---|
| **1** | Year | Present Value of 1 at 10% | Net Cash Flow | Present Value of Net Cash Flow |
| **2** | | | | |
| **3** | | | | |
| **4** | | | | |
| **5** | | | | |
| **6** | | | | |
| **7** | | | | |
| **8** | | | | |
| **9** | | | | |
| **10** | | | | |
| **11** | | | | |

**(2)** For each project, compute the net present value, assuming that Project 1 is adjusted to a 5-year life for purposes of analysis.

| | A | B | C | D |
|---|---|---|---|---|
| **1** | Year | Present Value of 1 at 10% | Net Cash Flow | Present Value of Net Cash Flow |
| **2** | | | | |
| **3** | | | | |
| **4** | | | | |
| **5** | | | | |
| **6** | | | | |
| **7** | | | | |
| **8** | | | | |
| **9** | | | | |
| **10** | | | | |
| **11** | | | | |
| **12** | | | | |

**(3)** Determine which of the two projects is more attractive based upon your findings in (2) above.

# 26 Cost Allocation and Activity-Based Costing

## QUIZ AND TEST HINTS

The following hints may be helpful to you in preparing for a quiz or a test over the material covered in Chapter 26.

1. This chapter introduces new terms related to cost allocation and activity-based costing. Instructors normally test this material using true/false and multiple-choice questions. Review the "Key Terms" section at the end of the chapter and be sure you understand each term. Do the Matching and Fill-in-the-Blank exercises included in this Study Guide.

2. The chapter focuses on demonstrating three different methods of allocating factory overhead: the plantwide rate method, the multiple production department rate method, and the activity-based costing method. Expect problems requiring you to determine product costs under these methods. You may be asked to compare and explain the difference in results obtained from using different methods with the same underlying information. The Illustrative Problem in the text is a good study aid.

3. Be prepared to explain the conditions that favor the use of the single plantwide rate method, the multiple production department rate method, and the activity-based costing method.

4. The activity-based costing method is illustrated in the chapter for factory costs, selling and administrative expenses, and service companies. Expect a problem using activity-based costing in one or more of these scenarios.

5. Be prepared to explain the difference between using activity-based costing and relative sales-volume allocation for selling and administrative expenses.

6. Expect some multiple-choice questions using the simpler plantwide rate allocation and the more complex activity-based costing approach.

7. Review the "At A Glance" section at the end of the chapter. Read and review each of the Key Points and related Learning Outcomes. For each Learning Outcome that has an Example Exercise, locate the Example Exercise in the chapter and be sure that you understand the solution and can work a similar item on a test. If you have any questions about an Example Exercise, read the section of the chapter immediately preceding the Example Exercise.

## MATCHING

**Instructions:**   Match each of the statements below with its proper term. Some terms may not be used.

A.   activity base
B.   activity-base usage quantity
C.   activity-based costing (ABC) method
D.   activity cost pools
E.   activity rate
F.   budgeted factory overhead rates

G.   cost distortion
H.   engineering change order
I.   multiple production department factory overhead rate method
J.   product costing
K.   setup
L.   single plantwide factory overhead rate method

_____   1.   The level of activity in determining the activity rate.

_____   2.   Determining the cost of a product.

_____   3.   An accounting framework based on determining the cost of activities and allocating these costs to products, customers, or other cost objects, using activity rates.

_____   4.   A document that initiates a change in the specification of a product or process.

_____   5.   A method that allocates all factory overhead to products by using a single factory overhead rate.

_____   6.   Cost accumulations that are associated with a given activity, such as machine usage, inspections, moving, and production setups.

_____   7.   The cost of an activity per unit of activity base, determined by dividing the activity cost pool by the activity base.

_____   8.   The amount of activity used by a particular product measured in activity-base terms.

_____   9.   Inaccurate product costs that are the result of applying a cost allocation method that is inappropriate for the situation.

_____   10.   A method that allocates factory overhead to products by using factory overhead rates for each production department.

_____   11.   Changing the characteristics of a machine to produce a different product.

# FILL IN THE BLANK—PART A

*Instructions:*  Answer the following questions or complete the statements by writing the appropriate words or amounts in the answer blanks.

1.  Determining the cost of a product is called _____ _____.

2.  The single plantwide factory overhead rate is determined by dividing

    _____ _____ _____ _____

    _____ by _____ _____ _____

    _____ _____.

3.  The factory overhead allocated to a product with 24 machine hours, using a single plantwide factory overhead rate of $12 per machine hour, is

    _____.

4.  Under the multiple production department factory overhead rate method there is a factory overhead rate for each _____

    _____.

5.  An Assembly Department has budgeted factory overhead of $420,000 and 7,000 estimated direct labor hours; thus, the Assembly Department factory overhead rate is _____.

6.  If the Packing Department has a departmental factory overhead rate of $32 per direct labor hour, then a product requiring 15 hours in the Packing Department will be allocated _____ of Packing Department factory overhead cost.

7.  When some products are allocated too much cost, while others are allocated too little cost, the cost allocation method is said to lead to product cost _____.

8.  The total factory overhead cost allocated by the single plantwide rate method is _____ (less than, equal to, or greater than) the cost allocated by the multiple production department rate method.

9.  One of the necessary conditions that indicates that the single plantwide factory overhead rate may lead to product cost distortion is _____ in production department factory overhead rates.

10.  One of the necessary conditions that indicates that the single plantwide factory overhead rate may lead to product cost distortion is differences in the _____ of allocation-base usage.

11.  Under activity-based costing, factory overhead costs are first accounted for in activity cost _____.

12.  Product L is set up 12 times, with each production run consisting of 10 units. If the setup activity rate is $400 per setup, then the setup cost per unit is _____.

13. The activity pool for the purchasing activity is $360,000, while there are 12,000 purchase orders estimated for the period; thus, the purchasing activity rate is _____.

14. Under activity-based costing, more factory overhead will be allocated to a(n) _____ product.

15. Under activity-based costing, an activity base used for the quality control inspection activity would be _____ _____ _____.

16. Under generally accepted accounting principles, selling and administrative expenses should be treated as _____ expenses; however, management may wish to treat them as _____ costs for management reporting purposes.

17. The traditional method of allocating selling and administrative expenses to products is based on product _____ volumes.

18–19. Product K had 150 sales orders and 10 returns, while Product L had 200 sales orders and 50 returns. The activity rate for the sales order processing activity is $36 per sales order, while the activity rate for the return processing activity is $145 per return.

18. The sales order and return processing activity cost of Product K is _____.

19. The sales order and return processing activity cost of Product L is _____.

20. Activity-based costing could be used by a hospital to determine the cost of services consumed by a(n) _____.

## FILL IN THE BLANK—PART B

*Instructions:* Answer the following questions or complete the statements by writing the appropriate words or amounts in the answer blanks.

1. An accounting framework based on relating the cost of activities to final cost objects is called _____-_____ _____.

2. The single plantwide factory overhead rate method's greatest advantage is _____.

3. Each department under the multiple production department rate method uses _____ (the same or different) factory overhead rates.

4. In activity-based costing, activity rates are determined by dividing the cost budgeted for each activity by an estimated _____ _____.

5. Under the single plantwide rate method, the total factory overhead allocated to products will be _____ (less than, equal to, or greater than) the total factory overhead allocated under the multiple production department rate method.

6. A method of allocating factory overhead to products by using factory overhead rates for each production department is termed the

   _____ _____ _____ _____ method.

7. A method of allocating factory overhead to products by using a single factory overhead rate is termed the _____ _____ _____ method.

8. A(n) _____ _____ _____ activates an administrative process to change the product design characteristics.

9. The activity of changing the characteristics of a machine to prepare for manufacturing a different product is termed a(n) _____.

10. The denominator used to determine a production department rate is termed a(n) _____ _____.

11–14. In each of the following independent cases assume a multiple-department, multi-product factory. Answer "yes" if using a plantwide factory overhead rate would likely distort product costs and "no" if it would not.

11. The factory overhead rates in Departments A and B are both $40 per machine hour. _____

12. The factory overhead rate in Department T is $32 per machine hour, in Department V it is $62 per machine hour, and the products use the same number of hours in each department. _____

13. One product consumes 12 direct labor hours at $18 per direct labor hour in Department L and 8 direct labor hours at $40 per direct labor hour in Department M. Another product consumes 6 direct labor hours at $18 per direct labor hour in Department L and 15 direct labor hours at $40 per hour in Department M. _____

14. One product consumes 20 direct labor hours at $30 per direct labor hour in Department D and 12 direct labor hours at $30 per direct labor hour in Department E. Another product consumes 12 direct labor hours at $30 per direct labor hour in Department D and 20 direct labor hours at $30 per hour in Department E. _____

15. The danger of product cost distortion is that it can lead to bad decisions and flawed _____.

16. If the reactor activity cost is estimated to be $850,000 for the year and the reactor is expected to run for 2,000 hours during the year, the activity rate per machine hour is _____.

17. Product T requires 12 hours in the Reaction Department. The reaction activity cost allocated to Product T using the activity rate in Question 16 is _____.

18. If the budgeted factory overhead is $1,400,000 and the direct labor hours budgeted is 50,000, the plantwide factory overhead rate per direct labor hour is _____.

19. Selling and administrative activities _____ (can or cannot) be allocated to products for management reporting purposes.

20. An appropriate activity base for the radiological testing activity in a hospital is _____ _____ _____.


## MULTIPLE CHOICE

*Instructions:*   Circle the best answer for each of the following questions.

1. Which of the following allocation bases would most likely be used under the single plantwide rate method?
   a. total direct labor hours
   b. number of setups
   c. number of engineering changes
   d. Packing Department direct labor hours

2. Hy-Gain Company manufactures two products—cellular phones and pagers. The budgeted factory overhead for Hy-Gain for the next period is $450,000. Hy-Gain expects to operate the plant for 10,000 machine hours during the next period. The cellular phone requires 1.2 machine hours, and the pager requires 0.8 machine hours. How much factory overhead per unit should be allocated to the pager under the single plantwide rate method?
   a. $36.00
   b. $45.00
   c. $54.00
   d. $56.25

3. Celebration Cards Inc. is a greeting card company that uses the multiple production department rate method to allocate factory overhead. Celebration Cards prints cards for two occasions—Valentine's Day and birthdays. The cards are manufactured through two departments—Printing and Cutting. The Printing Department has a factory overhead budget of $120,000 and 5,000 machine hours. The Cutting Department has a factory overhead budget of $80,000 and 8,000 direct labor hours. If a case of Valentine's Day cards requires 0.5 machine hours in the Printing Department and 0.25 direct labor hours in the Cutting Department, how much factory overhead should be allocated to the case?

   a. $11.55
   b. $12.00
   c. $14.50
   d. $15.40

4. Activity-based costing will generally have _____ activity (allocation) rates than the multiple production department rate method.

   a. fewer
   b. more
   c. the same number of
   d. either fewer or more

5. The multiple production department rate method will lead to more accurate factory overhead allocation than the single plantwide rate method when:

   a. there are significant differences between the production department rates
   b. there are differences in the ratios of allocation-base usage of the products across the departments
   c. either a or b
   d. both a and b

6. The activity rate is determined by dividing the estimated activity cost pool by:

   a. the activity-base usage quantity
   b. the total estimated activity base
   c. the total estimated allocation base
   d. the units of production

7. Luv 'N Stuff Company manufactures stuffed toy animals. Activities and the activity rates from the selling and administrative expenses include the following:

Sales order processing ........................... $45 per sales order
Customer service .................................. $125 per request
Customer return processing ................. $400 per returned item

How much selling and administrative expense should be allocated to the Benny the Bear toy if Benny had 60 sales orders, 5 customer requests for service, and 4 customer returns?

   a. $4,925

   b. $39,330

   c. $5,200

   d. $2,700

8. When should selling and administrative expenses be allocated using the relative sales volume method?

   a. when these expenses are proportional to sales volume

   b. never

   c. when sales are expected to be nearly the same for each product

   d. when these expenses are not proportional to sales volume

9–10. Portions of the Central Railroad Company's costs consist of crew salaries, fuel, and railcar loading and unloading. These costs are estimated for the year to be as follows:

Crew salaries ....................................... $360,000
Fuel ....................................................... 80,000
Railcar loading and unloading .............. 290,000

In addition, the Central Railroad Company estimates that their trains pull 2,900 railcars over the year. The trains will run a total of 25,000 miles. Train 102 consists of 60 railcars moved from Cincinnati to Kansas City— a distance of 550 miles.

9. What is the activity rate for "railcar loading and unloading"?

   a. $35 per railcar

   b. $75 per railcar

   c. $100 per railcar

   d. $11.60 per mile

10. What is the crew salary, fuel, and railcar loading and unloading cost for Train 102?

   a. $15,103

   b. $15,680

   c. $16,060

   d. $30,880

11. The controller says that the sum of activity-based factory allocations to all your products is greater than the sum of the single plantwide rate allocations to the same products. What is your conclusion?

   a. Activity-based costing must use more rates than the single plantwide rate method.

   b. Activity-based costing allocates more cost than the single plantwide rate method because there are more activity pools under activity-based costing.

   c. Activity-based costing has larger rates than the single plantwide rate method.

   d. Something is wrong with the controller's calculations.

12. The single plantwide factory overhead rate is $52 per direct labor hour. The company implements activity-based costing using four different activity bases, including direct labor hours (and three others). What can be said about the direct labor rate under activity-based costing relative to the single plantwide rate?

   a. The direct labor rate under activity-based costing must be greater than $52 per direct labor hour.

   b. The direct labor rate under activity-based costing must be less than $52 per direct labor hour.

   c. The direct labor rate under activity-based costing will be equal to $52 per direct labor hour.

   d. The direct labor rate under activity-based costing cannot be compared meaningfully to the $52 per direct labor hour rate.

## TRUE/FALSE

*Instructions:* Indicate whether each of the following statements is true or false by placing a check mark in the appropriate column.

| | **True** | **False** |
|---|---|---|

1. The advantage of the single plantwide factory overhead rate method is that it is simple to use............................  _____  _____

2. The production department overhead cost under the multiple production department rate method must be the same as a production activity pool under activity-based costing.........................................................................  _____  _____

3. The multiple production department rate method will lead to improved factory overhead cost allocation only if there are significant rate differences between the production departments. ..........................................................  _____  _____

4. The activity-based costing method uses activity pools to allocate factory overhead to products. ...............................  _____  _____

5. Activity-based costing should only be used by manufacturing companies..................................................................  _____  _____

6. An example of an activity is the plant manager's salary. .....  _____  _____

7. Engineering change orders are issued to change engineering personnel. ............................................................  _____  _____

8. Activity-based costing will lead to more accurate factory overhead allocations when products exhibit complexity that is unrelated to production volumes. ...........................  _____  _____

9. Selling and administrative expenses allocated to products under the relative sales volume method is based on the assumption that these expenses are proportional to sales volume..........................................................................  _____  _____

10. Service companies should not allocate overhead since they do not have product costs for determining inventory. ...  _____  _____

## EXERCISE 26-1

Peacock Apparel Company manufactures three styles of men's shirts: casual, work, and dress. The company has budgeted the following overhead expenses for the upcoming period:

| | |
|---|---:|
| Factory depreciation ..................................... | $    40,000 |
| Indirect labor ............................................... | 840,000 |
| Factory electricity ......................................... | 90,000 |
| Indirect materials ......................................... | 70,000 |
| Selling expenses ......................................... | 350,000 |
| Administrative expenses ........................... | 170,000 |
| Total .................................................... | $1,560,000 |

Factory overhead is allocated to the three products on the basis of direct labor hours. The products had the following production budget volume and direct labor hours per unit information:

| | Budgeted Production Volume | Direct Labor Hours per Unit |
|---|---|---|
| Casual ......................... | 450,000 | 0.1 |
| Work ............................ | 200,000 | 0.2 |
| Dress ........................... | 150,000 | 0.3 |
| | 800,000 | |

*Instructions:*

(1) Determine the single plantwide factory overhead rate.

(2) Use the factory overhead rate in (1) to determine the amount of total and per-unit factory overhead allocated to each of the three products under generally accepted accounting principles.

_____

_____

_____

_____

_____

_____

_____

_____

_____

_____

_____

_____

_____

_____

## EXERCISE 26-2

Sure-Stop Brake Company produces three types of brakes: auto, truck, and bus. A brake is first pressed in the Press Department. The pressed brakes are then sent to the Cure Department, where the final brake is cured for strength. Sure-Stop uses the multiple production department rate method of allocating factory overhead costs. Sure-Stop's factory overhead costs are budgeted as follows:

| | |
|---|---|
| Press Department overhead ...................... | $600,000 |
| Cure Department overhead ....................... | 240,000 |
| Total ................................................... | $840,000 |

The machine hours estimated for each production department are as follows:

| | Press Department | Cure Department | Total |
|---|---|---|---|
| Machine hours ............................. | 8,000 | 24,000 | 32,000 |

Machine hours are used to allocate the production department overhead to the products. The machine hours per set for each product for each production department were obtained from the engineering records as follows:

| | Auto Brake | Truck Brake | Bus Brake |
|---|---|---|---|
| Press Department .......................... | 0.30 | 0.5 | 1 |
| Cure Department ........................... | 2.25 | 2.5 | 3 |
| Machine hours per brake set ......... | 2.55 | 3.0 | 4 |

**Instructions:**

(1) Determine the production department factory overhead rates.

(2) Use the production department factory overhead rates to determine the factory overhead per set for each product.

_____

_____

_____

_____

_____

_____

_____

_____

_____

_____

_____

_____

_____

_____

_____

_____

_____

_____

_____

_____

_____

_____

_____

_____

_____

_____

_____

_____

## EXERCISE 26-3

Perfect Reflection Printer Company is estimating the activity cost associated with producing laser and ink jet printers. The indirect labor can be traced to four separate activity pools, based on time records provided by the indirect employees. The budgeted activity cost and activity-base information is provided below.

| Activity | Activity Cost Pool | Activity Base |
|---|---|---|
| Purchasing ..................... | $225,000 | Number of purchase orders |
| Inspecting ...................... | 140,000 | Number of inspections |
| Materials handling ........... | 70,000 | Number of moves |
| Product development ...... | 165,000 | Number of engineering change orders |
| Total ........................ | $600,000 | |

Estimated activity-base usage and unit information for Perfect Reflection's two product lines was determined from corporate records as follows:

| | Number of Purchase Orders | Number of Inspections | Number of Moves | Number of Engineering Changes | Units |
|---|---|---|---|---|---|
| Laser printer .......... | 4,000 | 5,500 | 20,000 | 800 | 4,000 |
| Ink jet printer ......... | 6,000 | 1,500 | 15,000 | 200 | 4,000 |
| Totals .............. | 10,000 | 7,000 | 35,000 | 1,000 | 8,000 |

### Instructions:

(1) Determine the activity rate for each activity cost pool.

**(2)** Determine the total and per-unit activity-based cost for each product.

Laser Printer:

| | A | B | C | D | E | F |
|---|---|---|---|---|---|---|
| 1 | | Activity-Base Usage | × | Activity Rate | = | Activity Cost |
| 2 | | | | | | |
| 3 | | | | | | |
| 4 | | | | | | |
| 5 | | | | | | |
| 6 | | | | | | |
| 7 | | | | | | |
| 8 | | | | | | |

Ink Jet Printer:

| | A | B | C | D | E | F |
|---|---|---|---|---|---|---|
| 1 | | Activity-Base Usage | × | Activity Rate | = | Activity Cost |
| 2 | | | | | | |
| 3 | | | | | | |
| 4 | | | | | | |
| 5 | | | | | | |
| 6 | | | | | | |
| 7 | | | | | | |
| 8 | | | | | | |

## EXERCISE 26-4

Swanson Wine Distribution, Inc., markets and distributes California and imported wine products. The controller prepared the following report showing the income from operations for both products:

Swanson Wine Distribution, Inc.
Statement of Operating Income—By Product
For the Year Ended December 31, 20--

|  | Imported Wines | California Wines | Total |
|---|---|---|---|
| Sales | $3,600,000 | $5,040,000 | $8,640,000 |
| Cost of goods sold | 2,160,000 | 3,024,000 | 5,184,000 |
| Gross profit | $1,440,000 | $2,016,000 | $3,456,000 |
| Selling and administrative expenses .. | 531,250 | 743,750 | 1,275,000 |
| Income from operations | $ 908,750 | $1,272,250 | $2,181,000 |
| Income from operations as a percent of sales | 25.2% | 25.2% | 25.2% |

When preparing the report, the controller allocated selling and administrative costs based on the relative sales volume (in dollars). The report shows that both categories of wine have the same income from operations as a percent of sales. The president of the company criticized the report for assuming that selling and administrative expenses were proportional to sales volume. The president believes this assumption is invalid and asks that a new report be prepared using activity-based costing to allocate the selling and administrative expenses. An activity analysis reveals that the following activities were performed in the selling and administrative areas:

| | |
|---|---|
| Sales order processing and collecting activities | $ 435,000 |
| Promotional activities | 525,000 |
| Importing and customs activities | 200,000 |
| Inventory carrying cost | 115,000 |
| Total selling and general administrative expenses | $1,275,000 |

In addition, the controller collects the following operating information:

|  | Imported Wines | Domestic Wines |
|---|---|---|
| Cases sold | 4,500 | 12,000 |
| Average order size (cases) | 2 | 8 |
| Number of days' sales in inventory | 120 | 40 |
| Number of promotional ads placed | 90 | 30 |

In the table above, *average order size* represents the average number of cases of wine associated with a customer order, *number of days' sales in inventory* is a measure of the relative inventory for the two types of wine, and *number of promotional ads placed* is the number of ads placed in a national life-style magazine.

### Instructions:

Use the financial and operational data to recast the "Statement of Operating Income—By Product" report using activity-based costing. Interpret your results.

*Swanson Wine Distribution, Inc.*

*Statement of Operating Income—By Product*

*For the Year Ended December 31, 20--*

| | IMPORTED WINES | CALIFORNIA WINES | TOTAL |
|---|---|---|---|
| | | | |
| | | | |
| | | | |
| | | | |
| | | | |
| | | | |
| | | | |
| | | | |
| | | | |
| | | | |
| | | | |
| | | | |
| | | | |

*Supporting Calculations and Interpretation:*

_____

_____

_____

_____

_____

_____

_____

_____

_____

_____

_____

_____

_____

_____

_____

_____

_____

## PROBLEM 26-1

Bon Voyage Luggage Company manufactures two products: suitcases and garment bags. The factory overhead is incurred as follows:

| | |
|---|---:|
| Indirect labor | $ 800,000 |
| Cutting Department | 800,000 |
| Assembly Department | 200,000 |
| Total | $1,800,000 |

The activity base associated with the two production departments is direct labor hours. The indirect labor can be assigned to two different activities as follows:

| Activity | Activity Cost Pool | Activity Base |
|---|---|---|
| Inspection | $600,000 | Number of inspections |
| Setup | 200,000 | Number of setups |
| Total | $800,000 | |

The activity-base information for the two products is shown below.

| | Number of Inspections | Number of Setups | Dir. Labor Hours— Cutting | Dir. Labor Hours— Assembly | Units Produced |
|---|---|---|---|---|---|
| Suitcase | 1,000 | 200 | 8,000 | 2,000 | 10,000 |
| Garment bag | 3,000 | 600 | 2,000 | 8,000 | 10,000 |
| Totals | 4,000 | 800 | 10,000 | 10,000 | 20,000 |

### Instructions:

(1) Determine the factory overhead rates under the multiple production department rate method. Assume that indirect labor is associated with the production departments, so that the total factory overhead is $1,200,000 and $600,000 for Cutting and Assembly, respectively.

**(2)** Determine the total and per-unit factory overhead costs allocated to each product using the multiple production department overhead rates in (1).

**(3)** Determine the activity rates, assuming that the indirect labor is associated with activities rather than with the production departments.

|  | A | B | C | D | E |
|---|---|---|---|---|---|
| 1 |  | Inspecting | Setup | Cutting | Assembly |
| 2 |  |  |  |  |  |
| 3 |  |  |  |  |  |
| 4 |  |  |  |  |  |

**(4)** Determine the total and per-unit factory overhead costs assigned to each product under activity-based costing.

Suitcase:

| | A | B | C | D | E | F |
|---|---|---|---|---|---|---|
| 1 | | Activity-Base Usage | × | Activity Rate | = | Activity Cost |
| 2 | | | | | | |
| 3 | | | | | | |
| 4 | | | | | | |
| 5 | | | | | | |
| 6 | | | | | | |
| 7 | | | | | | |
| 8 | | | | | | |

Garment Bag:

| | A | B | C | D | E | F |
|---|---|---|---|---|---|---|
| 1 | | Activity-Base Usage | × | Activity Rate | = | Activity Cost |
| 2 | | | | | | |
| 3 | | | | | | |
| 4 | | | | | | |
| 5 | | | | | | |
| 6 | | | | | | |
| 7 | | | | | | |
| 8 | | | | | | |

**(5)** Explain the difference in the per-unit factory overhead allocated to each product under the multiple production department rate and activity-based costing methods.

## PROBLEM 26-2

XCell Soft Inc. sells commercial software. The company incurs selling and administrative expenses of $21,600,000. The company wishes to assign these costs to its three major products: integrated accounting software, human resource (HR) software, and project management software. These expenses are related to three major activities: 1-800 customer support, customer return processing, and order processing. The activity cost pool and activity bases associated with these activities are provided below.

| Activity | Activity Cost Pool | Activity Base |
|---|---|---|
| 1-800 customer support ........... | $ 5,400,000 | Number of calls |
| Customer return processing .... | 7,200,000 | Number of returns |
| Order processing ..................... | 9,000,000 | Number of sales orders |
| Total ................................. | $21,600,000 | |

The following activity-base usage and units sold information for the three products is available from the corporate records:

| | Integrated Accounting | Human Resource | Project Management | Total |
|---|---|---|---|---|
| Number of 1-800 calls ..... | 20,000 | 20,000 | 10,000 | 50,000 |
| Number of returns ........... | 2,000 | 5,000 | 5,000 | 12,000 |
| Number of orders ............ | 20,000 | 15,000 | 10,000 | 45,000 |
| Unit volume .................... | 50,000 | 40,000 | 10,000 | 100,000 |

In addition, the price and the cost of goods sold per unit for the three products are as follows:

| | Per Unit |
|---|---|
| Price ..................................... | $500 |
| Cost of goods sold .............. | 50 |
| Gross profit .......................... | $450 |

### Instructions:

**(1)** Determine the activity rates for each of the three activity pools.

**(2)** Determine the activity costs allocated to the three products using the activity rates in (1).

**(3)** Construct product profitability reports for the three products using the activity costs in (2). The reports should disclose the gross profit and operating profit associated with each product.

**(4)** Provide recommendations to management based on the profit reports in (3).

# 27

# Cost Management for Just-in-Time Environments

## QUIZ AND TEST HINTS

The following hints may be helpful to you in preparing for a quiz or a test over the material covered in Chapter 27.

1. This chapter has two major sections: the just-in-time philosophy and the impact of the just-in-time philosophy on management accounting. You should expect multiple-choice questions about the just-in-time philosophy. In addition, you may be asked to compare and contrast the just-in-time philosophy with traditional manufacturing approaches.

2. Be prepared to define and calculate the lead time for a product.

3. You should be able to provide some simplified journal entries for a just-in-time manufacturer. In addition, you may have multiple-choice or short-answer questions asking you to identify the unique features of management accounting in a just-in-time environment.

4. Be prepared to answer multiple-choice questions about quality cost definitions. In addition, be able to prepare a cost of quality report, a Pareto chart of quality costs, and a value-added/nonvalue-added analysis.

5. The specialized terms associated with a just-in-time environment are introduced in this chapter. You should be prepared to answer true/false or multiple-choice questions about these terms. Review the "Key Terms" section at the end of the chapter and be sure you understand each term. Do the Matching and Fill-in-the-Blank exercises included in this Study Guide.

6. Review the "At A Glance" section at the end of the chapter. Read and review each of the Key Points and related Learning Outcomes. For each Learning Outcome that has an Example Exercise, locate the Example Exercise in the chapter and be sure that you understand the solution and can work a similar item on a test. If you have any questions about an Example Exercise, read the section of the chapter immediately preceding the Example Exercise.

# MATCHING

***Instructions:*** Match each of the statements below with its proper term. Some terms may not be used.

| | | | |
|---|---|---|---|
| A. | activity analysis | O. | nonvalue-added lead time |
| B. | appraisal costs | P. | Pareto chart |
| C. | backflush accounting | Q. | prevention costs |
| D. | cost of quality report | R. | process |
| E. | costs of quality | S. | process-oriented layout |
| F. | electronic data interchange (EDI) | T. | product-oriented layout |
| G. | employee involvement | U. | pull manufacturing |
| H. | enterprise resource planning (ERP) | V. | push manufacturing |
| | | W. | raw and in process (RIP) inventory |
| I. | external failure costs | X. | radio frequency identification device (RFID) |
| J. | internal failure costs | | |
| K. | just-in-time manufacturing | Y. | six-sigma |
| L. | lead time | Z. | supply chain management |
| M. | nonfinancial measure | AA. | value-added activities |
| N. | nonvalue-added activities | BB. | value-added lead time |
| | | CC. | value-added ratio |

_____ 1. A bar chart that shows the totals of a particular attribute for a number of categories, ranked left to right from the largest to smallest totals.

_____ 2. A business philosophy that focuses on eliminating time, cost, and poor quality within manufacturing processes.

_____ 3. The coordination and control of materials, services, information, and finances as they move in a process from supplier, through the manufacturing, wholesaler, and retailer to the consumer.

_____ 4. A just-in-time method wherein customer orders signal the release of finished goods, which signals production, which signals the release of materials from suppliers.

_____ 5. A performance measure that has not been stated in dollar terms.

_____ 6. A philosophy that grants employees the responsibility and authority to make their own decisions about their operations.

_____ 7. A report summarizing the costs, percent of total, and percent of sales by appraisal, prevention, internal failure, and external failure cost of quality categories.

_____ 8. A sequence of activities that converts an input into an output.

_____ 9. An information technology that allows different business organizations to use computers to communicate orders, relay information, and make or receive payments.

_____ 10. Costs incurred to prevent defects from occurring during the design and delivery of products or services.

____ 11. Costs to detect, measure, evaluate, and audit products and processes to ensure that they conform to customer requirements and performance standards.

____ 12. Materials are released into production and work in process is released into finished goods in anticipation of future sales.

____ 13. Organizing work in a plant or administrative function around processes (tasks).

____ 14. Organizing work in a plant or administrative function around products; sometimes referred to as product cells.

____ 15. The capitalized cost of direct materials purchases, labor, and overhead charged to the production cell.

____ 16. The cost of activities that are needed to meet customer requirements.

____ 17. The cost of activities that are perceived as unnecessary from the customer's perspective and are thus candidates for elimination.

____ 18. The costs associated with controlling quality (prevention and appraisal) and failing to control quality (internal and external failure).

____ 19. The costs associated with defects that are discovered by the organization before the product or service is delivered to the consumer.

____ 20. The costs incurred after defective units or services have been delivered to consumers.

____ 21. The elapsed time between starting a unit of product into the beginning of a process and its completion.

____ 22. The ratio of the value-added lead time to the total lead time.

____ 23. The study of employee effort and other business records to determine the cost of activities.

____ 24. The time required to manufacture a unit of product or other output.

____ 25. The time that units wait in inventories, move unnecessarily, and wait during machine breakdowns.

____ 26. The transfer of costs from raw and in process accounts directly to finished production without the use of intermediate work in process accounts.

____ 27. A quality improvement process developed by Motorola Corporation consisting of five steps: Define, Measure, Analyze, Improve, and Control (DMAIC).

____ 28. Electronic tags (chips) placed on or embedded within products that can be read by radio waves that allow instant monitoring of product location.

____ 29. An integrated business and information system used by companies to plan and control both internal and supply chain operations.

# FILL IN THE BLANK—PART A

*Instructions:* Answer the following questions or complete the statements by writing the appropriate words or amounts in the answer blanks.

1. Another term for lean (or short-cycle) manufacturing is _____-\_\_\_\_-_____ _____.

2. A company embracing just-in-time manufacturing will _____ (reduce or increase) inventory.

3. _____ _____ is a measure of the time that elapses between starting a unit of product into the beginning of a process and completing the unit of product.

4. The amount of lead time associated with actually converting materials to a finished unit is called _____-_____ _____ _____.

5. Long setup times result in larger inventories and longer _____ _____.

6–7. A batch of 50 units of a product moves sequentially through three machining operations that require 16 minutes per unit of total machine time. The total time to move the batch between the three machines is 12 minutes.

6. The total value-added lead time is _____.

7. The total nonvalue-added lead time is _____.

8. The effort necessary to change a machine's characteristics to prepare for production of a new product is termed a(n) _____.

9. A(n) _____-_____ _____ occurs when work is organized around processes.

10. Allowing employees to evaluate each other is an example of _____ _____.

11. Pull manufacturing uses _____ to signal production quantities to be used by the next stage of production.

12. _____ _____ _____ _____ are used to electronically monitor the location of product within the supply chain.

13–14. A product cell has budgeted conversion costs of $175,000 for the month. The cell is planned to be available for 250 hours during the month. Each unit requires 9 minutes in the cell. The materials cost is $110 per unit.

13. The budgeted conversion cost per unit is _____.

14. The cost debited to Raw and In Process Inventory for the period is _____.

15. Many companies are embracing _____-_____ in improving the quality of their products and processes.

16. Lead time, percent good quality, and orders filled on time are examples of _____ performance measures.

17. The budgeted cell conversion rate for a cell with a budgeted cost of $430,000 for 860 planned hours of production is _____.

18. The cost associated with correcting defects discovered by the customer is called a(n) _____ _____ cost.

19. A(n) _____ _____ is a graphical approach to identifying important problems or issues.

20. The cost of activities that are necessary to meet customer requirements, such as product design and conversion activities, are called _____-_____ activity costs.

21. A process is a sequence of activities linked together by common _____ and _____.

## FILL IN THE BLANK—PART B

*Instructions:*  Answer the following questions or complete the statements by writing the appropriate words or amounts in the answer blanks.

1. A business philosophy that focuses on eliminating time, cost, and poor quality within manufacturing and nonmanufacturing processes is called _____-_____-_____ _____.

2. The production approach based on producing goods to finished goods inventory rather than producing goods to fill a customer order is called _____ _____ _____.

3. The production scheduling approach in which work in process flows through the factory based on the actual demand of the customer is called _____ manufacturing.

4. A layout of the factory in which production processes are organized around product cells is called a(n) _____-_____ layout.

5. The time a product waits or moves unnecessarily is called _____-_____ _____ _____.

6–7. A batch of 24 units of a product moves sequentially through three machining operations that require 28 minutes per unit of total machine time. The total time to move the batch between the three machines is 15 minutes.

6. The total value-added lead time is _____.

7. The total nonvalue-added lead time is _____.

8. A bar chart that shows the totals of a particular attribute for a number of categories is a(n) _____ _____.

9. The accounting system in a just-in-time environment will frequently use a combined account for _____ and _____ ____
_____.

10. _____ _____ _____ software is used by companies to plan and control supply chain activities.

11. _____ _____ _____ is a method of using computers to electronically communicate orders, relay information, and make or receive payments from one organization to another.

12–13. A product cell has budgeted conversion costs of $360,000 for the month. The cell is planned to be available for 240 hours during the month. Each unit requires 18 minutes in the cell. The materials cost is $75 per unit.

12. The budgeted conversion cost per unit is _____.

13. The cost debited to Raw and In Process Inventory for the period is _____.

14. If $18,200 was budgeted to support 260 hours of production, the cell conversion cost rate would be _____.

15. Performance measures for a just-in-time manufacturer often include both financial and _____ measures.

16. The costs associated with correcting defects prior to shipment to a customer is called _____ _____ costs.

17. Employee training is an example of the _____ quality cost classification.

18. The cost of activities that are not required by the customer, such as errors, omissions, and failures, are called _____-_____ activity costs.

19. The relationship between the costs of quality is such that increasing investments in prevention and appraisal activities should reduce the cost of _____ and _____ activities.

20. A(n) _____ _____ _____ _____ identifies the activity cost associated with each quality cost classification and the percentage of total quality costs associated with each classification.

21. A process can be made more efficient by _____ unnecessary or wasteful work.

## MULTIPLE CHOICE

*Instructions:*   Circle the best answer for each of the following questions.

1.  Which of the following is not a characteristic of just-in-time manufacturing?
    a.   emphasizes pull manufacturing
    b.   emphasizes a process-oriented layout
    c.   reduces inventory
    d.   reduces setup time

2.  Which of the following is the best approach for reducing lead time?
    a.   supply chain management
    b.   employee involvement
    c.   reducing setup time
    d.   electronic data interchange

3.  Which of the following would be considered value-added lead time?
    a.   setup time
    b.   move time
    c.   waiting in inventory
    d.   machine time

4.  If a product is manufactured in batch sizes of 20 units and it takes 2 minutes to manufacture each unit within each of two operations, what is the within-batch wait time?
    a.   4 minutes
    b.   38 minutes
    c.   76 minutes
    d.   80 minutes

5.  A company using a just-in-time manufacturing system will likely debit materials purchases to:
    a.   Raw and In Process Inventory
    b.   Materials Inventory
    c.   Work in Process Inventory
    d.   Cost of Goods Sold

6–7.  The cell rate is $175 per hour. Each unit has $48 per unit of materials cost and requires 18 minutes of cell conversion time. The cell produces 300 units, of which 285 are sold.

6.  What is the debit to Raw and In Process Inventory?
    a.   $14,400
    b.   $15,750
    c.   $30,150
    d.   $66,900

7. What is the Finished Goods Inventory balance?
   a. $3,345
   b. $1,507.50
   c. $787.50
   d. $720

8. Which of the following is an example of external failure cost?
   a. scrap
   b. rework
   c. billing errors and correction
   d. quality control inspection

9. The purpose of a Pareto chart is to:
   a. visually highlight important categories
   b. provide trend information
   c. summarize profitability
   d. visually demonstrate how two variables are related to each other

10. An activity analysis shows the following quality cost activities:

| | |
|---|---|
| Warranty | $100,000 |
| Rework | 80,000 |
| Final inspection | 30,000 |
| Supplier certification | 60,000 |
| Employee training | 90,000 |
| Disposal of scrap | 40,000 |
| Total | $400,000 |

What is the percentage of prevention cost to total cost?
   a. 32.5%
   b. 37.5%
   c. 45%
   d. 47.5%

11. A product is produced in batches of 15 units in three departments. Each department requires 10 minutes processing time per unit. The move time between each department is 5 minutes. The move time from raw materials to the first department and the move time from the last department to the shipping department are also 5 minutes. What is the ratio of nonvalue-added time to total lead time?
   a. 91.2%
   b. 93.6%
   c. 95.6%
   d. 97.4%

12. A hospital using just-in-time principles would have which of the following characteristics?

   a. a centralized pharmacy in order to have better control over drugs

   b. extensive travel distance for various blood and chemistry tests

   c. patient transportation to centralized X-ray units

   d. cross-trained caregivers

13. If a company is using pull scheduling, how is it determined what a process will build at any given time?

   a. The production schedule will indicate the production requirements for a process.

   b. The process will produce according to what was produced by the feeder (upstream) department.

   c. The process will produce according to what is required by the next (downstream) operation.

   d. The process will produce according to a forecast.

14. Assume a customer service process costs $100,000 to serve 2,500 customers. If a planned process improvement requires a 20% increase in cost in order to eliminate $50,000 of activity cost, what would be the expected cost per customer served?

   a. $12

   b. $28

   c. $40

   d. $48

## TRUE/FALSE

*Instructions:*   Indicate whether each of the following statements is true or false by placing a check mark in the appropriate column.

|  | True | False |
|---|---|---|
| 1.  Just-in-time manufacturing is primarily an inventory reduction technique. | ____ | ____ |
| 2.  Lead time is equivalent to the amount of standard direct labor time needed to produce a product. | ____ | ____ |
| 3.  A product-oriented layout reduces the amount of materials movement. | ____ | ____ |
| 4.  Reducing setup time will increase within-batch wait time. | ____ | ____ |
| 5.  Pull manufacturing uses kanbans to signal materials movement and release. | ____ | ____ |
| 6.  A JIT environment will increase the number of accounting and control transactions due to kanbans. | ____ | ____ |
| 7.  JIT accounting combines materials and work in process into a single account. | ____ | ____ |
| 8.  JIT manufacturing often increases the need for cost allocation. | ____ | ____ |
| 9.  Prevention costs are value-added activities. | ____ | ____ |
| 10.  A Pareto chart is a line chart plotting quality costs over time. | ____ | ____ |

## EXERCISE 27-1

Twin Image Scanner Company is considering a new just-in-time product cell. The present manufacturing approach produces a scanner in four separate process steps. The production batch sizes are 40 units. The process time for each process step is as follows:

Process Step 1:  3 minutes          Process Step 3:  12 minutes
Process Step 2:  7 minutes          Process Step 4:    5 minutes

The time required to move each batch between each of the production steps is 15 minutes. In addition, the time to move raw materials to Process Step 1 and to move completed units from Process Step 4 to finished goods inventory is also 15 minutes each.

The new just-in-time layout will allow the company to reduce the batch sizes from 40 units to 3 units. The time required to move each batch between the production steps and inventory locations will be reduced to 5 minutes. The processing time in each process step will stay the same.

*Instructions:*  Determine the value-added, nonvalue-added, and total lead times under the present and proposed production approaches.

_____

_____

_____

_____

_____

_____

_____

_____

_____

_____

_____

_____

_____

_____

_____

_____

_____

_____

_____

_____

_____

_____

_____

_____

_____

_____

_____

_____

_____

_____

## EXERCISE 27-2

Clarity Audio Inc. uses a just-in-time strategy to manufacture CD players. The company manufactures CD players through a single product cell. The budgeted conversion cost for the year is $1,845,000 for 2,050 production hours. Each unit requires 10 minutes of cell process time. During April, 1,025 CD players are manufactured in the cell. The estimated materials cost per unit is $135. The following summary transactions took place during March:

**(a)** Materials are purchased to manufacture April production.
**(b)** Conversion costs were applied to production.
**(c)** 1,025 CD players are assembled and placed in finished goods.
**(d)** 1,000 CD players are sold for $480 per unit.

### Instructions:

**(1)** Determine the budgeted cell conversion cost per hour.

**(2)** Determine the budgeted cell conversion cost per unit.

**(3)** Journalize the summary transactions (a)–(d) for April.

## JOURNAL

PAGE

| | DATE | | DESCRIPTION | POST. REF. | DEBIT | CREDIT | |
|---|---|---|---|---|---|---|---|
| 1 | | | | | | | 1 |
| 2 | | | | | | | 2 |
| 3 | | | | | | | 3 |
| 4 | | | | | | | 4 |
| 5 | | | | | | | 5 |
| 6 | | | | | | | 6 |
| 7 | | | | | | | 7 |
| 8 | | | | | | | 8 |
| 9 | | | | | | | 9 |
| 10 | | | | | | | 10 |
| 11 | | | | | | | 11 |
| 12 | | | | | | | 12 |
| 13 | | | | | | | 13 |
| 14 | | | | | | | 14 |
| 15 | | | | | | | 15 |
| 16 | | | | | | | 16 |
| 17 | | | | | | | 17 |
| 18 | | | | | | | 18 |
| 19 | | | | | | | 19 |
| 20 | | | | | | | 20 |
| 21 | | | | | | | 21 |
| 22 | | | | | | | 22 |
| 23 | | | | | | | 23 |
| 24 | | | | | | | 24 |
| 25 | | | | | | | 25 |
| 26 | | | | | | | 26 |
| 27 | | | | | | | 27 |
| 28 | | | | | | | 28 |
| 29 | | | | | | | 29 |
| 30 | | | | | | | 30 |
| 31 | | | | | | | 31 |
| 32 | | | | | | | 32 |
| 33 | | | | | | | 33 |
| 34 | | | | | | | 34 |

## EXERCISE 27-3

Veracity Instruments Inc. manufactures instrument panels for the automotive industry. An activity analysis was conducted, and the following activity costs were identified with the manufacture and sale of instrument panels:

| Activity | Activity Cost |
|---|---|
| Emergency equipment maintenance ............... | $ 70,000 |
| Employee training ............................................. | 15,000 |
| Correcting shipment errors ............................... | 25,000 |
| Warranty claims ................................................ | 190,000 |
| Final inspection ................................................ | 50,000 |
| Supplier development ........................................ | 5,000 |
| Processing customer returns ............................ | 140,000 |
| Scrap reporting ................................................ | 22,000 |
| Disposing of scrap ............................................ | 160,000 |
| Inspecting materials ......................................... | 40,000 |
| Preventive equipment maintenance ................ | 10,000 |
| Total ............................................................. | $727,000 |

***Instructions:*** Prepare a Pareto chart of these activities.

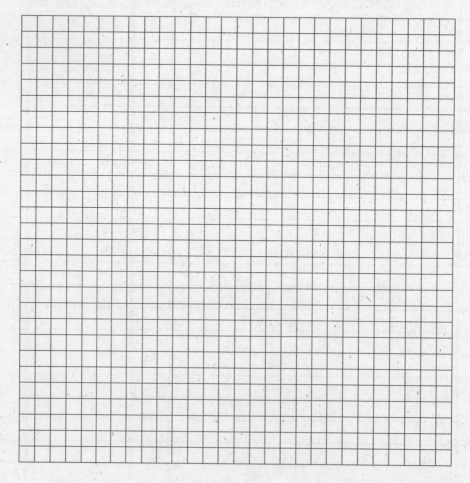

## EXERCISE 27-4

Hope Hospital performs diagnostic imaging services for patients admitted to the hospital. The process consists of the following activities with their associated activity costs (personnel costs only):

| Imaging Process Activities | Activity Cost |
|---|---|
| Prepare patient (radioactive tracer injection) ........... | $ 22,000 |
| Move patient to Imaging Department ..................... | 15,000 |
| Conduct imaging ..................................................... | 75,000 |
| Move patient back to room ..................................... | 15,000 |
| Doctor dictates diagnosis via tape recorder ............ | 50,000 |
| Transcribe report to hardcopy ............................... | 18,000 |
| File and retrieve report .......................................... | 45,000 |
| Total cost ...................................................... | $240,000 |

During the period, the hospital planned to perform 1,500 diagnostic images. In an effort to become more cost efficient, the hospital made some changes to this process. First, a policy was established that requires less critical procedures to be imaged prior to surgery on an "outpatient" basis. Second, the hospital purchased a digital voice recognition system that can automatically transcribe the doctor's voice into an electronic report. This report then can be electronically stored and retrieved by doctors in the area. These two changes are expected to have the following impact:

(a) It is estimated that 60% of the patients will use imaging services on an outpatient basis under the new policy.

(b) The new voice recognition technology will eliminate all of the transcription activity and 80% of the filing and retrieval activity.

(c) By scheduling patients for outpatient service, the Imaging Department will be able to use the imaging suites 20% more efficiently.

### Instructions:

(1) Determine the process cost per image under the current process.

(2) Determine the personnel process cost under the proposed process.

(3) Determine the personnel process cost per image under the proposed process.

_____

_____

_____

_____

_____

_____

_____

_____

_____

_____

_____

_____

_____

_____

_____

_____

_____

_____

_____

_____

_____

_____

_____

## PROBLEM 27-1

Memory Technologies Inc. manufactures electronic storage devices for computers, such as magnetic and optical drives. The manufacturing process includes printed circuit (PC) card assembly, final assembly, testing, and shipping. The PC card assembly operation includes a number of individuals responsible for assembling electronic components into the printed circuit boards. Each operator is responsible for soldering components according to a given set of instructions. Operators work on batches of 80 printed circuit boards. Each board requires 12 minutes of assembly time. After each batch is completed, the operator moves the assembled cards to the final assembly area. This move takes 10 minutes to complete. The final assembly for each storage device requires 18 minutes and is also done in batches of 80 devices. A batch of 80 devices is moved into the test building, which is across the street. This move takes 30 minutes. Before conducting the test, the test equipment must be set up for the particular device model. The test setup requires 45 minutes. In the final test, the 80-unit batch is tested one circuit board at a time. Each test requires 4 minutes. On average, the test equipment breaks down (fails) for 10% of the tests. The equipment maintenance averages 10 minutes per machine breakdown. The completed batch, after all testing, is sent to shipping for packaging and final shipment to customers. A complete batch of 80 units is sent from final assembly to shipping. The shipping department is located next to final assembly. Thus, there is insignificant move time between these two operations. Packaging and labeling requires 4 minutes per unit.

### Instructions:

(1) Determine the amount of value-added and nonvalue-added lead time in this process for an average storage device in a batch of 80 units. Categorize the nonvalue-added time into wait, move, and equipment breakdown time.

(2) How could this process be improved so as to reduce the amount of waste in the process?

_____

_____

_____

_____

_____

_____

_____

_____

_____

_____

_____

_____

_____

_____

_____

_____

_____

_____

_____

_____

_____

_____

_____

_____

_____

_____

_____

_____

_____

_____

_____

_____

_____

_____

_____

_____

_____

_____

_____

_____

_____

_____

_____

_____

_____

_____

## PROBLEM 27-2

The president of Kokimo Company has been concerned about the growth in costs over the last several years. The president asked the controller to perform an activity analysis to gain a better insight into these costs. The activity analysis revealed the following:

| Activity | Activity Cost |
| --- | --- |
| Preventive machine maintenance | $ 45,000 |
| Disposing of scrap | 125,000 |
| Correcting invoice errors | 30,000 |
| Final inspection | 38,000 |
| Expediting production | 65,000 |
| Disposing of materials with poor quality | 45,000 |
| Responding to customer quality complaints | 120,000 |
| Inspecting work in process | 22,000 |
| Producing product | 200,000 |
| Inspecting materials | 10,000 |
| Total | $700,000 |

The production process is complicated by quality problems, requiring the production manager to expedite production and dispose of scrap.

**Instructions:**

(1) Prepare a Pareto chart of the company's quality cost-related activities.

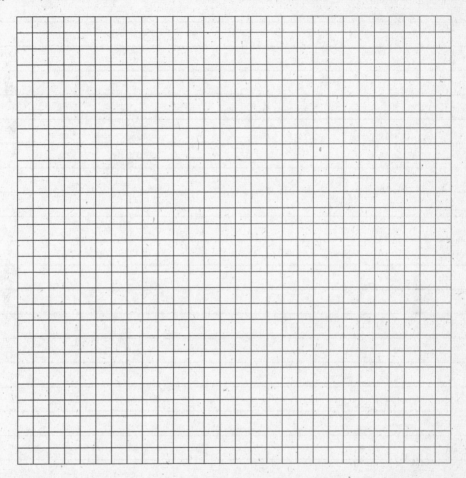

(2) Use the activity cost information to determine the percentage of total quality costs that are prevention, appraisal, internal failure, and external failure.

(3) Determine the percentage of total quality costs that are value-added and nonvalue-added.

(4) Interpret the information.

_____

_____

_____

_____

_____

_____

_____

_____

# CHAPTER 16

## MATCHING

| | | | | |
|---|---|---|---|---|
| 1. B | 8. D | 15. C | 22. Q | 29. CC |
| 2. R | 9. DD | 16. F | 23. T | 30. EE |
| 3. X | 10. II | 17. H | 24. U | 31. FF |
| 4. E | 11. Y | 18. J | 25. V | 32. GG |
| 5. P | 12. S | 19. K | 26. W | 33. HH |
| 6. N | 13. AA | 20. L | 27. Z | 34. I |
| 7. M | 14. A | 21. O | 28. BB | 35. G |

## FILL IN THE BLANK—PART A

1. financial
2. staff
3. directing
4. feedback
5. cost
6. direct labor
7. indirect
8. factory overhead (or factory burden, or manufacturing overhead)
9. prime
10. period
11. administrative
12. balance sheet
13. materials inventory
14. finished goods
15. cost of merchandise sold
16. cost of goods manufactured
17. less than
18. greater than
19. materials placed in production
20. cost of goods manufactured

## FILL IN THE BLANK—PART B

1. managerial
2. generally accepted accounting principles
3. line
4. controller
5. planning
6. controlling
7. continuous process improvement
8. factory overhead (or factory burden, or manufacturing overhead)
9. direct material
10. indirect costs
11. factory overhead (or factory burden, or manufacturing overhead)
12. conversion
13. product
14. selling
15. work in process
16. cost of goods sold
17. greater than
18. less than
19. work in process inventory
20. finished goods available for sale

## MULTIPLE CHOICE

1. a. Incorrect. Managerial accounting reports can be both objective or subjective, such as by using estimates or forecast.
   b. **Correct.** Managerial accounting reports need not be prepared according to GAAP. Rather, these reports can be developed according to management needs without reference to the rules required for external financial reporting needs.
   c. Incorrect. Managerial accounting reports can be prepared in any timeframe that is useful to management.
   d. Incorrect. Managerial accounting reports can be prepared for the company as a whole or any sub-segment required to support decision-making needs.

2. a. Incorrect. Managerial accounting reports need not strictly adhere to generally accepted accounting principles (GAAP).
   b. Incorrect. The focus of managerial accounting reports are on internal decision-making needs.
   c. **Correct.** Managerial accounting reports focus on the needs of management.
   d. Incorrect. Both a. and b. are incorrect.

3.  a. **Correct.**   The Accounting Department supports the manufacturing and sales functions, and thus, is a staff department.
    b. Incorrect.   The Assembly Department is a line department because it is directly involved in the objectives of the organization.
    c. Incorrect.   The Sales Department is a line department because it is directly involved in the objectives of the organization.
    d. Incorrect.   The Assembly Department is a line department because it is directly involved in the objectives of the organization.

4.  a. Incorrect.   The planning phase begins the management process and leads to the directing phase.
    b. Incorrect.   The directing phase is the result of the planning phase, and leads to the controlling phase.
    c. Incorrect.   The controlling phase assesses the execution of the plan.
    d. **Correct.**   The decision making is inherent to all of the phases of the management process, because management decisions are required in all phases.

5.  a. Incorrect.   Depreciation on the general offices is an administrative expense.
    b. **Correct.**   Utility and power costs of the factory are factory overhead costs.
    c. Incorrect.   The wages of a machine operator are direct labor costs.
    d. Incorrect.   Advertising costs are selling expenses.

6.  a. **Correct.**   Common stock is used for financing, not for generating revenues, so it would not generally be considered a cost object.
    b. Incorrect.   The product is a cost object, often to support product profitability analysis.
    c. Incorrect.   A sales territory can be cost object, often to support sales territory profitability analysis.
    d. Incorrect.   An organizational department can be a cost object, often to support budgeting.

7.  a. Incorrect.   Property taxes on a factory building are a factory overhead cost.
    b. Incorrect.   Insurance on a factory building is a factory overhead cost.
    c. **Correct.**   Sales salaries are part of selling expenses, not factory overhead cost.
    d. Incorrect.   Depreciation of factory plant and equipment is a factory overhead cost

8.  a. Incorrect.   Direct labor and direct materials are prime costs.
    b. Incorrect.   Direct material is not part of conversion cost because it is the item being converted.
    c. Incorrect.   Product and period costs are all of the costs, but are not conversion costs.
    d. **Correct.**   Conversion costs are direct labor and factory overhead costs, or the costs to convert materials into finished product.

9.  a. Incorrect.   The statement of cost of goods manufactured would include both material and work in process inventory changes in the determination of the cost of goods manufactured.
    b. Incorrect.   The statement of cost of goods manufactured would include both material and work in process inventory changes in the determination of the cost of goods manufactured.
    c. Incorrect.   The change in finished goods would be part of the income statement.
    d. **Correct.**   The statement of cost of goods manufactured would include both material and work in process inventory changes in the determination of the cost of goods manufactured.

10. a. Incorrect.
    b. Incorrect.
    c. **Correct.**   The correct calculation does not account for the change in material inventory, since the total manufacturing costs added to production already includes the impact of this change, thus the calculation is $110,000 + $5,000, or $115,000.
    d. Incorrect.

11. a. Incorrect.
    b. **Correct.**   The correct calculation does not account for the change in work in process inventory, since the cost of goods manufactured already includes the impact of this change, thus the calculation is $245,000 – $8,000, or $237,000.
    c. Incorrect.
    d. Incorrect.

## True/False

1. F  Managerial accounting reports are intended for use by management.
2. F  The sales department is directly involved in the objectives of the organization and is a line department.
3. T
4. T
5. F  The electrical cost for factory machinery would be classified as factory overhead cost.
6. F  The salary of the production engineer is not direct to the product, so would be classified as factory overhead cost.
7. T
8. F  The conversion cost is the direct labor and factory overhead cost.
9. T
10. T

## Exercise 16-1

(a) Direct labor

(b) Factory overhead

(c) Factory overhead

(d) Direct materials

(e) Direct materials

(f) Factory overhead

(g) Factory overhead

(h) Factory overhead

(i) Direct labor

(j) Direct materials

(k) Direct labor

(l) Direct materials

(m) Direct labor

(n) Factory overhead

## Exercise 16-2

(a) No, direct materials

(b) Yes

(c) Yes

(d) No, direct materials

(e) No, direct labor

(f) Yes

(g) Yes

(h) No, administrative expense

(i) No, direct labor

(j) No, direct materials

**(k)** No, direct labor

**(l)** Yes

**(m)** No, administrative expense

**(n)** Yes

## EXERCISE 16-3

**(a)** period

**(b)** period

**(c)** product

**(d)** period

**(e)** product

**(f)** product

**(g)** period

**(h)** product

**(i)** product

**(j)** product

**(k)** period

**(l)** period

**(m)** period

**(n)** product

## EXERCISE 16-4

**(1)**

Swift Manufacturing Company
Income Statement
For the Month Ended May 31, 20--

| | | |
|---|---:|---:|
| Revenues | | $195,000 |
| Cost of goods sold | | 114,000 |
| Gross profit | | $ 81,000 |
| Operating expenses: | | |
|    Selling expenses | $29,000 | |
|    Administrative expenses | 38,000 | |
| Total operating expenses | | 67,000 |
| Net income | | $ 14,000 |

**(2)** Inventory balances on May 31, 20--:

| | |
|---|---:|
| Materials ($80,000 − $55,000) | $25,000 |
| Work in process ($55,000 + $34,000 + $41,000 − $121,000) | 9,000 |
| Finished goods ($121,000 − $114,000) | 7,000 |

## PROBLEM 16-1

**(1)**   Scenario 1

    **(a)** $185,000 ($180,000 + $23,000 – $18,000)

    **(b)** $180,000 ($431,000 – $156,000 – $95,000)

    **(c)** $22,000 ($431,000 + $26,000 – $435,000)

    **(d)** $79,000 ($435,000 + $87,000 – $443,000)

    **(e)** $367,000 ($810,000 – $443,000)

    **(f)** $295,000 ($367,000 – $72,000)

Scenario 2

    **(a)** $40,000 ($245,000 + $42,000 – $247,000)

    **(b)** $577,000 ($247,000 + $128,000 + $202,000)

    **(c)** $570,000 ($610,000 – $40,000)

    **(d)** $563,000 ($570,000 + $102,000 – $109,000)

    **(e)** $537,000 ($1,100,000 – $563,000)

    **(f)** $170,000 ($537,000 – $367,000)

**(2)**

### Scenario 1
### Statement of Cost of Goods Manufactured
### For the Month Ended March 31, 20--

| | | |
|---|---:|---:|
| Work in process inventory, January 1 | | $ 26,000 |
|    Materials inventory, January 1 | $ 18,000 | |
|    Materials purchased | 185,000 | |
|    Cost of materials available for use | $203,000 | |
|    Less: Materials inventory, January 31 | 23,000 | |
| Materials placed into production | $180,000 | |
| Direct labor | 95,000 | |
| Factory overhead | 156,000 | |
| Total manufacturing costs added | | 431,000 |
| Total manufacturing costs | | $457,000 |
| Less: Work in process inventory, January 31 | | 22,000 |
| Cost of goods manufactured | | $435,000 |

**(3)**

### Scenario 1
### Income Statement
### For the Month Ended March 31, 20--

| | | |
|---|---:|---:|
| Sales | | $810,000 |
| Cost of goods sold | | |
|    Finished goods inventory, January 1 | $ 87,000 | |
|    Cost of goods manufactured | 435,000 | |
|    Cost of finished goods available for sale | $522,000 | |
|    Less: Finished goods inventory, December 31 | 79,000 | |
|      Cost of goods sold | | 443,000 |
| Gross profit | | $367,000 |
| Operating expenses | | 295,000 |
| Net income | | $ 72,000 |

**PROBLEM 16-2**

(1)
Ginza Manufacturing Company
Statement of Cost of Goods Manufactured
For the Month Ended October 31, 20--

| | | | |
|---|---|---|---|
| Work in process inventory, October 1 ............................ | | | $ 32,000 |
| Direct materials: | | | |
|     Materials inventory, October 1 .............................. | $ 19,000 | | |
|     Materials purchased ........................................... | 302,000 | | |
|     Cost of materials available for use ....................... | $321,000 | | |
|     Less: Materials inventory, October 31 ................... | 16,000 | | |
|         Cost of materials placed into production ........... | | $305,000 | |
| Direct labor .................................................................. | | 178,000 | |
| Factory overhead: | | | |
|     Depreciation expense – Factory equipment .............. | $ 48,000 | | |
|     Heat, light, and power – Factory ............................. | 26,000 | | |
|     Indirect labor ..................................................... | 112,000 | | |
|     Rent expense – Factory ........................................ | 67,000 | | |
|     Property taxes – Factory ....................................... | 36,000 | | |
|     Supplies – Factory .............................................. | 11,000 | | |
|     Miscellaneous cost – Factory................................. | 16,000 | | |
|         Total factory overhead cost ............................... | | 316,000 | |
| Total manufacturing costs added ................................ | | | 799,000 |
| Total manufacturing costs ......................................... | | | $831,000 |
| Less: Work in process inventory, October 31 ............... | | | 36,000 |
| Cost of goods manufactured ...................................... | | | $795,000 |

(2)
Ginza Manufacturing Company
Income Statement
For the Month Ended October 31, 20--

| | | | |
|---|---|---|---|
| Sales............................................................................ | | | $1,350,000 |
| Cost of goods sold: | | | |
|     Finished goods inventory, October 1...................... | $ 42,000 | | |
|     Cost of goods manufactured ............................... | 795,000 | | |
|     Cost of finished goods available for sale............... | $837,000 | | |
|     Less: Finished goods inventory, October 31 ......... | 40,000 | | |
|         Cost of goods sold......................................... | | | 797,000 |
| Gross profit................................................................... | | | $ 553,000 |
| Operating expenses: | | | |
|     Administrative expenses: | | | |
|         Depreciation expense – Office furniture ............... | $ 31,000 | | |
|         Office supplies expense...................................... | 189,000 | | |
|         Property taxes – Headquarters building ................ | 24,000 | | |
|         Total administrative expenses ......................... | | $244,000 | |
|     Selling expenses: | | | |
|         Advertising expense.............................................. | $ 97,000 | | |
|         Sales salaries expense ........................................ | 103,000 | | |
|         Total selling expenses ....................................... | | 200,000 | |
|     Total operating expenses........................................... | | | 444,000 |
| Net income .................................................................. | | | $ 109,000 |

# CHAPTER 17

## MATCHING

| | | | |
|---|---|---|---|
| **1.** G | **4.** H | **7.** D | **10.** J | **13.** K |
| **2.** F | **5.** N | **8.** A | **11.** B | **14.** M |
| **3.** I | **6.** O | **9.** L | **12.** E | |

## FILL IN THE BLANK—PART A

1. process cost
2. materials, work in process, finished goods
3. product
4. direct labor
5. factory overhead
6. factory overhead
7. job order
8. crediting, debiting
9. time tickets
10. allocation
11. $42
12. activity-based
13. overapplied (or overabsorbed)
14. rate
15. cost of goods sold
16. materials requisitions
17. stock ledger
18. period
19. administrative
20. service

## FILL IN THE BLANK—PART B

1. cost accounting
2. job cost
3. factory overhead
4. direct materials
5. indirect labor
6. product prices
7. debited, credited
8. requisitions
9. job cost
10. time tickets
11. activity base (or activity driver, or allocation base)
12. $5,625
13. $66
14. work in process
15. underapplied (or underabsorbed)
16. time tickets
17. finished goods
18. $100,975 {[($175,000 / 20,000) × (12,000 – 3,500)] + $26,600}
19. selling
20. cost of services

## MULTIPLE CHOICE

1. a. Incorrect. The building contractor should use a job order cost system to accumulate construction costs.
   b. **Correct.** The cookie processor should use a process cost system.
   c. Incorrect. The plumber should use a job order cost system to accumulate job costs.
   d. Incorrect. The textbook publisher should use a job order cost system to accumulate costs by textbook title.

2. a. Incorrect. A receiving report records the receipt of material to the storeroom.
   b. Incorrect. A purchase order is delivered to a supplier requesting the purchase of an item.
   c. Incorrect. A purchase requisition is not a term used in business.
   d. **Correct.** A materials requisition is used to request and release material from the storeroom for use in a job.

3. a. Incorrect. A clock card accumulates the amount of time an employee spends in the factory.
   b. **Correct.** A time ticket accumulates the amount of time an employee spends on a job.
   c. Incorrect. An in-and-out card accumulates the amount of time an employee spends in the factory.
   d. Incorrect. A labor requisition is not a term used in business.

4. a. Incorrect. An oil refinery would use a process cost system.
   b. Incorrect. A meat processor would use a process cost system.
   c. Incorrect. A hotel would accumulate costs by hotel property, which is not a "job."
   d. **Correct.** A textbook publisher would use a job order cost system.

5. a. Incorrect. The work in process ledger contains the individual accounts for the jobs (products) in process.
   b. **Correct.** The finished goods ledger includes the individual accounts of the products *produced*.
   c. Incorrect. The factory overhead ledger is not a term used in business.
   d. Incorrect. The materials ledger includes the individual accounts of the raw materials used to produce products.

6. a. Incorrect. The property taxes on the factory building are considered part of factory overhead costs.
   b. Incorrect. The insurance on the factory building is considered part of factory overhead costs.
   c. **Correct.** Sales salaries would be considered selling expenses, which are a period cost.
   d. Incorrect. Depreciation on the factory plant and equipment is considered part of factory overhead costs.

7. a. **Correct.** Factory overhead must be allocated to jobs using a predetermined factory overhead rate.
   b. Incorrect. The direct labor wage rate is used to associate direct labor with jobs.
   c. Incorrect. Material requisitions are used to associate direct materials with jobs.
   d. Incorrect.

8. a. **Correct.** If the actual factory overhead exceeds the amount applied, then the factory overhead is under-applied.
   b. Incorrect. This term is not used in business.
   c. Incorrect. Factory overhead is overapplied if the actual overhead incurred is less than the amount applied.
   d. Incorrect. Excess capacity is a different issue than determining under- or overapplied factory overhead.

9. a. Incorrect. Variable costing relates to the practice of including only variable cost in cost of goods sold.
   b. Incorrect. Flexible costing is a made-up term.
   c. **Correct.** Activity-based costing uses many overhead rates in allocating factory overhead to products.
   d. Incorrect. Service function allocation is a made-up term.

10. a. Incorrect. Controlling costs is one function of a job order cost system.
    b. Incorrect. Establishing product prices is one function of a job order cost system.
    c. Incorrect. Preparing financial statements is one function of a job order cost system.
    d. **Correct.** Management can use a job order cost system in all three functions.

11. a. Incorrect. This is the factory overhead rate ($360,000 / 15,000 hours).
    b. Incorrect. This is the direct labor ($12 per hour × 16 hours).
    c. **Correct.** ($360,000 / 15,000 hours) × 16 hours
    d. Incorrect. This is b and c summed together.

## TRUE/FALSE

1. T
2. F  The process cost system accumulates cost by department, not by separate jobs.
3. F  A publishing company would use a job cost system to accumulate costs for each title.
4. T
5. F  Materials are released to the factory floor in response to materials requisitions.
6. T
7. F  A debit balance in the factory overhead account means the factory overhead is underapplied.
8. T
9. F  There is no such restriction. Indeed, many companies use both the job order and process costs systems for different products within the company.
10. T

## EXERCISE 17-1

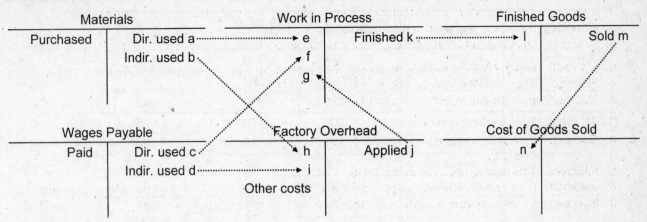

## EXERCISE 17-2

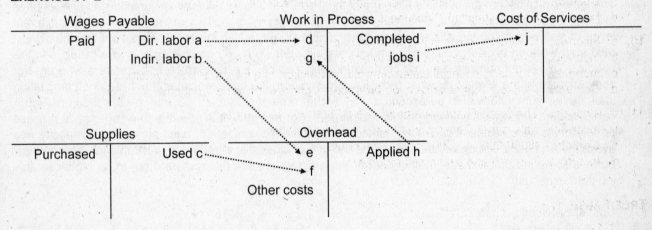

## EXERCISE 17-3

**(1)** $3.25 per machine hour ($65,000 / 20,000 hours)

**(2)** 42% of direct labor cost ($243,600 / $580,000)

**(3)**
| | | |
|---|---|---|
| Work in Process—Factory 1 .......................................... | 5,850 | |
| Factory Overhead—Factory 1 ................................... | | 5,850 |
| ($3.25 × 1,800) | | |
| Work in Process—Factory 2 ............................................ | 20,370 | |
| Factory Overhead—Factory 2 .................................. | | 20,370 |
| (42% × $48,500) | | |

**(4)** Factory 1—$200 debit (underapplied)
Factory 2—$270 credit (overapplied)

## EXERCISE 17-4

**(1)**

| Client | Service | Job Costs | Billable Hours | Job Cost per Billable Hour |
|--------|---------|-----------|----------------|----------------------------|
| Astor Co. | Audit | $11,040 | 240 | $46 |
| Brown, Inc. | Audit | 11,750 | 250 | 47 |
| Singhal Co. | Audit | 14,880 | 310 | 48 |
| Martinez Co. | Compilation | 1,875 | 75 | 25 |
| Ng, Inc. | Compilation | 2,040 | 85 | 24 |
| Wrigley Co. | Compilation | 2,185 | 95 | 23 |
| Zane, Inc. | Compilation | 4,950 | 110 | 45 |
| Howard Co. | Tax | 10,395 | 165 | 63 |
| McNelly Co. | Tax | 9,000 | 150 | 60 |

**(2)** The table indicates that tax services have the highest cost per billable hour, while compilation services have the lowest cost per billable hour. Since the professional labor cost is the largest part of the job cost, different levels of staff working on the different service assignments likely caused this result. It appears that the highest paid staff work on tax services, while the lowest paid staff work on compilation services (audit is in the middle). This is not surprising in that compilation services can be handled by bookkeepers who are not compensated at the level of experienced CPAs. In addition, the table indicates that the Zane compilation is an outlier from what would be expected. The higher cost per billable hour may be the result of higher compensated employees working on this assignment. For example, it is possible that some audit practice professionals were assigned to this job, either because the job was late or audit professional capacity was available. An alternative explanation would be the use of extensive overtime to finish this job. Regardless, there is some indication that something out of the ordinary caused the cost per hour to be higher for this job than expected.

**(3)** Cost of Services ............................................................... 68,115
     Work in Process........................................................               68,115

## PROBLEM 17-1

**(1)** Materials......................................................................... 60,000
     Prepaid Expenses ..................................................... 5,300
        Accounts Payable ...............................................               65,300

**(2)** Work in Process ............................................................ 23,200
     Factory Overhead....................................................... 1,200
        Materials ..............................................................               24,400

**(3)** Work in Process ............................................................ 35,900
     Factory Overhead....................................................... 2,700
        Wages Payable....................................................               38,600

**(4)** Factory Overhead............................................................ 12,200
     Selling Expenses........................................................ 21,950
     Administrative Expenses............................................ 15,300
        Accounts Payable ...............................................               49,450

| (5) | Factory Overhead | 5,000 | |
| | Selling Expenses | 800 | |
| | Administrative Expenses | 600 | |
| | Prepaid Expenses | | 6,400 |
| (6) | Work in Process | 25,130 | |
| | Factory Overhead | | 25,130 |
| (7) | Finished Goods | 53,000 | |
| | Work in Process | | 53,000 |
| (8) | Accounts Receivable | 160,000 | |
| | Sales | | 160,000 |
| | Cost of Goods Sold | 110,000 | |
| | Finished Goods | | 110,000 |

## PROBLEM 17-2

**Cash**

| Bal. | 135,400 | (1) | 78,000 |
| | | (4) | 12,500 |

**Finished Goods**

| Bal. | 50,800 | |
| (6) | 164,000 | |

**Work In Process**

| Bal. | 33,800 | (6) | 164,000 |
| (2) | 56,000 | | |
| (3) | 70,000 | | |
| (5) | 24,000 | | |

**Materials**

| Bal. | 18,000 | (2) | 58,400 |
| (1) | 78,000 | | |

**Factory Overhead**

| Bal. | 3,000 | (5) | 24,000 |
| (2) | 2,400 | | |
| (3) | 5,000 | | |
| (4) | 12,500 | | |

**Wages Payable**

| | | (3) | 75,000 |

# CHAPTER 18

## MATCHING

1. H
2. I
3. C
4. D
5. B
6. A
7. L
8. F
9. E
10. K

## FILL IN THE BLANK—PART A

1. job order
2. process
3. factory overhead
4. allocating
5. physical
6. credited
7. units to be assigned costs
8. 34,500  (58,500 – 24,000)
9. equivalent
10. 18,300  [(8,000 × 60%) + (18,500 – 8,000) + (7,500 × 40%)]
11. $98,820  ($32,500 + $66,320)
12. $56,700 ($5.40 × 10,500)
    ($98,820 / 18,300 = $5.40 per unit)
    (18,500 – 8,000 = 10,500; the units started and completed)
13. $16,200 ($5.40 × 7,500 × 40%)
14. cost per equivalent unit
15. $531.25 ($68,000 / 128)
16. 18,600  (solve for $99,510 / X = $5.35)
17. cost of production
18. yield
19. just-in-time
20. manufacturing cells

## FILL IN THE BLANK—PART B

1. process
2. job order
3. department
4. direct labor, factory overhead
5. conversion
6. fifo (first-in, first-out)
7. partially completed
8. ending in-process inventory
9. 600
10. whole
11. March
12. evenly
13. 510
14. $25
15. 8,800
16. multiplying
17. $10,350
18. $1,590
19. $11,940
20. kanbans

## MULTIPLE CHOICE

1.  a. Incorrect.
    b. Incorrect.
    c. **Correct.**  ($75,000 + $185,000) / 10,000 units
    d. Incorrect.

2.  a. Incorrect.
    b. Incorrect.
    c. Incorrect.
    d. **Correct.**  16,000 + 6,000; note that the total units to be accounted for are expressed as "whole units" and do not reflect equivalency.

3.  a. **Correct.**  The equivalent units for Material B include all 300 units of beginning inventory, since they are 50% complete. But the material is added at the 60% completion point, plus another 2,100 units started and completed during the period (2,400 – 300).
    b. Incorrect.
    c. Incorrect.
    d. Incorrect.

4.  a. Incorrect.
    b. **Correct.**  Beginning Inventory + Started and Completed + Ending Inventory, or (900 × 60%) + (9,000 – 900) + (600 × 10%)
    c. Incorrect.
    d. Incorrect.

5. a. **Correct.** Equivalent units are what could have been completed within a given accounting period. For a particular resource (material or conversion cost), equivalent units are what was incurred in production during the accounting period.
   b. Incorrect. This term is not used in business.
   c. Incorrect. This term may refer to the rated machine capacity of a particular process, but it is unrelated to what could have been completed.
   d. Incorrect. This term refers to the number units that have entered production, whether completed or not.

6. a. Incorrect. Prime cost is the direct labor and direct materials costs.
   b. Incorrect. The processing cost includes direct labor, direct materials, and factory overhead costs.
   c. **Correct.** The conversion cost per unit is the direct labor and factory overhead costs divided by the equivalent units of production.
   d. Incorrect. This is not a business term.

7. a. Incorrect. This is not a term used in business.
   b. Incorrect. This is not a term used in business.
   c. Incorrect. A capacity constraint is a machine or other resource that runs slower than the demand rate for the product.
   d. **Correct.** The yield is the ratio of the materials output quantity to the materials input quantity.

8. a. Incorrect. This is not a term used in business.
   b. **Correct.** Kanbans, a Japanese term for "cards," are used as material control signals in a just-in-time system.
   c. Incorrect. This is not a term used in business.
   d. Incorrect. This is not a term used in business.

9. a. Incorrect. This is not a term used in business.
   b. Incorrect. This is not a term used in business.
   c. Incorrect. This is not a term used in business.
   d. **Correct.** Work centers that are combined in just-in-time processing are termed manufacturing cells. None of the other terms in this question are typically used in business.

10. a. Incorrect.
    b. Incorrect.
    c. **Correct.** 2,000 + (22,000 − 3,000), or the beginning inventory plus the pounds started and completed.
    d. Incorrect.

11. a. Incorrect.
    b. **Correct.** $415,000 / [(3,000 × 70%) + 11,000 + (1,000 × 60%)]$
    c. Incorrect.
    d. Incorrect.

12. a. Incorrect.
    b. **Correct.** $(5,000 × 40% × \$6) + (5,000 × \$18)$
    c. Incorrect.
    d. Incorrect.

## TRUE/FALSE

1. T
2. T
3. T
4. F    The cost of production report is used to control costs.
5. F    Direct labor and factory overhead are referred to as conversion costs.
6. T
7. T
8. F    All the material will be introduced during the current period, since the material is introduced at the half-way point in production and the process is only 40% complete at the beginning of the period.
9. F    Work in process at the beginning of the period was started in the previous period but completed this period.
10. F    The units started and completed are the 1,600 started gallons, less the 300 gallons in process at the end of the period, or 1,300 gallons.

## EXERCISE 18-1

(a)    Purchases

(b)    Direct materials

(c)    Direct labor

(d)    Indirect materials

(e)    Factory overhead applied

(f)    Costs transferred out / Costs transferred in

(g)    Direct labor

(h)    Factory overhead applied

(i)    Costs transferred out to Finished Goods

(j)    Cost of goods sold

## EXERCISE 18-2

| Units | Total Whole Units | % Material to be Completed in April | % Conversion to be Completed in April | (1) Equivalent Units for Materials | (2) Equivalent Units for Conversion |
|---|---|---|---|---|---|
| Beginning Inventory | 12,000 | 0% | 70% | 0 | 8,400 |
| Started and Completed (66,000 – 12,000) | 54,000 | 100% | 100% | 54,000 | 54,000 |
| Transferred Out | 66,000 | | | 54,000 | 62,400 |
| Ending Inventory | 8,000 | 100% | 20% | 8,000 | 1,600 |
| Total Equivalent Units to Account for ............... | | | | 62,000 | 64,000 |

| Costs | (3) Direct Materials | (4) Conversion Costs | Total |
|---|---|---|---|
| Total Costs Incurred this Period | $148,800 | $326,400 | |
| Cost per Equivalent Unit | $2.40 ($148,800 ÷ 62,000) | $5.10 ($326,400 ÷ 64,000) | |
| Beginning Inventory—Balance | | | $ 47,000 |
| Beginning Inventory—Completed (Equiv. Units × Rate) | 0 | $ 42,840 | 42,840 |
| Started and Completed (Equiv. Units × Rate) | $129,600 | 275,400 | 405,000 |
| Transferred Out                           (6) | | | $494,840 |
| Ending Inventory (Equiv. Units × Rate)   (5) | $ 19,200 | $ 8,160 | 27,360 |
| Total Costs Charged to Department................ | | | $522,200 |

## EXERCISE 18-3

| | | Equivalent Units | |
|---|---|---|---|
| | Whole Units | Direct Materials | Conversion |
| Inventory in process, April 1 (40% completed) ............ | 4,200 | 0 | 2,520 |
| Started and completed in April...................... | 31,800 | 31,800 | 31,800 |
| Transferred to next department in April ...................... | 36,000 | 31,800 | 34,320 |
| Inventory in process, April 30 (75% complete) ............ | 3,200 | 3,200 | 2,400 |
| Total units........ | 39,200 | 35,000 | 36,720 |

| | Costs | |
|---|---|---|
| | Direct Materials | Conversion |
| Total costs for April in Cooking Department ....................................... | $647,500 | $449,820 |
| Total equivalent units (from above) ....................................................... | ÷ 35,000 | ÷ 36,720 |
| Cost per equivalent unit ........................................................................ | $ 18.50 | $ 12.25 |

## EXERCISE 18-4

(a)

|  | Direct Materials Cost per Equivalent Unit | Conversion Cost per Equivalent Unit |
|---|---|---|
| March | $18.00* | $12.00** |
| April (from Exercise 18-3) | $18.50 | $12.25 |

*March Direct Materials Cost per Equivalent Unit: $75,600 ÷ 4,200 equivalent units = $18
**March Conversion Cost per Equivalent Unit: $20,160 ÷ (4,200 × 40%) equivalent units = $12

(b) Both the materials and conversion costs per equivalent unit have increased from March to April. The materials cost increased by $0.50, from $18.00 to $18.50. The conversion cost increased by $0.25, from $12.00 to $12.25. These increases should be investigated further by management in order to discover the underlying cause and make remedial actions.

## PROBLEM 18-1

(1) Materials ............................................................... 210,000
    Accounts Payable ........................................         210,000

(2) Factory Overhead—Department 10 ................................. 2,100
    Factory Overhead—Department 20 ................................. 600
    Work in Process—Department 10 .................................... 18,000
    Work in Process—Department 20 .................................... 24,000
        Materials ................................................................         44,700

(3) Factory Overhead—Department 10 ................................. 2,700
    Factory Overhead—Department 20 ................................. 2,700
    Work in Process—Department 10 .................................... 25,000
    Work in Process—Department 20 .................................... 20,000
        Wages Payable ......................................................         50,400

(4) Factory Overhead—Department 10 ................................. 1,500
    Factory Overhead—Department 20 ................................. 2,250
        Accounts Payable ..................................................         3,750

(5) Factory Overhead—Department 10 ................................. 4,200
    Factory Overhead—Department 20 ................................. 3,150
        Accumulated Depreciation—Fixed Assets .................         7,350

(6) Work in Process—Department 10 .................................... 25,500
    Work in Process—Department 20 .................................... 15,000
        Factory Overhead—Department 10 ..........................         25,500
        Factory Overhead—Department 20 ..........................         15,000

(7) Work in Process—Department 20 .................................... 68,500
        Work in Process—Department 10 .............................         68,500

(8) Finished Goods ......................................................... 115,000
        Work in Process—Department 20 .............................         115,000

(9) Accounts Receivable .................................................. 160,000
        Sales ...................................................................         160,000

    Cost of Goods Sold .................................................... 122,000
        Finished Goods .....................................................         122,000

## PROBLEM 18-2

(1)

|   | A | B | C | D |
|---|---|---|---|---|
| 1 | Ivy Inc. | | | |
| 2 | Cost of Production Report—Polishing Department | | | |
| 3 | For the Month Ended March 31, 20-- | | | |
| 4 | | | Equivalent Units | |
| 5 | Units | Whole Units | Direct Materials | Conversion |
| 6 | Units charged to production: | | | |
| 7 | Inventory in process, March 1 | 5,000 | | |
| 8 | Received from Cutting | 21,000 | | |
| 9 | Total units accounted for by Polishing Dept. | 26,000 | | |
| 10 | Units to be assigned costs: | | | |
| 11 | Inventory in process, March 1 (30% completed) | 5,000 | 0 | 3,500 |
| 12 | Started and completed in March | 15,000 | 15,000 | 15,000 |
| 13 | Transferred to finished goods in March | 20,000 | 15,000 | 18,500 |
| 14 | Inventory in process, March 31 (60% completed) | 6,000 | 6,000 | 3,600 |
| 15 | Total units to be assigned cost | 26,000 | 21,000 | 22,100 |

|  | A | B | C | D |
|---|---|---|---|---|
| 1 | Ivy Inc. | | | |
| 2 | Cost of Production Report—Polishing Department (Concluded) | | | |
| 3 | For the Month Ended March 31, 20-- | | | |
| 4 | | Costs | | |
| 5 | Costs | Direct Materials | Conversion | Total Costs |
| 6 | Unit costs: | | | |
| 7 | Total cost for March in Polishing | $105,000 | $296,140 | |
| 8 | Total equivalent units (from above) | ÷ 21,000 | ÷ 22,100 | |
| 9 | Cost per equivalent unit | $    5.00 | $    13.40 | |
| 10 | Costs charged to production: | | | |
| 11 | Inventory in process, March 1 | | | $  44,300 |
| 12 | Costs incurred in March | | | 401,140 |
| 13 | Total costs accounted for by Polishing Dept. | | | $445,440 |
| 14 | Costs allocated to completed and partially completed units: | | | |
| 15 | Inventory in process, March 1—balance | | | $  44,300 |
| 16 | To complete inventory in process, March 1 | $        0 | $ 46,900[a] | 46,900 |
| 17 | Started and completed in March | 75,000[b] | 201,000[c] | 276,000 |
| 18 | Transferred to finished goods in March | | | $367,200 |
| 19 | Inventory in process, March 31 | 30,000[d] | 48,240[e] | 78,240 |
| 20 | Total costs assigned by Polishing Dept. | | | $445,440 |
| 21 | | | | |
| 22 | [a]3,500 × $13.40 = $46,900 | | | |
| 23 | [b]15,000 × $5.00 = $75,000 | | | |
| 24 | [c]15,000 × $13.40 = $201,000 | | | |
| 25 | [d]6,000 × $5.00 = $30,000 | | | |
| 26 | [e]3,600 × $13.40 = $48,240 | | | |

(2)

|  | A | B | C | D |
|---|---|---|---|---|
| 1 | | Inventory in Process, March 1 | March Cost of Production Report | Difference |
| 2 | Cost per equivalent unit-direct materials | $  4.90 | $  5.00 | $0.10 |
| 3 | Cost per equivalent unit-conversion costs | $13.20 | $13.40 | $0.20 |

The cost for materials increased by 10 cents per equivalent unit and the cost for conversion increased by 20 cents per equivalent unit.

# CHAPTER 19

## MATCHING

| | | | |
|---|---|---|---|
| 1. S | 4. E | 7. J | 10. F |
| 2. D | 5. I | 8. C | 11. H |
| 3. B | 6. O | 9. G | 12. Q |

| | |
|---|---|
| 13. N | 16. P |
| 14. L | 17. M |
| 15. K | 18. R |

## FILL IN THE BLANK—PART A

1. activity bases (or activity drivers)
2. relevant range
3. variable costs
4. fixed
5. mixed
6. mixed
7. direct costing
8. cost-volume-profit
9. contribution margin ratio
10. 9,500
11. increase
12. increase
13. 7,500
14. break-even
15. horizontal
16. profit-volume
17. "what if" analysis (or sensitivity analysis)
18. sales mix
19. margin of safety
20. operating leverage

## FILL IN THE BLANK—PART B

1. activity drivers
2. variable costs
3. fixed
4. fixed costs
5. mixed
6. semifixed
7. variable cost per unit
8. contribution margin
9. profit-volume ratio
10. contribution margin
11. fixed costs
12. break-even point
13. increase
14. increase
15. decrease
16. sales, costs
17. sensitivity analysis
18. sales mix
19. 4
20. straight lines

## MULTIPLE CHOICE

1. a. Incorrect. The per unit fixed costs change with changes in the underlying activity base.
   b. Incorrect. This describes a variable cost.
   c. Incorrect. Costs that vary in total with changes in the activity base are variable costs.
   d. **Correct.** The total dollar amount of fixed costs remains constant with changes in the activity base.

2. a. Incorrect.
   b. Incorrect.
   c. **Correct.** A mixed cost has the characteristics of both a variable and fixed cost.
   d. Incorrect. A sunk cost is a cost that is not affected by subsequent decisions.

3. a. Incorrect.
   b. **Correct.** ($240,000 – $152,500) / (150,000 – 80,000)
   c. Incorrect.
   d. Incorrect.

4. a. Incorrect. A decrease in fixed costs would decrease the break-even point.
   b. Incorrect. A decrease in unit variable cost would decrease the break-even point.
   c. **Correct.** A decrease in the unit selling price would increase the break-even point.
   d. Incorrect.

5. a. Incorrect. Direct materials are a variable cost.
   b. **Correct.** Real estate taxes are a fixed cost in a break-even analysis.
   c. Incorrect. Direct labor is a variable cost.
   d. Incorrect. Supplies are a variable cost.

6. a. **Correct.** $400,000 / $16
   b. Incorrect.
   c. Incorrect.
   d. Incorrect.

7.  a. **Correct.** ($300,000 – $250,000) / $300,000
    b. Incorrect.
    c. Incorrect.
    d. Incorrect.

8.  a. Incorrect.
    b. Incorrect.
    c. **Correct.** $200,000 / $40,000
    d. Incorrect.

9.  a. Incorrect.
    b. Incorrect.
    c. Incorrect. Variable costs change in total with changes in the activity level.
    d. **Correct.** Variable costs per unit remain unchanged with changes in the activity level.

10. a. Incorrect.
    b. **Correct.** ($12 – $8) / $12
    c. Incorrect.
    d. Incorrect.

11. a. Incorrect.
    b. Incorrect.
    c. **Correct.** $120,000 / ($30 – $18)
    d. Incorrect.

12. a. Incorrect.
    b. Incorrect.
    c. Incorrect.
    d. **Correct.**

## TRUE/FALSE

1.  T
2.  F   Mixed costs have both fixed and variable cost elements, in no particular proportion.
3.  T
4.  F   Fixed costs will remain the same at the high and low levels of activity.
5.  T
6.  T
7.  F   Decreases in unit selling price will increase the unit break-even point.
8.  F   Decreases in fixed cost will reduce the unit break-even point.
9.  F   The operating leverage is determined by dividing the contribution margin by the income from operations.
10. T

## EXERCISE 19-1

**(1)** Difference in total costs: $300,000 ($550,000 – $250,000)

Difference in total units of production: 30,000 units (50,000 units – 20,000 units)

**(2)** Variable cost per unit: $10 ($300,000 / 30,000 units)

Fixed cost estimated at highest level of production:
Total Cost = Total Variable Cost + Fixed Cost
$550,000 = ($10 × 50,000 units) + Fixed Cost
$550,000 = $500,000 + Fixed Cost
Fixed Cost = $50,000

or

Fixed cost estimated at lowest level of production:
Total Cost = Total Variable Cost + Fixed Cost
$250,000 = ($10 × 20,000 units) + Fixed Cost
$250,000 = $200,000 + Fixed Cost
Fixed Cost = $50,000

**(3)** Total Cost = Total Variable Cost + Fixed Cost
Total Cost = ($10 × 80,000 units) + $50,000
Total Cost = $800,000 + $50,000
Total Cost = $850,000

## EXERCISE 19-2

**Chart:** Cost-Volume-Profit Chart

**(a)** fixed costs

**(b)** break-even point

**(c)** operating profit area

**(d)** total sales

**(e)** operating loss area

**(f)** total costs

## EXERCISE 19-3

**(1)** ($2,000,000 – $1,700,000) / $2,000,000 = 15%

**(2)** ($150,000 – $100,000) / $150,000 = 33%

**(3)** $300,000 / $175,000 = 1.71

**(4)**

| | |
|---|---|
| Sales...................................... | $700,000 |
| Variable costs......................... | 300,000 |
| Contribution margin............... | $400,000 |

$400,000 / $200,000 = 2

## EXERCISE 19-4

Weighted contribution margin: (55% × $20) + (45% × $26) = $22.70
Break-even (units): $213,380 ÷ $22.70 = 9,400 units
Break-even (units) K-100: 9,400 units × 55% = 5,170 units
Break-even (units) V-200: 9,400 units × 45% = 4,230 units

## PROBLEM 19-1

**(1)**  $700,000 / $50 = 14,000 units

**(2)**  $710,000 / $50 = 14,200 units

**(3)**  $700,000 / $49 = 14,286 units

**(4)**  $700,000 / $52 = 13,462 units

**(5)**  ($700,000 + $300,000) / $50 = 20,000 units

## PROBLEM 19-2

**(1)**  ($180 × .80) + ($280 × .20) = $200 unit selling price of E
($140 × .80) + ($190 × .20) = $150 unit variable cost of E
($40 × .80) + ($90 × .20) = $50 unit contribution margin of E
Break-even point (units): $400,000 / $50 = 8,000 units
Sales necessary in dollars: 8,000 × $200 = $1,600,000

**(2)**

| | Product A | Product B | Total |
|---|---|---|---|
| Sales: | | | |
| 6,400 units × $180 | $1,152,000 | | $1,152,000 |
| 1,600 units × $280 | | $448,000 | 448,000 |
| Total sales | $1,152,000 | $448,000 | $1,600,000 |
| Variable costs: | | | |
| 6,400 units × $140 | 896,000 | | 896,000 |
| 1,600 units × $190 | | 304,000 | 304,000 |
| Total variable costs | $ 896,000 | $304,000 | $1,200,000 |
| Contribution margin | | | $ 400,000 |
| Fixed costs | | | 400,000 |
| Operating profit | | | $          0 |

# CHAPTER 20

## MATCHING

| | | | | | | | | | |
|---|---|---|---|---|---|---|---|---|---|
| **1.** M | **3.** B | **5.** L | **7.** G | **9.** K | **11.** I |
| **2.** A | **4.** F | **6.** H | **8.** D | **10.** C | **12.** J |

## FILL IN THE BLANK—PART A

**1.** absorption
**2.** manufacturing margin
**3.** less than
**4.** fixed factory overhead
**5.** $18,000, greater than
**6.** $60,000  (12,000 × $5)
**7.** controllable costs
**8.** sales mix

**9.** $800,000  (20,000 × $40)
**10.** $1,370,000  [(8,000 × $40) + (15,000 × $70)]
**11.** $182,000  (3,500 × $52)
**12.** $196,000  (3,500 × $56)
**13.** $450,000
**14.** $101,250
**15.** $303,750

**16.** $86,250
**17.** price factor
**18.** $23,250 decrease in variable cost of goods sold
**19.** $10,000 increase in variable cost of goods sold
**20.** increase
**21.** $4,200 decrease

## FILL IN THE BLANK—PART B

1. absorption costing
2. contribution margin
3. gross profit
4. variable cost of goods sold
5. absorption
6. product
7. variable
8. absorption

9. included
10. excluded
11. $189,000
12. $308,000
13. $63,000
14. $53,000
15. $415,000  (5,000 × $83)
16. $455,000  (5,000 × $91)

17. quantity factor
18. $8,000 increase in variable cost of goods sold
19. $12,500 decrease in variable cost of goods sold
20. $517,500 decrease

## MULTIPLE CHOICE

1. a. Incorrect. Fixed manufacturing costs are not deducted in determining the manufacturing margin.
   b. Incorrect. Nonmanufacturing costs are not deducted in determining the manufacturing margin.
   c. **Correct.**
   d. Incorrect. Fixed manufacturing costs are not deducted in determining the manufacturing margin.

2. a. Incorrect. Direct materials is a variable manufacturing cost, so it is included in both.
   b. Incorrect. Direct labor is a variable manufacturing cost, so it is included in both.
   c. **Correct.**
   d. Incorrect. Variable factory overhead is a variable manufacturing cost, so it is included in both.

3. a. **Correct.**
   b. Incorrect.
   c. Incorrect. This cannot be true when the units manufactured are different than the units sold.
   d. Incorrect.

4. a. Incorrect.
   b. **Correct.** Fixed costs are not deducted when determining contribution margin.
   c. Incorrect.
   d. Incorrect.

5. a. Incorrect.
   b. **Correct.** (20,000 units + 15,000 units) × $32 per unit
   c. Incorrect.
   d. Incorrect.

6. a. Incorrect.
   b. **Correct.** (15,000 units × $32 per unit) + (11,000 units × $65 per unit)
   c. Incorrect.
   d. Incorrect.

7. a. Incorrect. Variable costs may be considered for short-term pricing situations.
   b. **Correct.** Company-level costs would include fixed costs, which must also be controlled.
   c. Incorrect.
   d. Incorrect.

8. a. **Correct.**
   b. Incorrect. Territory is an example of a market segment.
   c. Incorrect. Product is an example of a market segment.
   d. Incorrect. Customer is an example of a market segment.

9. a. **Correct.** (16,000 units – 15,400 units) × $105 per unit
   b. Incorrect.
   c. Incorrect.
   d. Incorrect.

**10.** a. Incorrect.
    b. **Correct.**  ($112 per unit – $105 per unit) × 15,400 units
    c. Incorrect.
    d. Incorrect.

**11.** a. Incorrect.
    b. Incorrect.
    c. **Correct.**  (2,800 units – 2,500 units) × $85 per unit
    d. Incorrect.

**12.** a. Incorrect.
    b. Incorrect.
    c. Incorrect.
    d. **Correct.**  ($80 per unit – $85 per unit) × 2,800 units

**13.** a. Incorrect.  The contribution margin ratio does not say anything about the relative total aggregate contribution margin between the salespersons.
    b. Incorrect.  The contribution margin ratio does not say anything about the relative aggregate advertising expenditures between the two salespersons. It's possible that Salesperson #1 used less advertising *as a percent of sales*.
    c. **Correct.**
    d. Incorrect.  If anything, this scenario might suggest that Salesperson #1 has a *smaller* sales commission as a percent of sales than Salesperson #2 does, but it is probably not enough to explain the difference of 20 percentage points.

**14.** a. Incorrect.
    b. Incorrect.
    c. Incorrect.
    d. **Correct.**  ($2.50 × 3,750) – ($2.40 × 3,500)

## TRUE/FALSE

**1.** F  Absorption costing also includes fixed manufacturing costs in the cost of goods manufactured.
**2.** T
**3.** F  Only variable manufacturing costs are deducted in determining the manufacturing margin.
**4.** F  The two numbers can be equal when the units sold equal the units produced for the period.
**5.** T
**6.** F  Variable cost of goods sold should not include fixed manufacturing costs.
**7.** T
**8.** F  Absorption costing is frequently used for long-term pricing decisions.
**9.** T
**10.** F  The quantity factor is the difference between the actual sales and the planned sales, multiplied by the planned unit sales price (or unit cost).

## EXERCISE 20-1

**(1)**

Power Racquet Inc.
Absorption Costing Income Statement
For the Month Ended March 31, 20--

| | |
|---|---:|
| Sales (42,000 units × $45) | $1,890,000 |
| Cost of goods sold (42,000 units × $26) | 1,092,000 |
| Gross profit | $ 798,000 |
| Selling and administrative expenses ($210,000 + $160,000) | 370,000 |
| Income from operations | $ 428,000 |

**(2)**

Power Racquet Inc.
Variable Costing Income Statement
For the Month Ended March 31, 20--

| | | |
|---|---|---|
| Sales | | $1,890,000 |
| Variable cost of goods sold (42,000 units × $18) | | 756,000 |
| Manufacturing margin | | $1,134,000 |
| Variable selling and administrative expenses | | 210,000 |
| Contribution margin | | $ 924,000 |
| Fixed costs: | | |
| Fixed manufacturing costs | $360,000 | |
| Fixed selling and administrative expenses | 160,000 | 520,000 |
| Income from operations | | $ 404,000 |

**(3)** The difference between the absorption and variable costing income from operations of $24,000 ($428,000 – $404,000) can be explained as follows:

| | |
|---|---|
| Change in inventory | 3,000 |
| Fixed overhead per unit | × $8.00 |
| Income from operations difference | $24,000 |

Under absorption costing, the fixed manufacturing cost included in the cost of goods sold is matched with the revenues. As a result, 3,000 units that were produced but unsold (inventory) include fixed manufacturing cost, which is not included in the cost of goods sold. Under variable costing, all of the fixed manufacturing cost is deducted in the period in which it is incurred, regardless of the amount of the inventory change. Thus, when the inventory increases, the absorption costing income statement will have a higher income from operations than will the variable costing income statement.

## EXERCISE 20-2

Jupiter Company
Variable Costing Income Statement
For the Month Ended May 31, 20--

| | | |
|---|---|---|
| Sales (46,000 units) | | $650,000 |
| Variable cost of goods sold: | | |
| Variable cost of goods manufactured | $210,000 [1] | |
| Less inventory, May 31 (4,000 units) | 16,800 [2] | |
| Variable cost of goods sold | | 193,200 |
| Manufacturing margin | | $456,800 |
| Variable selling and administrative expenses | | 84,000 |
| Contribution margin | | $372,800 |
| Fixed costs: | | |
| Fixed manufacturing costs | $140,000 | |
| Fixed selling and administrative expenses | 61,000 | 201,000 |
| Income from operations | | $171,800 |

[1] $350,000 – $140,000 (total manufacturing cost less fixed manufacturing cost)
[2] $210,000 / $350,000 × $28,000 = $16,800 (the ratio of variable to total manufacturing costs times the value of the ending inventory under absorption costing) *OR* $210,000 / 50,000 units manufactured = $4.20; $4.20 × 4,000 units = $16,800

## EXERCISE 20-3

**(1)**

Snow Glide Company
Contribution Margin by Sales Territory
For the Year Ended December 31, 2010

|  | Eastern | Western |
| --- | --- | --- |
| Sales | $19,000,000 | $18,000,000 |
| Variable cost of goods sold | 12,000,000 | 10,000,000 |
| Manufacturing margin | $ 7,000,000 | $ 8,000,000 |
| Selling expenses | 5,000,000 | 5,000,000 |
| Contribution margin | $ 2,000,000 | $ 3,000,000 |
| | | |
| Contribution margin ratio | 10.5% | 16.7% |

**(2)** The contribution margin ratios for the Alpine and Nordic skis are different. Alpine skis have a contribution margin ratio of 20%, while the contribution margin ratio of Nordic skis is only 5%. In addition, the Nordic skis appear to have a low manufacturing margin as a percent of sales compared to the Alpine skis. Either the Nordic skis are being sold for too low a price or the variable manufacturing costs are too high. The Eastern territory has a lower contribution margin ratio than does the Western territory. This is because the Eastern territory sells a higher proportion of the lower-margin Nordic skis than does the Western territory. Management may wish to emphasize sales of Alpine skis until the pricing or cost problems in the Nordic line are resolved.

## PROBLEM 20-1

**(1)**

QuickKey Company
Absorption Costing Income Statement
For the Month Ended June 30, 20--

| | | |
| --- | --- | --- |
| Sales | | $1,912,500 |
| Cost of goods sold: | | |
| Cost of goods manufactured | $1,396,800 | |
| Less inventory, June 30 (1,500 × $58.20*) | 87,300 | |
| Cost of goods sold | | 1,309,500 |
| Gross profit | | $ 603,000 |
| Selling and administrative expenses | | 393,750 |
| Income from operations | | $ 209,250 |

*$58.20 = $1,396,800 ÷ 24,000

**(2)** QuickKey Company

Variable Costing Income Statement
For the Month Ended June 30, 20--

| | | |
| --- | --- | --- |
| Sales | | $1,912,500 |
| Variable cost of goods sold: | | |
| Variable cost of goods manufactured | $1,264,800 | |
| Less inventory, June 30 (1,500 × $52.70*) | 79,050 | |
| Variable cost of goods sold | | 1,185,750 |
| Manufacturing margin | | $ 726,750 |
| Variable selling and administrative expenses | | 270,000 |
| Contribution margin | | $ 456,750 |
| Fixed costs: | | |
| Fixed manufacturing costs | $ 132,000 | |
| Fixed selling and administrative expenses | 123,750 | 255,750 |
| Income from operations | | $ 201,000 |

*$52.70 = $1,264,800 ÷ 24,000

(3) The income from operations reported under absorption costing exceeds the income from operations reported under variable costing by $8,250 ($209,250 – $201,000). This $8,250 is due to including $8,250 of fixed manufacturing cost in inventory under absorption costing (1,500 units × $5.50, or 1,500 / 24,000 × $132,000). The $8,250 was thus deferred to a future month under absorption costing, while it was included as an expense of June (part of fixed costs) under variable costing.

## PROBLEM 20-2

Ho Company
Contribution Margin Analysis
For the Year Ended December 31, 2010

| | | |
|---|---:|---:|
| Planned contribution margin ................................................. | | $198,000 |
| Effect of changes in sales: | | |
| Sales quantity factor | | |
| (45,000 units – 44,000 units) × $18.50 ........................... | $18,500 | |
| Unit price factor ($20.00 – $18.50) × 45,000 units .............. | 67,500 | |
| Total effect of changes in sales ..................................... | | 86,000 |
| | | |
| Effect of changes in variable cost of goods sold: | | |
| Variable cost quantity factor | | |
| (44,000 units × 45,000 units) × $8.40 ............................. | –$ 8,400 | |
| Unit cost factor ($8.40 – $8.50) × 45,000 units .................. | – 4,500 | |
| Total effect of changes in variable cost of goods sold ..... | | –12,900 |
| | | |
| Effect of changes in selling and administrative expenses: | | |
| Variable cost quantity factor | | |
| (44,000 units × 45,000 units) × $5.60 ............................. | –$ 5,600 | |
| Unit cost factor ($5.60 – $5.30) × 45,000 units ................... | 13,500 | |
| Total effect of changes in selling and | | |
| administrative expenses ................................................. | | 7,900 |
| Actual contribution margin....................................................... | | $279,000 |

## PROBLEM 20-3

(1)

Sleepy Hollow Hotel Company
Contribution Margin by Region
For the Period Ended December 31, 20--

| | East | West | South | Total |
|---|---:|---:|---:|---:|
| Revenues....................................... | $331,200 | $1,380,000 | $552,000 | $2,263,200 |
| Variable costs: | | | | |
| Registration and checkout cost .............. | 21,000 | 35,000 | 28,000 | 84,000 |
| Housekeeping cost.................................. | 64,800 | 270,000 | 108,000 | 442,800 |
| Contribution margin....................................... | $245,400 | $1,075,000 | $416,000 | $1,736,400 |
| | | | | |
| Contribution margin ratio............................. | 74.1% | 77.9% | 75.4% | |

Note: Hotels will often have high contribution margins since there are significant fixed costs in providing lodging services. The West has the largest contribution margin ratio because guests have a tendency to stay longer periods of time per arrival (three nights per arrival on average) compared to the other two regions. This would be consistent with hotels that cater to convention or vacation customers.

(2)

Sleepy Hollow Hotel
Contribution Margin Analysis
For the Period Ended December 31, 20--

| | | |
|---|---:|---:|
| Planned contribution margin ............................................... | | $1,350,000 |
| Effect of changes in sales: | | |
| Sales quantity factor | | |
| (24,600 room nights – 20,000 room nights) × $90 .......... | $414,000 | |
| Unit price factor ($92 – $90) × 24,600 room nights ............. | 49,200 | |
| Total effect of changes in sales....................................... | | 463,200 |
| | | |
| Effect of changes in variable housekeeping costs: | | |
| Variable cost quantity factor | | |
| (20,000 room nights × 24,600 room nights) × $19 ........... | –$87,400 | |
| Unit cost factor ($19 – $18) × 24,600 room nights .............. | 24,600 | |
| Total effect of changes in variable housekeeping costs... | | –62,800 |
| | | |
| Effect of changes in variable registration and checkout costs: | | |
| Variable cost quantity factor | | |
| (14,000 guests – 12,000 guests) × $5............................. | $10,000 | |
| Unit cost factor ($5 – $7) × 12,000 guests ......................... | –24,000 | |
| Total effect of changes in variable registration and | | |
| checkout costs ................................................................ | | –14,000 |
| Actual contribution margin....................................................... | | $1,736,400 |

# CHAPTER 21

## MATCHING

| | | | | | | | | | |
|---|---|---|---|---|---|---|---|---|---|
| 1. | K | 4. | A | 7. | F | 10. | I | 13. | B |
| 2. | E | 5. | H | 8. | L | 11. | D | 14. | G |
| 3. | P | 6. | C | 9. | O | 12. | M | | |

## FILL IN THE BLANK—PART A

1. budget
2. planning
3. responsibility centers
4. control
5. slack
6. goal conflict
7. fiscal year
8. Accounting
9. static
10. relevant activity levels
11. master budget
12. quantity of estimated sales
13. expected unit selling price
14. 164,000
15. production
16. balance sheet budgets
17. cash
18. capital expenditures
19. 84,000
20. $1,500,000

## FILL IN THE BLANK—PART B

1. directing
2. feedback
3. tightly
4. budgetary slack
5. goal conflict
6. continuous budgeting
7. zero-based
8. static budget
9. flexible budget
10. computerized
11. sales
12. factory overhead cost
13. cost of goods sold
14. capital expenditures
15. past sales volumes
16. production
17. direct labor cost
18. budgeted income statement
19. $56,000
20. $18,500

## MULTIPLE CHOICE

1. a. Incorrect. The direct materials purchases budget is not related to the direct labor cost budget.
   b. Incorrect. Part of the cash budget is influenced by the direct labor cost budget.
   c. **Correct.** The production budget is the starting point for the direct labor cost budget.
   d. Incorrect. The cost of goods sold budget is partially prepared from the direct labor cost budget.

2. a. **Correct.** The direct materials purchases budget provides data on the quantities of direct materials purchases necessary to meet production needs.
   b. Incorrect. The sales budget provides data on the quantity of estimated sales and expected unit selling price.
   c. Incorrect. The production budget is a budget of estimated production.
   d. Incorrect. The direct labor cost budget estimates the cost of labor involved in converting raw materials into finished product.

3. a. Incorrect. The budgeted balance sheet provides an estimate of all balance sheet items, not just plant and equipment.
   b. Incorrect. The production budget is a budget of estimated production.
   c. Incorrect. The cash budget estimates the expected receipts (inflows) and payments (outflows, including acquisition of plant and equipment) of cash for a period of time.
   d. **Correct.** The capital expenditures budget summarizes future plans for the acquisition of plant facilities and equipment.

4. a. Incorrect. Variable budget is not a business term.
   b. Incorrect. A continuous budget is a method of budgeting that provides for maintaining a continuous twelve-month projection into the future, month by month.
   c. **Correct.** A flexible budget is a budget that adjusts with levels of activity and is often used in production cost centers.
   d. Incorrect. A zero-based budget is used to critically evaluate all expenditures by estimating budget data as if there had been no previous activities in the unit.

5. a. Incorrect. This is not a business term.
   b. Incorrect. A zero-based budget is used to critically evaluate all expenditures by estimating budget data as if there had been no previous activities in the unit.
   c. **Correct.** A static budget is typically used in administrative functions.
   d. Incorrect. A flexible budget is a budget that adjusts with levels of activity and is often used in production cost centers.

6. a. Incorrect.
   b. **Correct.** (80% × $860,000) + (20% × $640,000)
   c. Incorrect.
   d. Incorrect.

7. a. **Correct.** Zero-based budgets are used to critically evaluate all expenditures by estimating budget data as if there had been no previous activities in the unit.
   b. Incorrect. Master budgeting is not a business term, although a master budget is a comprehensive budget plan encompassing all the individual budgets related to sales, cost of goods sold, operating expenses, capital expenses, and cash.
   c. Incorrect. Flexible budgets are budgets that adjust with levels of activity and are often used in production cost centers.
   d. Incorrect. Continuous budgeting is a method of budgeting that provides for maintaining a continuous twelve-month projection into the future, month by month.

8. a. Incorrect. Annual budgeting is not a term defined in the text.
   b. **Correct.** Continuous budgeting is a method of budgeting that provides for maintaining a continuous twelve-month projection into the future, month by month.
   c. Incorrect. This is not a business term.
   d. Incorrect. This is not a business term.

9.  a.  Incorrect.  This is not a business term.
    b.  Incorrect.  This is only one type of center wherein a manager has authority and responsibility for the unit's performance. It is not a general term for this definition.
    c.  Incorrect.  This term is not defined in the text.
    d.  **Correct.**  A responsibility center is one wherein a manager has authority and responsibility for the unit's performance.

10. a.  **Correct.**    280,000 – 25,000 + 35,000
    b.  Incorrect.
    c.  Incorrect.
    d.  Incorrect.

11. a.  Incorrect.
    b.  **Correct.**    ($1,200,000 + $45,000 – $40,000) + $650,000 + $900,000 + ($80,000 – $95,000)
    c.  Incorrect.
    d.  Incorrect.

12. a.  Incorrect.
    b.  Incorrect.
    c.  **Correct.**    ($330,000 × 40%) + ($420,000 × 60%)
    d.  Incorrect.

## TRUE/FALSE

1.  F   A series of budgets for varying rates of activity is a flexible budget.
2.  T
3.  F   Computers are widely used in most accounting functions, including budgeting.
4.  T
5.  T
6.  F   The expenditures for plant and equipment will vary from year to year, depending upon economic conditions, business conditions, and capital availability.
7.  T
8.  F   The budgeted balance sheet brings together budgeted cash, capital acquisitions, financing, and other investing activities. Profit-making activities are reflected on the budgeted income statement.
9.  F   The first budget prepared is usually the sales budget. The cash budget is usually determined from budgets that result in receipts and expenditures, such as sales and production budgets.
10. T

## EXERCISE 21-1

| | A | B | C | D |
|---|---|---|---|---|
| 1 | Texier Inc. | | | |
| 2 | Sales Budget | | | |
| 3 | For the Month of May, 20-- | | | |
| 4 | Product and Area | Unit Sales Volume | Unit Selling Price | Total Sales |
| 5 | Product C: | | | |
| 6 | East area | 60,000 | $15 | $ 900,000 |
| 7 | West area | 80,000 | 20 | 1,600,000 |
| 8 | Total | 140,000 | | $2,500,000 |
| 9 | Product Q: | | | |
| 10 | East area | 75,000 | $ 8 | $ 600,000 |
| 11 | West area | 50,000 | 10 | 500,000 |
| 12 | Total | 125,000 | | $1,100,000 |
| 13 | Total revenue from sales | | | $3,600,000 |

| | A | B | C |
|---|---|---|---|
| 1 | Texier Inc. | | |
| 2 | Production Budget | | |
| 3 | For the Month of May, 20-- | | |
| 4 | | Units | |
| 5 | | Product C | Product Q |
| 6 | Sales | 140,000 | 125,000 |
| 7 | Plus desired inventory, May 31 | 28,000 | 25,000 |
| 8 | Total | 168,000 | 150,000 |
| 9 | Less estimated inventory, May 1 | 8,000 | 21,000 |
| 10 | Total production | 160,000 | 129,000 |

## EXERCISE 21-2

| | A | B | C | D |
|---|---|---|---|---|
| 1 | Nathalie Inc. | | | |
| 2 | Factory Overhead Cost Budget | | | |
| 3 | For the Month of January, 20-- | | | |
| 4 | Units of product | 30,000 | 60,000 | 90,000 |
| 5 | Variable cost: | | | |
| 6 | Indirect factory wages | $ 24,000 | $ 48,000 | $ 72,000 |
| 7 | Indirect materials | 13,500 | 27,000 | 40,500 |
| 8 | Electric power | 18,000 | 36,000 | 54,000 |
| 9 | Total variable cost | $ 55,500 | $111,000 | $166,500 |
| 10 | Fixed cost: | | | |
| 11 | Supervisory salaries | $ 30,000 | $ 30,000 | $ 30,000 |
| 12 | Depreciation of plant and equipment | 18,000 | 18,000 | 18,000 |
| 13 | Property taxes | 12,000 | 12,000 | 12,000 |
| 14 | Insurance | 7,500 | 7,500 | 7,500 |
| 15 | Electric power | 4,500 | 4,500 | 4,500 |
| 16 | Total fixed cost | $ 72,000 | $ 72,000 | $ 72,000 |
| 17 | Total factory overhead cost | $127,500 | $183,000 | $238,500 |

## EXERCISE 21-3

**(1)**

| | A | B |
|---|---|---|
| 1 | Gyro Company | |
| 2 | Production Budget | |
| 3 | | Product A |
| 4 | Sales | 500,000 |
| 5 | Plus desired ending inventory | 10,000 |
| 6 | Total | 510,000 |
| 7 | Less estimated beginning inventory | 12,000 |
| 8 | Total production | 498,000 |

**(2)**

| | A | B | C |
|---|---|---|---|
| 1 | Gyro Company | | |
| 2 | Direct Materials Purchases Budget | | |
| 3 | | Material XX | Material ZZ |
| 4 | Pounds required for production | 249,000* | 597,600** |
| 5 | Plus desired ending inventory | 14,000 | 25,000 |
| 6 | Total | 263,000 | 622,600 |
| 7 | Less estimated beginning inventory | 8,000 | 20,000 |
| 8 | Total pounds to be purchased | 255,000 | 602,600 |
| 9 | Unit price per pound | ×    $4 | ×    $6 |
| 10 | Total direct materials purchases | $1,020,000 | $3,615,600 |
| 11 | | | |
| 12 | *498,000 × 0.5 lbs. = 249,000 pounds | | |
| 13 | **498,000 × 1.2 lbs. = 597,600 pounds | | |

## EXERCISE 21-4

| | A | B | C | D |
|---|---|---|---|---|
| 1 | Gyro Company | | | |
| 2 | Direct Labor Cost Budget | | | |
| 3 | | Assembly Dept. | Packing Dept. | Total |
| 4 | | | | |
| 5 | Hours required for production: | | | |
| 6 | Product A units (from Exercise 22-3) | 498,000 | 498,000 | |
| 7 | Product A hours per unit | × .40 hours | × .25 hours | |
| 8 | Total Product A hours | 199,200 hours | 124,500 hours | |
| 9 | Hourly rate | × $12 per hour | × $9 per hour | |
| 10 | Total direct labor cost | $2,390,400 | $1,120,500 | $3,510,900 |

PROBLEM 21-1

| | A | B | C |
|---|---|---|---|
| 1 | Amant Inc. | | |
| 2 | Cash Budget | | |
| 3 | For Two Months Ending April 30, 20-- | | |
| 4 | | March | April |
| 5 | Estimated cash receipts from: | | |
| 6 | Cash sales | $ 96,000 | $ 80,000 |
| 7 | Collection of accounts receivable | 160,200 | 124,800 |
| 8 | Total cash receipts | $256,200 | $204,800 |
| 9 | Estimated cash disbursements for: | | |
| 10 | Merchandise costs | $130,000 | $140,000 |
| 11 | Operating expenses | 34,000 | 28,000 |
| 12 | Capital expenditures | — | 125,000 |
| 13 | Property taxes | 5,000 | — |
| 14 | Total cash disbursements | $169,000 | $293,000 |
| 15 | Cash increase or (decrease) | $ 87,200 | $ (88,200) |
| 16 | Cash balance at beginning of month | 24,000 | 111,200 |
| 17 | Cash balance at end of month | $111,200 | $ 23,000 |
| 18 | Minimum cash balance | 50,000 | 50,000 |
| 19 | Excess or (deficiency) | $ 61,200 | $ (27,000) |

PROBLEM 21-2

(1)

| | A | B | C |
|---|---|---|---|
| 1 | Fernandez Furniture Company | | |
| 2 | Production Budget | | |
| 3 | | Product A | Product B |
| 4 | Sales | 168,000 | 324,000 |
| 5 | Plus desired ending inventory | 8,000 | 36,000 |
| 6 | Less estimated beginning inventory | (12,000) | (24,000) |
| 7 | Total production | 164,000 | 336,000 |

(2)

| | A | B | C | D | E |
|---|---|---|---|---|---|
| 1 | Fernandez Furniture Company | | | | |
| 2 | Direct Materials Purchases Budget | | | | |
| 3 | | Material X | Material Y | Material Z | Total |
| 4 | Pounds required for production: | | | | |
| 5 | Product A | 98,400 | | 196,800 | |
| 6 | Product B | 604,800 | 1,142,400 | | |
| 7 | Plus desired ending inventory | 14,500 | 8,700 | 9,800 | |
| 8 | Total | 717,700 | 1,151,100 | 206,600 | |
| 9 | Less estimated beginning inventory | (16,000) | (5,600) | (12,400) | |
| 10 | Total pounds to be purchased | 701,700 | 1,145,500 | 194,200 | |
| 11 | Price per pound | × $0.40 | × $0.50 | × $0.60 | |
| 12 | Total direct materials purchases | $280,680 | $ 572,750 | $116,520 | $969,950 |

(3)

| | A | B | C | D |
|---|---|---|---|---|
| 1 | Fernandez Furniture Company | | | |
| 2 | Direct Labor Cost Budget | | | |
| 3 | | Department 1 | Department 2 | Total |
| 4 | Product A hours | 32,800 | 24,600 | |
| 5 | Product B hours | 16,800 | 33,600 | |
| 6 | Total hours | 49,600 | 58,200 | |
| 7 | Hourly departmental rate | × $14.00 | × $18.00 | |
| 8 | Total direct labor cost | $694,400 | $1,047,600 | $1,742,000 |

# CHAPTER 22

## MATCHING

| | | | | | | | | | |
|---|---|---|---|---|---|---|---|---|---|
| 1. E | | 5. P | | 9. H | | 12. Q | | 15. N | | 18. R |
| 2. I | | 6. T | | 10. D | | 13. M | | 16. B | | 19. J |
| 3. A | | 7. G | | 11. F | | 14. K | | 17. S | | 20. O |
| 4. L | | 8. C | | | | | | | | |

## FILL IN THE BLANK—PART A

1. standard cost systems
2. principle of exceptions
3. ideal
4. currently attainable (or normal)
5. quantity
6. purchasing
7. cost variance
8. total manufacturing
9. direct materials quantity variance
10. $700 favorable
11. direct labor time variance
12. $1,900 unfavorable
13. controllable
14. $3,000 favorable
15. volume variance
16. total factory overhead cost
17. factory overhead cost variance report
18. Direct Materials Quantity Variance
19. cost of goods sold
20. nonfinancial performance
21. input, output
22. process
23. unfavorable

## FILL IN THE BLANK—PART B

1. standard cost system
2. engineers
3. ideal standards
4. currently attainable (or normal)
5. budgetary performance evaluation
6. budget performance
7. unfavorable
8. direct materials price variance
9. unfavorable materials quantity variance
10. purchasing department
11. $320 unfavorable
12. direct labor rate variance
13. $1,100 favorable
14. production supervisors
15. flexible
16. controllable variance
17. controllable variance
18. $1,000 favorable
19. Direct Materials Price Variance
20. nonfinancial
21. linked
22. manufacturing cost variance

## MULTIPLE CHOICE

1. a. **Correct.** Standard costs are a method for measuring efficiency.
   b. Incorrect. Standard costs are a financial measure of performance.
   c. Incorrect. Standard costs can be used to measure volume variances, but they are not used to measure "volume."
   d. Incorrect. Standard costs can be used to measure direct material quantity variances, but not just "quantity."

2. a. Incorrect.
   b. Incorrect.
   c. **Correct.** [4,800 − (6,000 × 0.75 hours)] × $10 per standard labor hour; the variance is unfavorable because the standard hours allowed is less than the actual hours required.
   d. Incorrect.

3. a. Incorrect.
   b. **Correct.** (5,100 pounds − 5,000 pounds) × $2 per pound; the variance is unfavorable because the standard pounds are less than the actual pounds used.
   c. Incorrect.
   d. Incorrect.

4. a. Incorrect.
   b. Incorrect.
   c. Incorrect.
   d. **Correct.** 700 hours × $2

5. a. Incorrect.
   b. **Correct.** $18,900 − [(5,000 × 0.25) × $12]
   c. Incorrect.
   d. Incorrect.

6. a. **Correct.** The difference between the actual and the standard quantity of direct materials, multiplied by the standard price, is the direct materials quantity variance.
   b. Incorrect. The direct materials price variance measures the difference between the actual price and the standard price, multiplied by the actual quantity used.
   c. Incorrect. Direct materials volume variance is not a business term.
   d. Incorrect. Controllable materials variance is not a business term.

**7.** a. Incorrect.  Direct labor quantity variance is not a business term.
   b. Incorrect.  Direct labor volume variance is not a business term.
   c. Incorrect.  The direct labor rate variance measures the difference between the actual labor rate and the standard labor rate, multiplied by the actual hours worked.
   d. **Correct.**  The direct labor time variance is the difference between the actual and the standard labor hours, multiplied by the standard labor rate.

**8.** a. Incorrect.  Efficiency variance is not a term defined in this text.
   b. Incorrect.  The controllable variance is the difference between the actual variable overhead incurred and the budgeted variable overhead for actual production.
   c. **Correct.**  The volume variance is the difference between the budgeted fixed overhead at 100% of normal capacity and the standard fixed overhead for the actual production achieved during the period.
   d. Incorrect.  The total overhead variance is the difference between the standard factory overhead applied to production and the actual factory overhead.

**9.** a. Incorrect.
   b. Incorrect.
   c. Incorrect.
   d. **Correct.**

**10.** a. **Correct.**  Number of customer complaints is a nonfinancial performance measure.
   b. Incorrect.  Direct labor time variance is a financial performance measure.
   c. Incorrect.  Controllable (variable) overhead variance is a financial performance measure.
   d. Incorrect.

**11.** a. Incorrect.  Accounts Payable would be credited for $5,400.
   b. **Correct.**  Direct Materials Price Variance would be debited because it is unfavorable.
   c. Incorrect.
   d. Incorrect.  Materials would be debited for $4,800.

**12.** a. Incorrect.
   b. **Correct.**  $32,000 – (2,500 units × 2 hours per unit × $6 per hour)
   c. Incorrect.
   d. Incorrect.

## TRUE/FALSE

**1.** T
**2.** F  This would be a price variance.
**3.** T
**4.** F  This is the factory overhead cost variance.
**5.** T
**6.** F  Variances are usually transferred to the cost of goods sold account.
**7.** F  An ideal standard assumes perfect operating conditions; "reasonable effort" would be a normal standard.
**8.** T
**9.** F  Standards can also be applied in selling, administrative, and service settings in some cases.
**10.** T

## EXERCISE 22-1

**(1)** Price variance:
   Direct Materials Price Variance: (Actual Price – Standard Price) × Actual Quantity
   Direct Materials Price Variance: ($1.82 – $1.80) × 77,000 = $1,540 Unfavorable

   Quantity variance:
   Direct Materials Quantity Variance: (Actual Quantity – Standard Quantity) × Standard Price
   Direct Materials Quantity Variance: (77,000 lbs. – 75,000 lbs.) × $1.80 = $3,600 Unfavorable

   Total direct materials cost variance:
   Total Direct Materials Cost Variance: Actual Cost – Standard Cost
   Total Direct Materials Cost Variance: $140,140 – $135,000 = $5,140 Unfavorable

**(2)** Rate variance:
   Direct Labor Rate Variance: (Actual Rate – Standard Rate) × Actual Quantity
   Direct Labor Rate Variance: ($19.75 – $20.00) × 42,500 = –$10,625 Favorable

   Time variance:
   Direct Labor Time Variance: (Actual Time – Standard Time) × Standard Price
   Direct Labor Time Variance: (42,500 hrs. – 42,000 hrs.) × $20.00 = $10,000 Unfavorable

   Total direct labor cost variance:
   Total Direct Labor Cost Variance: Actual Cost – Standard Cost
   Total Direct Labor Cost Variance: $839,375 – $840,000 = –$625 Favorable

## EXERCISE 22-2

Volume variance:

| | | |
|---|---:|---:|
| 100% of normal capacity | 40,000 hours | |
| Standard for amount produced | 30,000 hours | |
| Productive capacity not used | 10,000 hours | |
| Standard fixed factory overhead rate | × $3 | |
| Variance—unfavorable | | $30,000 |

Controllable variance:

| | | |
|---|---:|---:|
| Actual variable factory overhead | $153,500 | |
| Budgeted variable factory overhead for 30,000 hours | 150,000 | |
| Variance—unfavorable | | 3,500 |
| Total factory overhead cost variance—unfavorable | | $33,500 |

## EXERCISE 22-3

| | A | B | C | D | E |
|---|---|---|---|---|---|
| 1 | Nathalie Inc. | | | | |
| 2 | Budget Performance Report—Factory Overhead Cost | | | | |
| 3 | For the Month Ended January 31, 20-- | | | | |
| 4 | | Budget | Actual | Unfavorable | Favorable |
| 5 | Variable cost: | | | | |
| 6 | Indirect factory wages | $ 48,000 | $ 50,500 | $2,500 | |
| 7 | Indirect materials | 27,000 | 27,600 | 600 | |
| 8 | Electric power | 36,000 | 35,000 | | $1,000 |
| 9 | Total variable cost | $111,000 | $113,100 | | |
| 10 | Fixed cost: | | | | |
| 11 | Supervisory salaries | $ 30,000 | $ 30,000 | | |
| 12 | Depreciation of plant and equipment | 18,000 | 18,000 | | |
| 13 | Property taxes | 12,000 | 12,000 | | |
| 14 | Insurance | 7,500 | 7,500 | | |
| 15 | Electric power | 4,500 | 4,500 | | |
| 16 | Total fixed cost | 72,000 | 72,000 | | |
| 17 | Total factory overhead cost | $183,000 | $185,100 | $3,100 | $1,000 |

## EXERCISE 22-4

(1)       30 employees
    ×     40 hours per week
      1,200 total hours worked
    ×   $16 labor rate per hour
$19,200 IRS labor cost

(2)  Flexible budget:
       No. of traditional paper returns processed......... 1,300 × 45 min. =  58,500 min.
       No. of electronic returns processed................... 225 × 8 min. =   1,800 min.
                                                                                                60,300 min.

       60,300 / 60 = 1,005 hours flexible budget

(3)  Time variance:
       Direct Labor Time Variance: (Actual Time – Standard Time) × Standard Price
       Direct Labor Time Variance: (1,200 hrs. – 1,005 hrs.) × $16.00 = $3,120 Unfavorable

# PROBLEM 22-1

**(1)**                          Direct Materials Cost Variances

Price variance:

Direct Materials Price Variance: (Actual Price – Standard Price) × Actual Quantity

Direct Materials Price Variance: ($6.20 – $6.00) × 250,000 = $50,000 Unfavorable

Quantity variance:

Direct Materials Quantity Variance: (Actual Quantity – Standard Quantity) × Standard Price

Direct Materials Quantity Variance: (250,000 lbs. – 255,000 lbs.) × $6.00 = –$30,000 Favorable

Total direct materials cost variance:

Total Direct Materials Cost Variance: Actual Cost – Standard Cost

Total Direct Materials Cost Variance: $1,550,000 – (25,500 units × $60) = $20,000 Unfavorable

**(2)**                          Direct Labor Cost Variances

Rate variance:

Direct Labor Rate Variance: (Actual Rate – Standard Rate) × Actual Quantity

Direct Labor Rate Variance: ($14.60 – $15.00) × 77,400 = –$30,960 Favorable

Quantity variance:

Direct Labor Time Variance: (Actual Time – Standard Time) × Standard Price

Direct Labor Time Variance: (77,400 hrs. – 76,500 hrs.) × $15.00 = $13,500 Unfavorable

Total variance:

Total Direct Labor Cost Variance: Actual Cost – Standard Cost

Total Direct Labor Cost Variance: $1,130,040 – (25,500 units × $45) = –$17,460 Favorable

**(3)**                          Factory Overhead Cost Variances

|  |  | Variance |
|---|---|---|
| Controllable variance: |  |  |
| Actual variable factory overhead cost incurred............................. | $160,000 |  |
| Budgeted variable factory overhead for actual product produced ................................................................................ | 153,000 |  |
| Variance............................................................................. |  | $ 7,000 U |
| Volume variance: |  |  |
| Budgeted hours at 100% of normal capacity............................... | 90,000 hrs. |  |
| Standard hours for amount produced........................................ | 76,500 hrs. |  |
| Productive capacity not used................................................. | 13,500 hrs. |  |
| Standard fixed factory overhead cost rate................................. | × $1.50 |  |
| Variance............................................................................. |  | 20,250 U |
| Total factory overhead cost variance ................................................................................... |  | $27,250 U |

## Alternative Computation of Overhead Variances

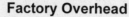

### Factory Overhead

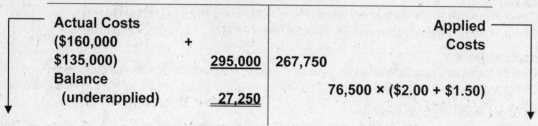

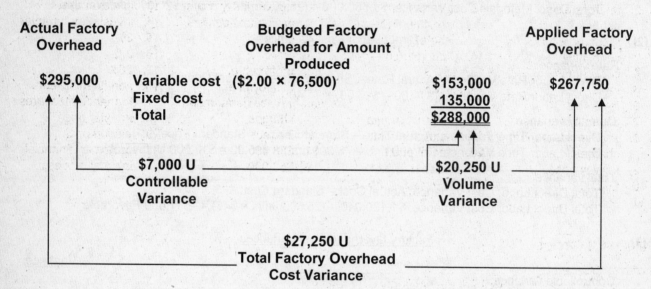

| Actual Factory Overhead | Budgeted Factory Overhead for Amount Produced | | | Applied Factory Overhead |
|---|---|---|---|---|
| $295,000 | Variable cost ($2.00 × 76,500) | | $153,000 | $267,750 |
| | Fixed cost | | 135,000 | |
| | Total | | $288,000 | |

$7,000 U
Controllable
Variance

$20,250 U
Volume
Variance

$27,250 U
Total Factory Overhead
Cost Variance

## PROBLEM 22-2

Piazza Company, Inc.
Income Statement
For the Month Ended January 31, 20--

| | Favorable | Unfavorable | |
|---|---|---|---|
| Sales | | | $995,000 |
| Cost of goods sold—at standard | | | 812,000 |
| Gross profit—at standard | | | $183,000 |
| Less variances from standard cost: | | | |
| Direct materials price | | $  500 | |
| Direct materials quantity | | 1,500 | |
| Direct labor rate | | 1,200 | |
| Direct labor time | $3,000 | | |
| Factory overhead controllable | 4,000 | | |
| Factory overhead volume | | 10,000 | 6,200 |
| Gross profit | | | $176,800 |
| Operating expenses: | | | |
| Selling expenses | | $68,000 | |
| Administrative expenses | | 42,000 | 110,000 |
| Income before income tax | | | $ 66,800 |

# CHAPTER 23

## MATCHING

| | | | | | |
|---|---|---|---|---|---|
| 1. O | 5. E | 8. L | 11. F | 14. Q | 17. A |
| 2. K | 6. I | 9. N | 12. P | 15. D | 18. C |
| 3. H | 7. B | 10. S | 13. M | 16. J | 19. G |
| 4. R | | | | | |

## FILL IN THE BLANK—PART A

1. centralized
2. responsibility centers
3. responsibility accounting
4. cost center
5. more
6. revenues
7. controllable
8. service department charges
9. activity base
10. $48,000
11. $53,000
12. investment center
13. rate of return on investment (or on assets)
14. profit margin
15. 8%
16. 3.125
17. 25%
18. DuPont formula
19. residual income
20. market price
21. negotiated price
22. balanced scorecard

## FILL IN THE BLANK—PART B

1. decentralization
2. responsibility center
3. investment centers
4. costs
5. more
6. profit center
7. controllable
8. service department charges
9. indirect
10. $38,400
11. $68,000
12. residual income
13. invested assets
14. investment turnover
15. 8%
16. 2.5
17. 20%
18. non-financial performance measures
19. transfer price
20. market price
21. customer, financial, internal process

## MULTIPLE CHOICE

1. a. *Correct.*
   b. Incorrect. A profit center has authority over revenue.
   c. Incorrect. An investment center has authority over revenues and assets.
   d. Incorrect.

2. a. Incorrect. Market price is an appropriate transfer price when the selling division has no excess capacity.
   b. *Correct.*
   c. Incorrect.
   d. Incorrect.

3. a. Incorrect. This term is the return on investment.
   b. Incorrect. This term is the investment turnover.
   c. *Correct.*
   d. Incorrect.

4. a. Incorrect. A cost center manager has authority over only costs.
   b. Incorrect. A profit center manager has authority over costs and revenues.
   c. Incorrect. A data center is a function department, not a type of responsibility center.
   d. *Correct.* An investment center manager has authority over costs, revenues, and assets.

5. a. Incorrect.
   b. Incorrect.
   c. Incorrect.
   d. *Correct.* ($750,000 − $450,000 − $228,000) / $300,000

6. a. Incorrect.
   b. *Correct.* $750,000 / $300,000
   c. Incorrect.
   d. Incorrect.

7. a. Incorrect.
   b. Incorrect.
   c. **Correct.**   15% × 1.2
   d. Incorrect.

8. a. **Correct.**
   b. Incorrect. Some bad decisions will not positively affect overall profitability.
   c. Incorrect. This is a possible disadvantage of decentralization.
   d. Incorrect.

9. a. Incorrect.
   b. Incorrect.
   c. Incorrect.
   d. **Correct.**   All of these departments provide internal services to other departments.

10. a. Incorrect. This is a financial measure.
    b. Incorrect. This is a financial measure.
    c. **Correct.**
    d. Incorrect. This is a financial measure.

11. a. Incorrect.
    b. **Correct.**   [$130,000 / (100 × 52)] × 30 employees × 4 weeks
    c. Incorrect.
    d. Incorrect.

12. a. Incorrect.
    b. **Correct.**   [$180,000 / (10,000 × 12 months)] × 4,000 invoices; the invoices represented in the accounts receivable balance are part of the monthly invoices, so they should not be counted twice.
    c. Incorrect.
    d. Incorrect.

## TRUE/FALSE

1. T
2. T
3. F   The amount of budget detail will be greater in responsibility centers at the lowest level of the organization.
4. F   A cost center would not be responsible for revenues, which are included in an income statement.
5. T
6. T
7. F   Sales divided by invested assets is the investment turnover.
8. F   The profit margin is 18% / 3 = 6%
9. T
10. F   The negotiated price (greater than variable cost, but less that market price) is a more appropriate transfer price for a selling division that has excess capacity.

## EXERCISE 23-1

(1)  (a) $280,000       (c) $520,000
     (b) $120,000       (d) $135,000

(2)  Division M:  16% ($120,000 / $750,000)
     Division N:  22% ($110,000 / $500,000)

(3)  Division M

(4)  Division N

## EXERCISE 23-2

**(1)** Division M:

| | |
|---|---:|
| Income from operations | $120,000 |
| Minimum income ($750,000 × 12%) | 90,000 |
| Residual income | $ 30,000 |

Division N:

| | |
|---|---:|
| Income from operations | $110,000 |
| Minimum income ($500,000 × 12%) | 60,000 |
| Residual income | $ 50,000 |

**(2)** Division N

## EXERCISE 23-3

**(a)** 1.6

**(b)** 12.5%

**(c)** 18.9%

**(d)** 18%

**(e)** 1.5

## EXERCISE 23-4

Increase in Estes (Purchasing) Division's Income from Operations =
   (Market Price – Transfer Price) × Units Transferred
Increase in Estes (Purchasing) Division's Income from Operations =
   ($50 – $44) × 16,000 units = $96,000

Increase in Sierra Division (Supplying) Division's Income from Operations =
   (Transfer Price – Variable Cost per Unit) × Units Transferred
Increase in Sierra Division (Supplying) Division's Income from Operations =
   ($44 – $32) × 16,000 units = $192,000

## PROBLEM 23-1

Budget Performance Report—Supervisor, Department F, Plant 7
For the Month Ended July 31, 20--

| | Budget | Actual | Over | Under |
|---|---:|---:|---:|---:|
| Factory wages | $ 65,000 | $ 73,600 | $8,600 | |
| Materials | 39,500 | 37,700 | | $1,800 |
| Supervisory salaries | 15,000 | 15,000 | | |
| Power and light | 8,900 | 9,600 | 700 | |
| Dept. of plant and equipment | 7,500 | 7,500 | | |
| Maintenance | 4,300 | 3,900 | | 400 |
| Insurance and property taxes | 2,000 | 2,000 | | |
| | $142,200 | $149,300 | $9,300 | $2,200 |

## PROBLEM 23-2

Firefly Co.
Income Statement—Divisions J and K
For the Year Ended May 31, 20--

| | Division J | Division K | Total |
|---|---|---|---|
| Net sales | $280,000 | $420,000 | $700,000 |
| Cost of goods sold | 122,500 | 227,500 | 350,000 |
| Gross profit | $157,500 | $192,500 | $350,000 |
| Operating expenses | 48,000 | 72,000 | 120,000 |
| Income from operations before service department charges | $109,500 | $120,500 | $230,000 |
| Less service department charges: | | | |
| Payroll accounting | $ 24,000 | $ 36,000 | $ 60,000 |
| Purchasing | 48,400 | 39,600 | 88,000 |
| Brochure advertising | 31,250 | 18,750 | 50,000 |
| Total service department charges | $103,650 | $ 94,350 | $198,000 |
| Income from operations | $ 5,850 | $ 26,150 | $ 32,000 |

Supporting Schedules:

| | Number of Payroll Checks | Number of Requisitions | Number of Brochure Pages |
|---|---|---|---|
| Division J | 400 | 2,200 | 500 |
| Division K | 600 | 1,800 | 300 |
| Total | 1,000 | 4,000 | 800 |
| Relative percentages: | | | |
| Division J | 40.00% | 55.00% | 62.50% |
| Division K | 60.00% | 45.00% | 37.50% |
| Service department costs | $60,000 | $88,000 | $50,000 |
| Percentages multiplied by service department costs: | | | |
| Division J | $24,000 | $48,400 | $31,250 |
| Division K | $36,000 | $39,600 | $18,750 |

## PROBLEM 23-3

(1)  (a)  no effect

(b)  no effect

(2)  (a)  increase by $30,000

Increase in Division X's (Purchasing) Income from Operations =
(Market Price – Transfer Price) × Units Transferred
Increase in Division X's (Purchasing) Income from Operations =
($30 – $27) × 10,000 units = $30,000

(b)  increase by $50,000

Increase in Divisions Y's (Supplying) Income from Operations =
(Transfer Price – Variable Cost per Unit) × Units Transferred
Increase in Division Y's (Supplying) Income from Operations =
($27 – $22) × 10,000 units = $50,000

**(3)** **(a)** increase by $100,000

Increase in Division X's (Purchasing) Income from Operations =
  (Market Price – Transfer Price) × Units Transferred
Increase in Division X's (Purchasing) Income from Operations =
  ($30 – $20) × 10,000 units = $100,000

**(b)** decrease by $20,000

Increase in Division Y's (Supplying) Income from Operations =
  (Transfer Price – Variable Cost per Unit) × Units Transferred
Increase in Division Y's (Supplying) Income from Operations =
  ($20 – $22) × 10,000 units = $(20,000)

# CHAPTER 24

## MATCHING

| | | | | | |
|---|---|---|---|---|---|
| 1. F | 4. I | 6. M | 8. A | 10. K | 12. J |
| 2. H | 5. B | 7. D | 9. C | 11. G | 13. E |
| 3. L | | | | | |

## FILL IN THE BLANK—PART A

1. differential revenue
2. differential cost
3. sunk cost
4. income tax differential
5. $68,000
6. $5
7. opportunity cost
8. further processing
9. variable
10. variable costs
11. demand-based
12. competition-based
13. total costs
14. total fixed costs
15. 10%
16. 65%
17. 83.3%
18. drift
19. activity-based costing
20. production bottle-neck (or constraint)
21. theory of constraints

## FILL IN THE BLANK—PART B

1. differential analysis
2. sunk costs
3. differential income (or loss)
4. differential revenues
5. $79,000
6. capacity
7. opportunity cost
8. $0.30
9. Robinson-Patman Act
10. total cost
11. product cost
12. variable cost
13. total cost
14. total cost
15. total manufacturing costs
16. 12.5%
17. 80%
18. 50%
19. target costing
20. production bottle-neck (or constraint)

## MULTIPLE CHOICE

1. a. Incorrect. Although not defined in the text, gross profit analysis would be a type of vertical analysis of gross profit as a percent of sales compared with other companies in an industry.
   b. Incorrect. Capital investment analysis is the process by which management evaluates capital projects (as explained in the next chapter).
   c. **Correct.**
   d. Incorrect. CVP analysis is an analysis used to determine the break-even point.

2. a. **Correct.** ($18 – $16 variable cost) × 10,000 units
   b. Incorrect.
   c. Incorrect.
   d. Incorrect.

**3.** a. Incorrect. A sunk cost is incurred in the past and is not relevant to a decision impacting a future course of action.
b. **Correct.**
c. Incorrect. A differential cost is the amount of increase or decrease in cost that is expected from a course of action as compared with an alternative.
d. Incorrect. This is not a term defined in this text, nor is it commonly used in business.

**4.** a. Incorrect. Under the total cost concept, only the desired profit is allowed for determining the markup.
b. **Correct.**
c. Incorrect. Under the variable cost concept, the desired profit and total fixed costs are allowed for determining the markup.
d. Incorrect.

**5.** a. Incorrect.
b. Incorrect.
c. Incorrect.
d. **Correct.** (5,000 gallons × 2 batches × 90% × $5 per gallon) – (2 batches × $7,800) – (5,000 gallons × 2 batches × $3 per gallon)

**6.** a. Incorrect. Product cost is used for cost-plus pricing.
b. Incorrect. Total cost is used for cost-plus pricing.
c. Incorrect. Variable cost is used for cost-plus pricing.
d. **Correct.**

**7.** a. Incorrect. The total cost plus markup approach assumes the market will accept the cost-plus price.
b. Incorrect. The variable cost plus markup approach assumes the market will accept the cost-plus price.
c. **Correct.** The target cost approach begins with an assumed market price and works backwards to the markup.
d. Incorrect. The product cost plus markup approach assumes the market will accept the cost-plus price.

**8.** a. Incorrect.
b. **Correct.** The most profitable product is determined by dividing the contribution margin per unit by the process hours in the constraint resource; thus, Product B is the most profitable ($70 / 3 hours).
c. Incorrect.
d. Incorrect.

**9.** a. **Correct.**
b. Incorrect. Total cost-based is a cost-plus method.
c. Incorrect. Variable cost-based is a cost-plus method.
d. Incorrect. Product cost-based is a cost-plus method.

**10.** a. Incorrect. This cost is relevant to this decision.
b. Incorrect. This cost is relevant to this decision.
c. **Correct.** A sunk cost is incurred in the past and is not relevant to a decision impacting a future course of action. The book value of previously purchased equipment is such a cost.
d. Incorrect. This cost is relevant to this decision.

**11.** a. **Correct.** [($40 + $4) – ($50 – $9)] × 5,000 units = $15,000
b. Incorrect.
c. Incorrect.
d. Incorrect.

**12.** a. **Correct.** $25,000 loss from operations + (30% × $50,000) depreciation = ($10,000) contribution margin; the small speaker line has a negative contribution margin, which could be avoided if the line were dropped.
b. Incorrect.
c. Incorrect.
d. Incorrect.

**13.** a. Incorrect.
   b. Incorrect.
   c. **Correct.**   [$60 price – ($50 variable cost + $6 export fee)] × 1,000 units = $4,000
   d. Incorrect.

## TRUE/FALSE

**1.** T

**2.** F  This is called a differential cost.

**3.** F  The special price may be less than all costs (including fixed costs), but greater than all variable costs and still produce differential income if accepted.

**4.** F  Many common fixed costs will not be eliminated by discontinuing an unprofitable business segment. For example, the plant and equipment depreciation that is common to many products will not be eliminated if one product is discontinued.

**5.** F  This is called an opportunity cost.

**6.** T

**7.** T

**8.** T

**9.** T

**10.** F  The best way to evaluate profitability of products in production-constrained environments is to measure contribution margin per unit of bottleneck resource.

## EXERCISE 24-1

### Walden Transportation Inc.
### Proposal to Lease or Sell Truck

| | | |
|---|---:|---:|
| Differential revenue from alternatives: | | |
| Revenue from lease | $20,000 | |
| Revenue from sale | 18,000 | |
| Differential revenue from lease | | $2,000 |
| Differential cost of alternatives: | | |
| License expenses during lease | $ 1,100 | |
| Repainting expense on sale | 900 | |
| Differential cost of leasing | | 200 |
| Net differential income (loss) from lease alternative | | $1,800 |

## EXERCISE 24-2

### Tran Inc.
### Proposal to Manufacture Metal Blades

| | | |
|---|---:|---:|
| Purchase price of blades | | $14.00 |
| Differential cost to manufacture blades: | | |
| Direct materials | $6.75 | |
| Direct labor | 5.10 | |
| Variable factory overhead | 0.80 | 12.65 |
| Cost savings (increase) from manufacturing blades | | $ 1.35 |

## EXERCISE 24-3

English Chairs Inc.
Proposal to Discontinue Rocking Chairs
December 31, 20--

| | | |
|---|---:|---:|
| Differential revenue from sales of rocking chairs: | | |
| Revenue from sales.................................................................. | | $350,000 |
| Differential cost of sales of rocking chairs: | | |
| Variable cost of goods sold ................................................. | $180,000 | |
| Variable operating expenses................................................ | 75,000 | 255,000 |
| Differential income (loss) from sales of rocking chairs ......................... | | $ 95,000 |

The rocking chairs section probably <u>should</u> be continued.

## EXERCISE 24-4

Golub Inc.
Proposal to Replace Machine
December 31, 20--

| | | |
|---|---:|---:|
| Annual variable costs—present machine............................................. | $ 65,000 | |
| Annual variable costs—new machine ................................................. | 30,000 | |
| Annual differential decrease (increase) in variable costs ...................... | $ 35,000 | |
| Number of years applicable ............................................................. | × 7 | |
| Total differential decrease (increase) in variable costs......................... | $245,000 | |
| Proceeds from sale of present machine ............................................. | 83,000 | $328,000 |
| Cost of new machine ..................................................................... | | 370,000 |
| Net differential decrease (increase) in cost, seven-year total................ | | $ (42,000) |
| Annual net differential decrease (increase) in cost—new machine ....... | | $ (6,000) |

## PROBLEM 24-1

**(1)** $60,000  ($500,000 × 12%)

**(2) (a)** Total costs:

| | | |
|---|---|---:|
| Variable ($5 × 50,000 units)..................... | | $250,000 |
| Fixed ($35,000 + $15,000)....................... | | 50,000 |
| Total.................................................... | | $300,000 |

Cost amount per unit:  $300,000 / 50,000 units = $6

**(b)** Markup Percentage = Desired Profit / Total Costs
Markup Percentage = $60,000 / $300,000
Markup Percentage = 20%

**(c)**

| | |
|---|---:|
| Cost amount per unit ...................................... | $6.00 |
| Markup ($6 × 20%) ........................................ | 1.20 |
| Selling price .................................................. | $7.20 |

## PROBLEM 24-2

**(1)** Total manufacturing costs:

| | |
|---|---|
| Variable ($4 × 50,000 units) | $200,000 |
| Fixed factory overhead | 35,000 |
| Total | $235,000 |

Cost amount per unit: $235,000 / 50,000 units = $4.70

**(2)** Markup Percentage = (Desired Profit + Total Selling and Administrative Expenses) / Total Manufacturing Costs

Markup Percentage = [$60,000 + $15,000 + ($1 × 50,000 units)] / $235,000

Markup Percentage = $125,000 / $235,000

Markup Percentage = 53.2%

**(3)**

| | |
|---|---|
| Cost amount per unit | $4.70 |
| Markup ($4.70 × 53.2%) | 2.50 |
| Selling price | $7.20 |

## PROBLEM 24-3

**(1)** Total variable costs: $5 × 50,000 units = $250,000

Cost amount per unit: $250,000 / 50,000 units = $5

**(2)** Markup Percentage = Desired Profit + Total Fixed Costs / Total Variable Costs

Markup Percentage = ($60,000 + $35,000 + $15,000) / $250,000

Markup Percentage = $110,000 / $250,000

Markup Percentage = 44%

**(3)**

| | |
|---|---|
| Cost amount per unit | $5.00 |
| Markup ($5 × 44%) | 2.20 |
| Selling price | $7.20 |

## PROBLEM 24-4

First, determine the contribution margin per bottleneck hour for each product.

| | Product D | Product E | Product F |
|---|---|---|---|
| Sales price per unit | $750 | $600 | $400 |
| Variable cost per unit | 300 | 350 | 200 |
| Contribution margin per unit | $450 | $250 | $200 |
| Furnace hours per unit | ÷ 15 | ÷ 10 | ÷ 8 |
| Contribution margin per furnace hour (CM ÷ furnace hours) | $ 30 | $ 25 | $ 25 |

Product D is more profitable in per furnace hour terms than either Products E or F. Products E and F would need to increase prices enough to make their contribution margin per furnace hour equal to $30.

Product E:   (X − $350) / 10 furnace hours = $30

$$X − \$350 = \$300$$
$$X = \$650$$

Product F:   (X − $200) / 8 furnace hours = $30

$$X − \$200 = \$240$$
$$X = \$440$$

# CHAPTER 25

## MATCHING

| | | | | | |
|---|---|---|---|---|---|
| **1.** H | **4.** E | **6.** I | **8.** C | **10.** J | **12.** B |
| **2.** K | **5.** M | **7.** L | **9.** G | **11.** D | **13.** F |
| **3.** A | | | | | |

## FILL IN THE BLANK—PART A

1. capital investment analysis (or capital budgeting)
2. internal rate of return
3. short
4. 3.3%  [($53,500 – 46,500) / ($400,000 + $28,000 / 2)]
5. average rate of return
6. cash payback
7. 6 years  [$300,000 / ($65,000 – $15,000)]
8. cash payback
9. annuity
10. net present value (or discounted cash flow)
11. $9,550  [($50,000 × 3.791) – $180,000]
12. index
13. net present value (or discounted cash flow)
14. annual net cash flows
15. highest
16. uncertainty
17. same
18. strategic
19. qualitative
20. minimum

## FILL IN THE BLANK—PART B

1. present values
2. cash payback
3. time value
4. average rate of return (or accounting rate of return)
5. 25%  [($270,000 ÷ 3) / ($680,000 + $40,000) ÷ 2]
6. net cash flow
7. cash payback period
8. timing
9. present value of an annuity
10. net present value
11. $12,060  [($30,000 × .893) + ($30,000 × .797) + ($30,000 × .712)] – $60,000 or ($30,000 × 2.402) – $60,000
12. 1.44  ($72,000 / $50,000)
13. internal rate of return (or time-adjusted rate of return)
14. $5,200  [($10,000 × 3.170) – $26,500]
15. 4.975  ($79,600 / $16,000)
16. internal rate of return
17. leasing
18. inflation
19. rationing
20. strategic investments

## MULTIPLE CHOICE

1.  a. **Correct.**
    b. Incorrect.  The discounted cash flow method uses present values.
    c. Incorrect.  The discounted internal rate of return method uses present values.
    d. Incorrect.

2.  a. Incorrect.  The average rate of return method does not use present values.
    b. Incorrect.  The cash payback method does not use present values.
    c. Incorrect.  The discounted internal rate of return method computes the rate of return from the net cash flows expected from the proposals.
    d. **Correct.**

3.  a. Incorrect.  The average rate of return method does not use present values.
    b. Incorrect.  The cash payback method does not use present values.
    c. **Correct.**
    d. Incorrect.  The net present value method determines the total present value of cash flows expected from investment proposals and compares these values with the amounts to be invested.

**4.** a. Incorrect.
b. **Correct.**   $360,000 / $120,000 = 3 years
c. Incorrect.
d. Incorrect.

**5.** a. Incorrect.
b. **Correct.**   ($600,000 / 6 years) / ($800,000 / 2)
c. Incorrect.
d. Incorrect.

**6.** a. **Correct.**
b. Incorrect.   Expected net cash inflows is a quantitative factor.
c. Incorrect.   Amounts of cash to be invested is a quantitative factor.
d. Incorrect.   Timing of cash inflows is a quantitative factor.

**7.** a. Incorrect.
b. Incorrect.
c. **Correct.**   ($50,000 × 3.17 annuity factor) / $145,000
d. Incorrect.

**8.** a. Incorrect.
b. Incorrect.   Time-adjusted rate of return method is another term for the internal rate of return method.
c. Incorrect.   Average rate of discounted return method is a meaningless term.
d. **Correct.**

**9.** a. Incorrect.   This is an advantage of the cash payback method.
b. Incorrect.   The cash payback method does not emphasize accounting income.
c. **Correct.**
d. Incorrect.   The cash payback method can be used when cash flows are not equal.

**10.** a. Incorrect.
b. Incorrect.
c. Incorrect.
d. **Correct.**

**11.** a. **Correct.**   [($70,000 + $20,000) × 3.605 present value factor] – $320,000
b. Incorrect.
c. Incorrect.
d. Incorrect.

**12.** a. Incorrect.
b. Incorrect.
c. **Correct.**   $83,200 / $20,000 = 4.16, which is the present value of an annuity factor from Exhibit 2 that is for seven periods at 15%.
d. Incorrect.

**13.** a. Incorrect.
b. Incorrect.
c. **Correct.**   [($15,000 × 2.991) + ($8,000 × .402)] – $45,000
d. Incorrect.

## TRUE/FALSE

1.  T
2.  T
3.  F   This time period is called the cash payback period.
4.  F   Longer investment horizons should take into account the time value of money.
5.  F   The net present value method determines the total present value of cash flows expected from investment proposals and compares these values with the amounts to be invested.
6.  F   The present value index is computed by dividing the total present value of net cash flows by the amount to be invested.
7.  T
8.  T
9.  T
10. F   This is an advantage of the cash payback period.

## EXERCISE 25-1

(1)   $48,000 / $310,000 = 15.48%

(2)   $620,000 / $200,000 = 3.1 years

(3)   Yes. The proposal meets the minimum rate of return desired.

(4)   No. The proposal does not meet the minimum cash payback period desired.

## EXERCISE 25-2

Proposal 1:  $250,000 / $60,000 = 4.17 years

Proposal 2:

| Year | Net Cash Flow | Cumulative Net Cash Flow |
|------|---------------|--------------------------|
| 1 | $100,000 | $100,000 |
| 2 | 80,000 | 180,000 |
| 3 | 70,000 | 250,000 |
| 4 | 45,000 | 295,000 |
| 5 | 45,000 | 340,000 |
| 6 | 20,000 | 360,000 |

The cumulative net cash flow at the end of three years equals the amount of the investment, $250,000, so the payback period is three years.

## EXERCISE 25-3

Proposal 1:  The factor for the present value of an annuity for 6 years at 10%:  4.355

| | |
|---|---|
| $60,000 × 4.355............................ | $261,300 |
| Less amount invested................... | 250,000 |
| Net present value ........................ | $ 11,300 |

Proposal 2:

| | A | B | C | D |
|---|---|---|---|---|
| 1 | Year | Present Value of 1 at 10% | Net Cash Flow | Present Value of Net Cash Flow |
| 2 | 1 | 0.909 | $100,000 | $ 90,900 |
| 3 | 2 | 0.826 | 80,000 | 66,080 |
| 4 | 3 | 0.751 | 70,000 | 52,570 |
| 5 | 4 | 0.683 | 45,000 | 30,735 |
| 6 | 5 | 0.621 | 45,000 | 27,945 |
| 7 | 6 | 0.564 | 20,000 | 11,280 |
| 8 | Total | | $360,000 | $279,510 |
| 9 | | | | |
| 10 | Amount to be invested in equipment | | | 250,000 |
| 11 | | | | |
| 12 | Excess of present value over amount to be invested | | | $ 29,510 |

## EXERCISE 25-4

(1)  Present Value Factor for an Annuity of $1 = Amount to be Invested / Annual Net Cash Flow
Present Value Factor for an Annuity of $1 = $358,900 / $120,000
Present Value Factor for an Annuity of $1 = 2.991

(2)  20%

## PROBLEM 25-1

(1)

| | A | B | C | D |
|---|---|---|---|---|
| 1 | Year | Present Value of 1 at 12% | Net Cash Flow | Present Value of Net Cash Flow |
| 2 | 1 | 0.893 | $ 80,000 | $ 71,440 |
| 3 | 2 | 0.797 | 60,000 | 47,820 |
| 4 | 3 | 0.712 | 60,000 | 42,720 |
| 5 | 4 | 0.636 | 60,000 | 38,160 |
| 6 | 5 | 0.567 | 60,000 | 34,020 |
| 7 | Total | | $320,000 | $234,160 |
| 8 | | | | |
| 9 | Amount to be invested in equipment | | | 180,000 |
| 10 | | | | |
| 11 | Excess of present value over amount to be invested | | | $ 54,160 |

(2)  1.30  ($234,160 / $180,000)

(3)  yes

## PROBLEM 25-2

**(1)** Project 1:

| | A | B | C | D |
|---|---|---|---|---|
| 1 | Year | Present Value of 1 at 10% | Net Cash Flow | Present Value of Net Cash Flow |
| 2 | 1 | 0.909 | $ 55,000 | $ 49,995 |
| 3 | 2 | 0.826 | 50,000 | 41,300 |
| 4 | 3 | 0.751 | 45,000 | 33,795 |
| 5 | 4 | 0.683 | 40,000 | 27,320 |
| 6 | 5 | 0.621 | 40,000 | 24,840 |
| 7 | 6 | 0.564 | 30,000 | 16,920 |
| 8 | 7 | 0.513 | 15,000 | 7,695 |
| 9 | Total | | $275,000 | $201,865 |
| 10 | | | | |
| 11 | Amount to be invested | | | 180,000 |
| 12 | | | | |
| 13 | Net present value | | | $ 21,865 |

Project 2:

| | A | B | C | D |
|---|---|---|---|---|
| 1 | Year | Present Value of 1 at 10% | Net Cash Flow | Present Value of Net Cash Flow |
| 2 | 1 | 0.909 | $ 55,000 | $ 49,995 |
| 3 | 2 | 0.826 | 55,000 | 45,430 |
| 4 | 3 | 0.751 | 55,000 | 41,305 |
| 5 | 4 | 0.683 | 55,000 | 37,565 |
| 6 | 5 | 0.621 | 55,000 | 34,155 |
| 7 | Total | | $275,000 | $208,450 |
| 8 | | | | |
| 9 | Amount to be invested | | | 180,000 |
| 10 | | | | |
| 11 | Net present value | | | $ 28,450 |

**(2)**   Project 1:

| | A | B | C | D |
|---|---|---|---|---|
| 1 | Year | Present Value of 1 at 10% | Net Cash Flow | Present Value of Net Cash Flow |
| 2 | 1 | 0.909 | $ 55,000 | $ 49,995 |
| 3 | 2 | 0.826 | 50,000 | 41,300 |
| 4 | 3 | 0.751 | 45,000 | 33,795 |
| 5 | 4 | 0.683 | 40,000 | 27,320 |
| 6 | 5 | 0.621 | 40,000 | 24,840 |
| 7 | 5 Res. Value | 0.621 | 60,000 | 37,260 |
| 8 | Total | | $290,000 | $214,510 |
| 9 | | | | |
| 10 | Amount to be invested | | | 180,000 |
| 11 | | | | |
| 12 | Net present value | | | $ 34,510 |

**(3)**   Using a 5-year analysis, Project 1's net present value, $34,510, is greater than Project 2's, $28,450; thus Project 1 is more attractive.

# CHAPTER 26

## MATCHING

| | | | | | |
|---|---|---|---|---|---|
| **1.** A | **3.** C | **5.** L | **7.** E | **9.** G | **11.** K |
| **2.** J | **4.** H | **6.** D | **8.** B | **10.** I | |

## FILL IN THE BLANK—PART A

1. product costing
2. total budgeted factory overhead cost, total budgeted plantwide allocation base
3. $288  (24 machine hours × $12 per machine hour)
4. production department.
5. $60 per direct labor hour ($420,000 ÷ 7,000 direct labor hours)
6. $480  ($32 × 15 hours)
7. distortion
8. equal to
9. differences
10. ratio
11. pools
12. $40 per unit  ($400 × 12 setups) / (12 setups × 10 units), or $400 / 10 units
13. $30 per purchase order ($360,000 ÷ 12,000 purchase orders)
14. complex
15. number of inspections
16. period, product
17. sales
18. $6,850  ($36 × 150) + ($145 × 10)
19. $14,450  ($36 × 200) + ($145 × 50)
20. patient

## FILL IN THE BLANK—PART B

1. activity-based costing
2. simplicity
3. different
4. activity base
5. equal to
6. multiple production department rate
7. single plantwide rate
8. engineering change order
9. setup
10. allocation base
11. no
12. no
13. yes
14. no
15. strategies
16. $425
17. $5,100
18. $28
19. can
20. number of images

## MULTIPLE CHOICE

1. a. **Correct.**
   b. Incorrect.  Number of setups would be used for the setup activity under activity-based costing.
   c. Incorrect.  Number of engineering changes would be used for the engineering change activity under activity-based costing.
   d. Incorrect.  Packing Department direct labor hours are only for a single department, not the complete plant.

2. a. **Correct.**  ($450,000 / 10,000 machine hours) × 0.8 machine hours
   b. Incorrect.
   c. Incorrect.
   d. Incorrect.

3. a. Incorrect.
   b. Incorrect.
   c. **Correct.**  [($120,000 / 5,000 machine hours) × .5 machine hours] + [($80,000 / 8,000 direct labor hours) × .25 direct labor hours]
   d. Incorrect.

**4.** a. Incorrect.
   b. **Correct.**
   c. Incorrect.
   d. Incorrect.

**5.** a. Incorrect.
   b. Incorrect.
   c. Incorrect.
   d. **Correct.**

**6.** a. Incorrect. The activity-base usage quantity is multiplied by the activity rate to determine a product's activity cost.
   b. **Correct.**
   c. Incorrect. An allocation base is not related to the activity and is used in plantwide and multiple department rates.
   d. Incorrect. Units of production may be an example of an estimated activity base, but it is not a generalized answer.

**7.** a. **Correct.** (60 sales orders × $45) + (5 requests × $125) + (4 returns × $400)
   b. Incorrect.
   c. Incorrect.
   d. Incorrect.

**8.** a. **Correct.**
   b. Incorrect.
   c. Incorrect.
   d. Incorrect.

**9.** a. Incorrect.
   b. Incorrect.
   c. **Correct.** ($290,000 ÷ 2,900 railcars)
   d. Incorrect.

**10.** a. Incorrect.
   b. **Correct.** [($290,000 / 2,900 railcars) × 60 railcars] + {[($360,000 + $80,000) / 25,000 miles] × 550 miles} = ($100 per railcar × 60 railcars) + ($17.60 per mile × 550 miles)
   c. Incorrect.
   d. Incorrect.

**11.** a. Incorrect. Using more rates does not necessarily mean that the sum of the allocations will be different.
   b. Incorrect. Using more activity pools does not necessarily mean that the sum of the allocations will be different.
   c. Incorrect. Activity-based costing rates cannot be compared meaningfully to single plantwide rates.
   d. **Correct.** The sum of the allocations across all products under both methods must be equal.

**12.** a. Incorrect.
   b. **Correct.** There is less cost in the direct labor cost pool under activity-based costing because the three other activities use cost out of the single plantwide pool.
   c. Incorrect.
   d. Incorrect.

## TRUE/FALSE

1. T
2. F  Often the production overhead cost under activity-based costing (rather than under the production department method) will include costs that are more closely aligned to the production department.
3. F  There must be significant differences in the production department rates *and* differences in the ratios of allocation base usage across the product.
4. T
5. F  Activity-based costing can be used by any type of business (manufacturing, merchandising, or service), governmental, or not-for-profit entity.
6. F  This is not an activity, but it is considered an element of plant factory overhead cost. An activity performed by the plant manager might be "Perform performance reviews."
7. F  Engineering change orders are issued to initiate a change in the design of the product.
8. T
9. T
10. F  Service companies should allocate activities to the cost of services in order to better manage the profitability of a service line.

## EXERCISE 26-1

**(1)**  Total factory overhead is $1,040,000. The selling and administrative expenses are not *factory* overhead and should not be included in determining the plantwide rate.

Total direct labor hours:

| | Budgeted Production Volume | × | Direct Labor Hours per Unit | = | Direct Labor Hours |
|---|---|---|---|---|---|
| Casual | 450,000 | | 0.1 | | 45,000 |
| Work | 200,000 | | 0.2 | | 40,000 |
| Dress | 150,000 | | 0.3 | | 45,000 |
| | 800,000 | | | | 130,000 |

Single plantwide factory overhead rate: $\dfrac{\$1,040,000}{130,000 \text{ direct labor hours}}$ = $8 per direct labor hour

**(2)**

| | Direct Labor Hours | × | Single Plantwide Factory Overhead Rate per Direct Labor Hour | = | Factory Overhead | Factory Overhead per Unit (Factory Overhead ÷ Budgeted Production Volume) |
|---|---|---|---|---|---|---|
| Casual | 45,000 | | $8 | | $ 360,000 | ÷ 450,000 units = $0.80 |
| Work | 40,000 | | 8 | | 320,000 | ÷ 200,000 units =  1.60 |
| Dress | 45,000 | | 8 | | 360,000 | ÷ 150,000 units =  2.40 |
| Total | 130,000 | | | | $1,040,000 | |

## EXERCISE 26-2

**(1)**  Production department factory overhead rates:

| | Press Department | Cure Department |
|---|---|---|
| Total factory overhead ....................... | $600,000 | $240,000 |
| Machine hours ............................... | ÷  8,000 mh | ÷ 24,000 mh |
| Departmental overhead rate ............. | $     75/mh | $     10/mh |

**(2)**   Auto Brake

| | | | | | |
|---|---|---|---|---|---|
| Press Department | 0.3 dir. mach. hr. | × | $75/dmh | = | $22.50 |
| Cure Department | 2.25 dir. mach. hr. | × | $10/dmh | = | 22.50 |
| Total factory overhead per set (unit) | | | | | $45.00 |

Truck Brake

| | | | | | |
|---|---|---|---|---|---|
| Press Department | 0.5 dir. mach. hr. | × | $75/dmh | = | $37.50 |
| Cure Department | 2.5 dir. mach. hr. | × | $10/dmh | = | 25.00 |
| Total factory overhead per set (unit) | | | | | $62.50 |

Bus Brake

| | | | | | |
|---|---|---|---|---|---|
| Press Department | 1.0 dir. mach. hr. | × | $75/dmh | = | $ 75.00 |
| Cure Department | 3.0 dir. mach. hr. | × | $10/dmh | = | 30.00 |
| Total factory overhead per set (unit) | | | | | $105.00 |

## EXERCISE 26-3

**(1)**

| | Purchasing | Inspecting | Materials Handling | Product Engineering |
|---|---|---|---|---|
| Activity cost pool | $225,000 | $140,000 | $70,000 | $165,000 |
| Activity base | ÷ 10,000 POs | ÷ 7,000 insp. | ÷35,000 moves | ÷ 1,000 ECOs |
| Activity rate | $ 22.50/PO | $ 20/insp. | $ 2/move | $ 165/ECO |

**(2)**   Laser Printer:

| | A | B | C | D | E | F |
|---|---|---|---|---|---|---|
| | | Activity-Base Usage | × | Activity Rate | = | Activity Cost |
| 1 | Purchasing | 4,000 purch. orders | | $22.50/purch. order | | $ 90,000 |
| 2 | Inspecting | 5,500 inspections | | $20/inspection | | 110,000 |
| 3 | Materials handling | 20,000 moves | | $2/move | | 40,000 |
| 4 | Product development | 800 ECOs | | $165/ECO | | 132,000 |
| 5 | Total activity cost | | | | | $372,000 |
| 6 | Unit volume | | | | | ÷ 4,000 |
| 7 | Activity cost per unit | | | | | $ 93 |

Ink Jet Printer:

| | A | B | C | D | E | F |
|---|---|---|---|---|---|---|
| | | Activity-Base Usage | × | Activity Rate | = | Activity Cost |
| 1 | Purchasing | 6,000 purch. orders | | $22.50/purch. order | | $135,000 |
| 2 | Inspecting | 1,500 inspections | | $20/inspection | | 30,000 |
| 3 | Materials handling | 15,000 moves | | $2/move | | 30,000 |
| 4 | Product development | 200 ECOs | | $165/ECO | | 33,000 |
| 5 | Total activity cost | | | | | $228,000 |
| 6 | Unit volume | | | | | ÷ 4,000 |
| 7 | Activity cost per unit | | | | | $ 57 |

## EXERCISE 26-4

Swanson Wine Distribution, Inc.
Statement of Operating Income—By Product
For the Year Ended December 31, 20--

| | Imported Wines | California Wines | Total |
|---|---|---|---|
| Sales | $3,600,000 | $5,040,000 | $8,640,000 |
| Cost of goods sold | 2,160,000 | 3,024,000 | 5,184,000 |
| Gross profit | $1,440,000 | $2,016,000 | $3,456,000 |
| Sales order activities | 261,000 | 174,000 | 435,000 |
| Promotional activities | 393,750 | 131,250 | 525,000 |
| Import and customs activities | 200,000 | — | 200,000 |
| Inventory carrying cost | 86,250 | 28,750 | 115,000 |
| Total selling and general administrative activities | $ 941,000 | $ 334,000 | $1,275,000 |
| Income from operations | $ 499,000 | $1,682,000 | $2,181,000 |
| Income from operations as a percent of sales | 13.9% | 33.4% | 25.2% |

Supporting Calculations:

Sales order activities

| | Imported Wines | California Wines | Total |
|---|---|---|---|
| Quantity (cases) | 4,500 | 12,000 | |
| ÷ Average order size (cases) | ÷ 2 | ÷ 8 | |
| Number of orders | 2,250 | 1,500 | 3,750 |

Sales order activity rate: $\dfrac{\text{Sales order activity cost}}{\text{Number of sales orders}}$, or $\dfrac{\$435,000}{3,750}$ = $116 per order

Imported wines:   2,250 orders × $116 per order = $261,000
Domestic wines:   1,500 orders × $116 per order = $174,000

Promotional activities

Promotional activity rate: $\dfrac{\text{Promotional activity cost}}{\text{Number of ad placements}}$, or $\dfrac{\$525,000}{120}$ = $4,375 per placement

Imported wines:   90 ads × $4,375 per placement = $393,750
Domestic wines:   30 ads × $4,375 per placement = $131,250

Importing and customs activities
By definition, 100% is associated with imported wines.

Inventory carrying cost

Inventory carrying cost rate: $\dfrac{\text{Inventory carrying cost}}{\text{Number of days' inventory}}$, or $\dfrac{\$115,000}{160}$ = $718.75 per day

Imported wines:   120 days × $718.75 per day = $86,250
Domestic wines:    40 days × $718.75 per day = $28,750

As can be seen in the revised report, the imported wines have less operating income and the domestic wines have more operating income as a percent of sales (operating margin) than indicated in the first report. This is because the two types of wine utilize selling and administrative activities in proportions different than their sales volumes. Specifically, the imported wine product category uses more relative sales order activity because the average order sizes are smaller than those for domestic wines. The promotional activities are greater for imported wines because more relative promotional effort is directed toward these products. In addition, the cost of importation and customs should be associated only with the imported wines. Lastly, the inventory carrying cost is proportionally greater for the imported wines because the number of days' sales in inventory is greater for the imported category. After allocating these activities using activity-based costing, the imported wines produce only a 13.9% operating margin, while the domestic wines produce a 33.4% operating margin.

## PROBLEM 26-1

**(1)** Production department rates:

| | Cutting Department | Assembly Department |
|---|---|---|
| Factory overhead .............................. | $1,200,000 | $600,000 |
| Direct labor hours ............................. | ÷ 10,000 dlh | ÷ 10,000 dlh |
| Production department rate .............. | $ 120/dlh | $ 60/dlh |

**(2)** Suitcase:

| | Direct Labor Hours | × | Production Department Rate | = | Factory Overhead |
|---|---|---|---|---|---|
| Cutting | 8,000 | | $120/dlh | | $ 960,000 |
| Assembly | 2,000 | | $60/dlh | | 120,000 |
| Total factory overhead | | | | | $1,080,000 |
| Number of units | | | | | ÷ 10,000 |
| Factory overhead per unit | | | | | $ 108 |

Garment Bag:

| | Direct Labor Hours | × | Production Department Rate | = | Factory Overhead |
|---|---|---|---|---|---|
| Cutting | 2,000 | | $120/dlh | | $240,000 |
| Assembly | 8,000 | | $60/dlh | | 480,000 |
| Total factory overhead | | | | | $720,000 |
| Number of units | | | | | ÷ 10,000 |
| Factory overhead per unit | | | | | $ 72 |

**(3)** Activity-based rates:

| | A | B | C | D | E |
|---|---|---|---|---|---|
| 1 | | Inspecting | Setup | Cutting | Assembly |
| 2 | Activity cost pool | $600,000 | $200,000 | $800,000 | $200,000 |
| 3 | Activity base | ÷ 4,000 insp. | ÷ 800 setups | ÷ 10,000 dlh | ÷ 10,000 dlh |
| 4 | Activity rate | $ 150/insp. | $ 250/setup | $ 80/dlh | $ 20/dlh |

**(4)** Suitcase:

| | A | B | C | D | E | F |
|---|---|---|---|---|---|---|
| 1 | | Activity-Base Usage | × | Activity Rate | = | Activity Cost |
| 2 | Inspecting | 1,000 inspections | | $150/inspection | | $150,000 |
| 3 | Setup | 200 setups | | $250/setup | | 50,000 |
| 4 | Cutting | 8,000 dlh | | $80/dlh | | 640,000 |
| 5 | Assembly | 2,000 dlh | | $20/dlh | | 40,000 |
| 6 | Total | | | | | $880,000 |
| 7 | Number of units | | | | | ÷ 10,000 |
| 8 | Activity cost per unit | | | | | $    88 |

Garment Bag:

| | A | B | C | D | E | F |
|---|---|---|---|---|---|---|
| 1 | | Activity-Base Usage | × | Activity Rate | = | Activity Cost |
| 2 | Inspecting | 3,000 inspections | | $150/inspection | | $450,000 |
| 3 | Setup | 600 setups | | $250/setup | | 150,000 |
| 4 | Cutting | 2,000 dlh | | $80/dlh | | 160,000 |
| 5 | Assembly | 8,000 dlh | | $20/dlh | | 160,000 |
| 6 | Total | | | | | $920,000 |
| 7 | Number of units | | | | | ÷ 10,000 |
| 8 | Activity cost per unit | | | | | $    92 |

**(5)** The activity-based overhead assignment reveals that garment bags are more costly than suitcases on a per unit basis. The multiple production department rate method does not show this because the method assumes that all factory overhead is proportional to direct labor hours. Since each product consumes the same total direct labor hours, the factory overhead assignment is nearly equal. The activity-based method separately accounts for the inspecting and setup activity costs. Garment bags have more inspecting and setup activities than do suitcases Thus, garment bags are shown to have higher activity costs per unit than do suitcases.

## PROBLEM 26-2

**(1)**

| | 1-800 Support | Return Processing | Order Processing |
|---|---|---|---|
| Activity cost ..................................... | $5,400,000 | $7,200,000 | $9,000,000 |
| Activity base ..................................... | ÷ 50,000 calls | ÷ 12,000 returns | ÷ 45,000 orders |
| Activity rate ..................................... | $ 108/call | $ 600/return | $ 200/order |

**(2)**

| | Integrated Accounting | Human Resource | Project Management |
|---|---|---|---|
| Number of customer 1-800 calls | 20,000 | 20,000 | 10,000 |
| Activity rate per call | × $108 | × $108 | × $108 |
| 1-800 support cost | $2,160,000 | $2,160,000 | $1,080,000 |
| Number of returns | 2,000 | 5,000 | 5,000 |
| Activity rate per return | × $600 | × $600 | × $600 |
| Product return processing cost | 1,200,000 | 3,000,000 | 3,000,000 |
| Number of sales orders | 20,000 | 15,000 | 10,000 |
| Activity rate per order | × $200 | × $200 | × $200 |
| Sales order processing cost | 4,000,000 | 3,000,000 | 2,000,000 |
| Total nonmanufacturing activity costs | $7,360,000 | $8,160,000 | $6,080,000 |

**(3)**

| | Integrated Accounting | Human Resource | Project Management |
|---|---|---|---|
| Revenues ..................................... | $25,000,000 | $20,000,000 | $ 5,000,000 |
| Less cost of goods sold ................. | 2,500,000 | 2,000,000 | 500,000 |
| Gross profit ..................................... | $22,500,000 | $18,000,000 | $ 4,500,000 |
| Less: | | | |
|    1-800 support ........................... | $ 2,160,000 | $ 2,160,000 | $ 1,080,000 |
|    Return processing ..................... | 1,200,000 | 3,000,000 | 3,000,000 |
|    Sales order processing ............. | 4,000,000 | 3,000,000 | 2,000,000 |
|      Total activity cost ................. | $ 7,360,000 | $ 8,160,000 | $ 6,080,000 |
| Operating income .......................... | $15,140,000 | $ 9,840,000 | $(1,580,000) |

**(4)** Project management software is unprofitable, while the other two products have healthy margins. This is because the project management software has excessive 1-800 support calls, product returns (approximately 50% of unit volume!), and sales order activities relative to its volume. For example, the project management software averages one 1-800 call per unit sold, sells only one unit per order, and has half of the units returned. The company's options include the following:

**a.** Drop project management software. This does not necessarily mean that all the costs can be avoided. The costs will only go away if the reduced activity translates into lower expenditures. Thus, the company should evaluate the contribution margin of this product before making this decision.

**b.** Increase the price on the project software. Charge customers a higher price to compensate for the higher activities required to serve this software. However, the customers may not accept the price increase required to make this a profitable product.

**c.** Redesign the instructions to the software to reduce the amount of 1-800 call support for this product. Also, improve the product to reduce the high percentage of returns and 1-800 support calls. Apparently this software is having trouble in the field.

**d.** Price 1-800 customer support as a separate service. In other words, unbundle the pricing of goods from the support services.

**e.** Improve the efficiency of order processing. Each order costs $200 to process. For a $500 product, this seems excessive. There should be some opportunity for some process savings in this area.

**f.** Move the support and ordering to the Internet.

# CHAPTER 27

## MATCHING

| | | | |
|---|---|---|---|
| 1. P | 6. G | 11. B | 15. W | 19. J | 23. A | 27. Y |
| 2. K | 7. D | 12. V | 16. AA | 20. I | 24. BB | 28. X |
| 3. Z | 8. R | 13. S | 17. N | 21. L | 25. O | 29. H |
| 4. U | 9. F | 14. T | 18. E | 22. CC | 26. C | |
| 5. M | 10. Q | | | | | |

## FILL IN THE BLANK—PART A

1. just-in-time manufacturing
2. reduce
3. lead time
4. value-added lead time
5. lead time
6. 16 minutes
7. 796 minutes (49 units × 16 minutes) + 12 minutes
8. setup
9. process-oriented layout
10. employee involvement
11. kanban
12. radio frequency identification devices
13. $105 ($175,000 ÷ 250 hours) × (9 min. ÷ 60 min.)
14. $358,333 [(250 hours × 60 min.) ÷ 9 min.] × ($105 + $110)
15. six-sigma
16. nonfinancial
17. $500 per hour
18. external failure
19. Pareto chart
20. value-added
21. inputs, outputs

## FILL IN THE BLANK—PART B

1. just-in-time manufacturing
2. make to stock
3. pull
4. product-oriented
5. nonvalue-added lead time
6. 28 minutes
7. 659 minutes (23 units × 28 minutes) + 15 minutes
8. Pareto chart
9. materials, work in process
10. enterprise resource planning
11. electronic data interchange
12. $450 ($360,000 ÷ 240 hours) × (18 min. ÷ 60 min.)
13. $420,000 [(240 hours × 60 min.) ÷ 18 min.] × ($450 + $75)
14. $70
15. nonfinancial
16. internal failure
17. prevention
18. nonvalue-added
19. internal, external
20. cost of quality report
21. eliminating

## MULTIPLE CHOICE

1.  a. Incorrect. Emphasizing pull manufacturing is a characteristic of just-in-time manufacturing.
    b. **Correct.**
    c. Incorrect. Reducing inventory is a characteristic of just-in-time manufacturing.
    d. Incorrect. Reducing setup time is a characteristic of just-in-time manufacturing.

2.  a. Incorrect. Although supply chain management is a just-in-time principle, it is not the most direct way to reduce lead time.
    b. Incorrect. Although employee involvement is a just-in-time principle, it is not the most direct way to reduce lead time.
    c. **Correct.** Reducing setup time allows a company to reduce batch sizes, which will lead to shorter lead times.
    d. Incorrect. Although electronic data interchange is a just-in-time principle, it is not the most direct way to reduce lead time.

3.  a.  Incorrect.  Setup time would be considered nonvalue-added lead time.
    b.  Incorrect.  Move time would be considered nonvalue-added lead time.
    c.  Incorrect.  Waiting in inventory would be considered nonvalue-added lead time.
    d.  **Correct.**

4.  a.  Incorrect.  This is the value-added time.
    b.  Incorrect.
    c.  **Correct.**  (20 units – 1) × 4 minutes
    d.  Incorrect.

5.  a.  **Correct.**
    b.  Incorrect.  Materials Inventory is not often used by just-in-time manufacturers.
    c.  Incorrect.
    d.  Incorrect.  Cost of Goods Sold should only be debited upon sale of the item.

6.  a.  Incorrect.
    b.  Incorrect.
    c.  **Correct.**  {[$175 per hour × (18 min. / 60 min.)] + $48 per unit} × 300 units
    d.  Incorrect.

7.  a.  Incorrect.
    b.  **Correct.**  {[$175 per hour × (18 min. / 60 min.)] + $48 per unit} × 15 units
    c.  Incorrect.
    d.  Incorrect.

8.  a.  Incorrect.  Scrap is an internal failure cost.
    b.  Incorrect.  Rework is an internal failure cost.
    c.  **Correct.**
    d.  Incorrect.  Quality control inspection is an appraisal cost.

9.  a.  **Correct.**
    b.  Incorrect.  Line charts provide trend information.
    c.  Incorrect.
    d.  Incorrect.  Scatterplot diagrams visually demonstrate how two variables are related to each other.

10. a.  Incorrect.
    b.  **Correct.**  ($60,000 + $90,000) / $400,000
    c.  Incorrect.
    d.  Incorrect.

11. a.  Incorrect.
    b.  **Correct.**  {[(15 units – 1) × 10 min. × 3 depts.] + (4 moves × 5 min.)} / (420 min. + 20 min. + 30 min.)
    c.  Incorrect.
    d.  Incorrect.

12. a.  Incorrect.  The pharmacy would be decentralized to the various units.
    b.  Incorrect.  The tests would not need to travel far because the chemistry lab would be located directly within the unit.
    c.  Incorrect.  The patient would not move to a centralized X-ray department, but instead would use the X-ray suite located within the unit.
    d.  **Correct.**

13. a.  Incorrect.  This occurs in push scheduling.
    b.  Incorrect.  This occurs in push scheduling.
    c.  **Correct.**  In pull scheduling the schedule is based on replenishing what was consumed by the next (downstream) operation.
    d.  Incorrect.  This occurs in push scheduling.

**14.** a. Incorrect.  This is the per customer savings.
　　b. **Correct.**  [($100,000 × 1.20) – $50,000] / 2,500.
　　c. Incorrect.
　　d. Incorrect.

## TRUE/FALSE

**1.** F  This is a common misconception. Just-in-time is primarily a process improvement technique. The inventory can be reduced only after making the improvements.

**2.** F  Lead time also includes nonvalue-added wait and move time.

**3.** T

**4.** F  Reducing setup time will reduce the batch size and *reduce* within-batch wait time.

**5.** T

**6.** F  A JIT environment should *reduce* the number of accounting and control transactions.

**7.** T

**8.** F  Since many factory overhead items are assigned directly to product cells, there is less need for factory overhead allocation in JIT environments.

**9.** T

**10.** F  A Pareto chart is a bar chart that shows the totals of an attribute (such as cost) for a number of categories (such as activities).

## EXERCISE 27-1

|  | Traditional | JIT |
|---|---|---|
| Process Step 1 | 3 | 3 |
| Process Step 2 | 7 | 7 |
| Process Step 3 | 12 | 12 |
| Process Step 4 | 5 | 5 |
| Total value-added time | 27 | 27 |
|  |  |  |
| Number of moves | 5 | 5 |
| Minutes per move | × 15 | × 5 |
| Move time | 75 | 25 |
|  |  |  |
| Units waiting their turn (Batch size – 1) | 39 | 2 |
| Total processing minutes per unit | × 27 | × 27 |
| Within-batch wait time | 1,053 | 54 |

|  | Traditional | | JIT | |
|---|---|---|---|---|
|  | Time | Percent of Total Lead Time | Time | Percent of Total Lead Time |
| Total nonvalue-added time (move time + within-batch wait time) | 1,128 | 97.7% | 79 | 74 5% |
| Value-added process time per unit | 27 | 2.3% | 27 | 25.5% |
| Total lead time per unit | 1,155 | | 106 | |

## EXERCISE 27-2

**(1)** Cell conversion cost per hour:

$$\frac{\$1,845,000}{2,050 \text{ hours}} = \$900 \text{ per hour}$$

**(2)** Cell conversion cost per unit:

$$\frac{10 \text{ minutes}}{60 \text{ minutes}} \times \$900 \text{ per hour} = \$150 \text{ per unit}$$

**(3)** **(a)** Raw and In Process Inventory ......................... 138,375

Accounts Payable .......................................                      138,375

(1,025 units × $135)

**(b)** Raw and In Process Inventory ......................... 153,750

Conversion Cost ..........................................                      153,750

(1,025 units × $150)

**(c)** Finished Goods .............................................. 292,125

Raw and In Process Inventory ....................                      292,125

[1,025 units × ($135 + $150)]

**(d)** Accounts Receivable ...................................... 480,000

Sales .............................................................                      480,000

Cost of Goods Sold (1,000 × $285) .................. 285,000

Finished Goods ...........................................                      285,000

## EXERCISE 27-3

### Pareto Chart of Quality Costs—Veracity Instruments

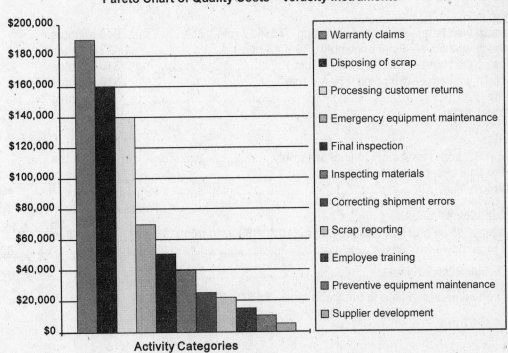

## EXERCISE 27-4

**(1)** Process cost per image: $\dfrac{\$240,000}{1,500 \text{ images}}$ = $160 per image

**(2) and (3)**

|  | Current Process | Percent Savings | Savings | Proposed Process |
|---|---|---|---|---|
| Prepare patient (radioactive tracer injection) | $ 22,000 | 0% | $ — | $ 22,000 |
| Move patient to Imaging Department | 15,000 | 60% | 9,000 | 6,000 |
| Conduct imaging | 75,000 | 20% | 15,000 | 60,000 |
| Move patient back to room | 15,000 | 60% | 9,000 | 6,000 |
| Doctor dictates diagnosis via tape recorder | 50,000 | 0% | — | 50,000 |
| Transcribe report to hardcopy | 18,000 | 100% | 18,000 | — |
| File and retrieve report | 45,000 | 80% | 36,000 | 9,000 |
| Total cost | $240,000 | | $87,000 | $153,000 |
| ÷ Number of images | ÷ 1,500 | | | ÷ 1,500 |
| Cost per image | $ 160 | | | $ 102 |

## PROBLEM 27-1

**(1)** Value-added time:

| | |
|---|---|
| Hand soldering of PC board | 12 minutes |
| Device final assembly | 18 minutes |
| Time to inspect one unit | 4 minutes |
| Pack and label | 4 minutes |
| Total | 38 minutes |

Nonvalue-added time:

Wait time:

| | | |
|---|---|---|
| Within-batch wait time—PC board soldering (79 × 12 min.) | 948 minutes | |
| Within-batch wait time—Final assembly (79 × 18 min.) | 1,422 minutes | |
| Within-batch wait time—Testing (79 × 4 min.) | 316 minutes | |
| Within-batch wait time—Shipping (79 × 4 min.) | 316 minutes | |
| Test setup | 45 minutes | |
| Total wait time | | 3,047 minutes |

Move time:

| | | |
|---|---|---|
| Move from PC board assembly to final assembly | 10 minutes | |
| Move from final assembly to testing | 30 minutes | |
| Total move time | | 40 minutes |

Machine breakdown time:

| | | |
|---|---|---|
| Average breakdown and maintenance time (10% × 80 × 10 min.) | 80 minutes | |
| Total breakdown wait time | | 80 minutes |

| | |
|---|---|
| Total nonvalue-added time | 3,167 minutes |

Ratio of nonvalue-added time to total lead time: 3,167 ÷ 3,205 = 98.81%

**(2)** The existing process is very wasteful. The company could improve the process by changing the layout from a process orientation to a product orientation. Each storage device type could be formed into a production cell. Each cell would have PC card assembly, final assembly, and shipping next to each other. In this way, the batch sizes could be reduced significantly. Workers could practice one-at-a-time processing and merely pass a single completed assembly through the cell. As a result, the move time and within-batch wait time would be eliminated. The company could also initiate total quality principles. Moving toward zero defects would allow the company to reduce testing activities (and time), and as a result the setup time for the test area might be eliminated or reduced. In addition, the company should use more preventive maintenance on the testing machines in order to reduce the amount of unexpected machine downtime.

## PROBLEM 27-2

**(1)**

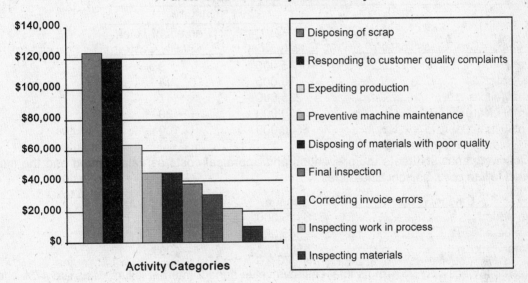

Pareto Chart of Quality Cost Activity

Legend:
- Disposing of scrap
- Responding to customer quality complaints
- Expediting production
- Preventive machine maintenance
- Disposing of materials with poor quality
- Final inspection
- Correcting invoice errors
- Inspecting work in process
- Inspecting materials

Activity Categories

**(2)** The following quality cost classifications were used in developing the cost of quality report:

| | | |
|---|---:|---|
| Preventive machine maintenance ........................... | $ 45,000 | Prevention |
| Disposing of scrap ................................................. | 125,000 | Internal failure |
| Correcting invoice errors ....................................... | 30,000 | External failure |
| Final inspection ..................................................... | 38,000 | Appraisal |
| Expediting production ............................................ | 65,000 | Internal failure |
| Disposing of materials with poor quality ............... | 45,000 | Internal failure |
| Responding to customer quality complaints .......... | 120,000 | External failure |
| Inspecting work in process ................................... | 22,000 | Appraisal |
| Producing product ................................................. | 200,000 | Not a cost of quality |
| Inspecting materials ............................................. | 10,000 | Appraisal |
| Total ................................................................. | $700,000 | |

Kokimo Company
Cost of Quality

| | Cost Summary | |
|---|---|---|
| Quality Cost Classification | Quality Cost | Percent of Total Quality Cost |
| Prevention ...................................... | $ 45,000 | 9% |
| Appraisal ....................................... | 70,000 | 14 |
| Internal failure .............................. | 235,000 | 47 |
| External failure ............................. | 150 000 | 30 |
| Total ......................................... | $500,000 | 100% |

**(3)** The following analysis treats the prevention and appraisal costs as value-added and the internal and external failure costs as nonvalue-added:

| Category | Amount | Percent |
|---|---|---|
| Value-added .................................. | $115,000 | 23% |
| Nonvalue-added ............................ | 385,000 | 77 |
| Total ........................................ | $500,000 | 100% |

**(4)** The company has only 23% of its total costs as value-added. Internal failure costs are 47% and external failure costs are 30% of total quality costs. Prevention activities are only 9% of the total quality cost effort. Kokimo should shift much more of its attention toward prevention and appraisal activities in order to eliminate the internal and external failure costs before they occur. There is significant room for improvement.